Cultural Differences and Improving Performance

This book is dedicated to my wife, Helen.

With so many thanks for encouragement, practical advice and boundless wisdom.

Cultural Differences and Improving Performance

How Values and Beliefs Influence Organizational Performance

BRYAN HOPKINS

Routledge
Taylor & Francis Group

LONDON AND NEW YORK

First published in paperback 2024

First published 2009 by Gower Publishing

Published 2016 by Routledge
4 Park Square, Milton Park, Abingdon, Oxon OX14 4RN

and by Routledge
605 Third Avenue, New York, NY 10158

Routledge is an imprint of the Taylor & Francis Group, an informa business

British Library Cataloguing in Publication Data
Hopkins, Bryan.
  Cultural differences and improving performance : how values
  and beliefs influence organizational performance.
  1. Industrial management--Social aspects. 2. National
  characteristics. 3. Diversity in the workplace.
  4. Intercultural communication. 5. International business
  enterprises--Personnel management.
  I. Title
  658.3'008-dc22

Library of Congress Cataloging-in-Publication Data
Hopkins, Bryan, 1954-
  Cultural differences and improving performance : how values and beliefs influence
organizational performance / by Bryan Hopkins.
      p. cm.
  Includes bibliographical references and index.
  ISBN 978-0-566-08907-7 (hbk.) 1. Diversity in the workplace--Management.
  2. Cultural awareness. 3. Intercultural communication. 4. Organizational behavior.
  5. Performance. I. Title.
  HF5549.5.M5H668 2009
  658.3'14--dc22

                                                                    2009025332

ISBN: 978-0-566-08907-7 (hbk)
ISBN: 978-1-03-283825-0 (pbk)
ISBN: 978-1-315-57525-4 (ebk)

DOI: 10.4324/9781315575254

Contents

List of Figures

List of Tables

Acknowledgements

Writing a book is never easy, especially when you are fitting it in amongst the demands of running a small training consultancy business and getting married. After all, it is not paid work, and every day spent sitting in a library, searching the Internet and trying to write something that makes any sense is time taken away from activities that put food on the table, pay the mortgage and ensure domestic harmony.

So during those lonely hours it has been important to know that there are people who have been providing support and encouragement, and from time to time looking at what I have produced, noting down nonsense, spotting lacunae in my logic and otherwise helping me to turn the manuscript into what I hope will be a useful guide to managers everywhere.

I should therefore like to thank specifically Phil Green of Optimum Learning Ltd, Mike Sleight of workstream.biz, Rachel Manser, Jeanie Fraser, Chief Civilian Personnel Officer in the UN Mission to Liberia, Juliana Ribeiro and Julia Howson for their invaluable help in getting this book to the publishers. And, of course, a special mention to my eternally patient wife Helen, who not only encouraged me but, as an expert in the field of diversity, provided great advice and encouragement.

Finally, I would like to thank the library staff at the University of Sheffield for helping me find my way around the stacks and, most importantly, for their enlightened access policy, which has made it possible for a non-academic like myself to make use of their resources.

Preface

In the early summer of 1976, innocently clutching my newly acquired degree in mechanical engineering in one hand and a 'go–no go' gauge in the other, I started work for the nuclear power construction division of what was then called the General Electric Company. By September of that year, as the leaves were turning on the trees and the long days beginning to rapidly shorten, I realized that I had spent the whole of that hot summer inside the cold, dark and empty core of what was to become Hartlepool nuclear power station, measuring screw threads with that 'go–no go' gauge.

I felt that there had to be more to life and the world. I therefore applied to Voluntary Service Overseas asking for a teaching position somewhere that the sun would shine on me.

So it was that in late 1977 I found myself looking out the window of a Boeing 707 as it descended over the outskirts of Khartoum, looking in naive astonishment and some trepidation at men in white jellabahs and women covered from head to toe in black robes walking through the dusty streets beneath me. My VSO posting took me to Atbara, a small town in the northern Sudan where I then spent two years teaching in a technical college, slowly getting to grips with the culture, the traditions and the language.

I followed that with a Master's degree in development studies and then several more years working on a local salary as an instructor in a technical college in the Gambia, once more immersing myself in the local culture.

Eventually returning to the United Kingdom to get 'a proper job' seemed very strange. Why did people do what they did? Why was that important? My homeland did not seem quite so familiar or much like home any more.

Proper jobs eventually turned into training consultancy, and I started to read more about current management thinking, exploring latest ideas on motivation, leadership, decision-making and the like. However, whenever I thought back to my experiences in Africa much of what I read did not seem to be altogether relevant, and this became even more apparent when I started to work with various United Nations agencies, the ultimate in diverse workplaces.

And so the idea for this book was born. That is, how can you improve the performance of people who do not fit into the template for workers, as assumed by those who frequent the business schools of American and European universities? I hope that this book provides some answers.

Bryan Hopkins

Introduction

Then said a teacher, speak to us of teaching.

And he said:

No man can reveal to you aught but that which already lies half asleep in the dawning of your knowledge.

The teacher who walks in the shadow of the temple, among his followers, it is not of his wisdom but rather of his faith and his lovingness.

If he is indeed wise he does not bid you enter the house of his wisdom, but rather leads you to the threshold of your own mind.

The astronomer may speak to you of his understanding of space but he cannot give you his understanding.

The musician may sing to you of the rhythm which is in all space, but he cannot give you the ear which arrests the rhythm, nor the voice that echoes it.

And he who is versed in the science of numbers can tell of the regions of weight and measure, but he cannot conduct you thither.

For the vision of one man lends not its wings to another man.

And even as each one of you stands alone in God's knowledge, so must each one of you be alone in his knowledge of God and in his understanding of the Earth.

From *The Prophet*, Kahlil Gibran, 1883–1931

Culture, performance – two words that can each have many meanings. So, before going any further, I think it would be a good idea to explain how I am going to be using these words in this book. Then you will be able to decide whether or not this book is going to answer your questions.

In this book culture is about the pattern of behaviour shown by people who share a similar national origin. So, for example, we can talk about a Brazilian culture, a British culture or a Bengali culture. People do not necessarily need to be living within that particular country to display their national culture, and naturally people of Brazilian or Bengali origin working in Britain, say, will bring their beliefs and values to their offices and factories.

The other element of the title, performance, is about how well people do what they do in those offices and factories or, more precisely, how quickly, accurately, reliably and so on they can carry out their tasks. Note that this definition places performance as a *result* not as a process. This is important, because there is a whole body of human resource management literature and practice covering the subject of 'performance management'. In my opinion this focuses on the *process* aspects of performance, in terms of, for example, the behaviours that people display or their competencies. This is an extremely important subject to consider, but it can lead the unwary to assume that the only factor contributing to how well a task is carried out is the quality of the behaviour that has gone into the task. Once someone has made that assumption, it then becomes almost inevitable that they will think that the solution to any output quality problem must be to refine the behaviours of the people involved – in other words, to train them.

This book challenges that assumption. Many other factors contribute to poor outcomes, such as the quality of information available about the task and the incentives provided for satisfactory completion, and the aim of this book is to show how to identify these and take them into consideration.

Putting these two definitions together, the book looks at how the beliefs and values that people bring to their workplace affects the quality of what they do. This is not to say that beliefs and values negatively affect its quality, because very often they contribute positively to what the organization is trying to achieve. However, things become more complicated when people holding different beliefs and values come to work together, particularly when this is within an organization that might have its own different set of beliefs and values.

Understanding what factors affect how well people can carry out everyday jobs and knowing how to make effective changes – sometimes known as performance engineering – is a well-developed discipline, but many of the underlying assumptions used to evaluate the significance of these factors come from a single cultural perspective. This book aims to combine current thinking on different cultural beliefs and values with the process of performance engineering so that managers working in culturally diverse settings will have some understanding of the issues involved and of the tools they can use to identify effective and culturally-sensitive solutions.

What This Book is – and is Not

Now, before carrying on it would be useful to clarify two things, what this book is and what it is not.

This book is an attempt at explaining how different cultural characteristics may affect how people behave and perform in their workplace, leading to ideas about how diverse workforces can be managed effectively.

This book is *not* about how to promote cultural diversity in the workplace, although I would like to think that this is implicit within what it says.

Everyone, regardless of their cultural background, has something to bring to the workplace, and this book looks at how a manager can harness people's strengths and help them with problems. There are many books available that look at how to promote cultural diversity in the workplace, and I suspect that many people reading this book will have their own favourites. However, when we start to discuss the characteristics of different cultures we do walk into a very sensitive and complex area. It is very difficult for any of us to not have stereotyped views about how other cultures behave or 'are', because stereotyping is what we do to try to make sense of the complexities of the world around us. But stereotypes can also be big obstacles, stopping us from seeing the true essence of people around us, and holding them can prejudice our opinions, making it difficult for us to think about, and deal rationally with, any issue in the workplace that seems to have a cultural dimension.

So at this point, before going any further, stop and think about your own prejudices about people who are different from you – and you will have such prejudices because we all have, myself included. I cannot do any better here than to quote from Peter Senge's book *The Fifth Discipline*:

> *Once a person begins to accept a stereotype of a particular group, that 'thought' becomes an active agent, 'participating' in shaping how he or she interacts with another person who falls into that stereotyped class. In turn, the tone of their interaction influences the other person's behaviour. The prejudiced person can't see how his prejudice shapes what he 'sees' and how he acts. In some sense, if he did, he would no longer be prejudiced. To operate, the 'thought' of prejudice must remain hidden to its holder.*

Senge, 1990, p. 241

Only when we are able to put up our hands and say, 'Yes, I have my prejudices', can we break this cycle and move on to become effective managers and, dare I say it, decent human beings.

Who is This Book For?

The first car that I ever owned was a 1968 Mark 1 Ford Escort. By the time that I came to be its proud owner it had covered over 70,000 miles, which for a mass-produced car of that era was definitely high mileage. However, it was mechanically simple, and I had some basic car maintenance skills, so felt that I could keep it on the road fairly cheaply.

For a while it ran very well, but then I found that at high speed (well, at 50 miles per hour) it started misfiring. I checked my maintenance manual, and it suggested that the spark plugs might be the problem. So I went to my local car parts shop, explained the situation and the assistant said that I needed a complete set of new plugs. Off I went, and fitted the new plugs. I went for a test drive and what did I find? No change; it still misfired.

Back to the car parts shop and I explained the symptoms again to the shop assistant.

'It sounds to me like it's the rotor arm,' he said. 'After that many miles the contacts get worn. That'll be the problem.'

So he sold me a brand-new rotor arm, and off I went again. Installing it was a breeze, and, full of optimism, I set off down the dual carriageway. Still misfiring.

I left it a few weeks and went back to the parts shop.

'Hmm', he said, scratching his chin. 'Well, the only other thing it can be is your high tension leads.'

Now, high tension leads were significantly more expensive than the previous solutions, but he was confident that this would solve the problem, so I handed over my cash. Home I went again and spent a little while fitting the new leads. Off down the dual carriageway again, only to discover that yet more money had been wasted.

I had now come to realize that my diagnostic skills were not sufficiently advanced and that my helpful car parts shop assistant did not actually know much more than me. It was time to take it to the experts. A little while after leaving it at the garage, the mechanic rang me. 'I can see what your problem is, Mr Hopkins. Your distributor cap has got a hairline crack in it. I've just put a new one on and it runs perfectly.'

So my love affair with my Ford Escort resumed, and it covered quite a few more miles before I passed it on to someone else. Years later I reflected on the bigger significance of what had happened. I really didn't know much about cars and had tried to solve the problem by going to somebody who only had solutions – in other words, spark plugs, rotor arms and high tension leads. But they didn't solve the problem. This only happened when I went to somebody who could analyse what was happening and could then identify exactly what I needed. We have talked about cars here, but the same thing happens in the workplace: people have a problem and look for the likely solutions, which might be sending people for training, running team-building events or signing up for leadership courses, to name but a few. And there are many people and organizations in the human relations industry who are very happy to sell solutions that, like my spark plugs and other miscellaneous car parts, are not actually solutions to that particular problem.

This book is therefore aimed at anyone in a managerial role who finds themselves having to do something to improve performance, and it should be of particular interest to people working in Human Relations departments or training, who are often the people asked to provide the solutions. All too often, solutions commissioned are ineffectual, but, as training is rarely evaluated in any meaningful way, these deficiencies remain undetected. Analysis that is done tends to be within the self-limiting constraints of a training needs analysis, which starts off with the assumption that training is needed and that the solution must lie in finding the right blend of training approaches, rather than in questioning any organizational factors having a negative impact on performance.

'But I don't have time to do all this analysis,' the cry goes up. Well, after my experience with the Ford Escort I realized that, had I invested more time early on when the car first started to misfire, I would have saved considerable time poking around underneath the bonnet and, of course, quite a bit of money spent on solutions that weren't actually solutions. The same applies in the business world. Managers may not have the time to do a thorough analysis, but they will have plenty of time to reflect on the solutions that do not work.

And while it might take some time to work through the problem-solving process described in this book in great detail, you can achieve a considerable amount quite quickly by just following the basics. However little you can manage, an early investment of time in analysis always brings good returns.

Before continuing it would be useful to refer to the extract from Kahlil Gibran's beautiful poem *The Prophet* quoted at the beginning of this Introduction. He writes, 'For the vision of one man lends not its wings to another man', and I want to say that it is not my intention in this book to make definitive statements about how different cultures in the world behave or how you, as a manager, should go about taking consideration of this into your daily working practices.

What I have attempted to do instead is to tie together the knowledge and wisdom of many other people in a way that hopefully make sense and will be useful for others. In my experience, problem-solving is not a linear process that can be resolved by a prescriptive approach: instead, it is an activity where a broad understanding of many different issues and techniques helps you identify ideas that may well be of value.

So take what you find in this book as a starting-point, and use it to help to further shape your understanding of your particular workplace and its cultural richness.

Diversity and Management Theory

Management is '... the application of skill or care in the manipulation, use, treatment, or control of things or persons, or in the conduct of an enterprise, operation, etc.' (*Oxford English Dictionary*). Or, to put it another way, it is to do what is necessary to get the best out of people and processes in a workplace situation.

If you are reading this book, you are presumably interested in finding out how you can do this and, to that end, may well have read many other books dealing with different aspects of management. You will probably also have some interest in what I have called working in 'global and culturally diverse organizations', so let us just pause to clarify what this means. I would take this definition to include someone working in:

- a foreign country, so that most of their colleagues are of a different culture;
- their home country, but in a team that includes people from different cultures dispersed around the world;
- their home country, in an organization with a culturally diverse workforce.

So you see that what I regard as a global or culturally diverse organization covers perhaps the majority of modern businesses. But if you are managing in such an organization, applying your skill to manipulate things and persons (to paraphrase the *OED*), you may feel that much of the management literature readily found on the shelves of the bookseller near you is somewhat limited, in that the prescriptions you read do not necessarily resonate with your own workplace experience.

For example, imagine that you are interested in finding out more about performance management. The standard books on the subject may have somewhat different perspectives, but they do generally have a consensus around certain points. For example:

- Performance management involves an ongoing dialogue between a manager and someone who reports to them.
- The quality of someone's performance is judged against their progress in achieving goals and objectives that are developed from some combination of organizational goals and personal development needs.
- There is a reliance on a mutual exchange of feedback.

Now, this may work perfectly well in an American or British workplace, but when you introduce people from different cultures certain cracks may begin to appear. For example:

- A subordinate may not be prepared to contribute to an open and honest dialogue about their performance, because in their culture what the boss says is right and it is therefore impertinent for them to express an opinion.
- Measuring performance by looking at what somebody has done is pointless because their progress through the organization is determined solely by their kinship with other people in the organization.
- Providing direct feedback to someone about their performance may be culturally completely unacceptable because that could lead to a loss of face.

All of a sudden, that impulse purchase of *Performance Management in Five Easy Steps* or *Performance Management for Beginners* (not, I hasten to add, real book titles) does not seem like such a good buy.

So why do we need a book of this sort, exploring both performance improvement and cultural differences? Well, in the second half of the twentieth century the United States of America stood astride the world like an economic colossus. Its power enabled it to export technology, culture and knowledge around the world. The drive to put people on the moon in 1969 led to massive developments in electronic technology, and, by the time the century drew to an end, this had developed to such an extent that global communications had been totally revolutionized. The hand-held communicators that *Star Trek's* Jim Kirk carried with him as he beamed down to yet another planet in the 1960s were now consumer items, enabling people to make telephone calls, exchange messages and watch video virtually anywhere in the world.

By the early years of twenty-first century the watchword was globalization. Improvements in communication technologies and air transport meant that people now worked globally by physically locating in another country or as part of a virtual team, working in their home country but communicating and collaborating with people spread around the world. In 1901 people could only readily communicate with the other inhabitants of their own village or town – people who would, by and large, share the same set of beliefs and values. By 2001 the village was global, and instant communication with people from completely different cultural backgrounds in more or less any corner of the world was no longer a cause of wonderment.

And yet, as the global executives travelled from departure lounge to departure lounge, the management texts on sale in the bookshops, wherever they went, stayed largely the same, with the same, almost exclusively American, management gurus advising on leadership, motivation, negotiation and every other topic of interest to the modern businessperson. This is because, as well as the technological developments that it has created, the United States has also made huge contributions to thinking in many other areas – particularly, as far as this book is concerned, in social sciences and occupational psychology.

Most management theories have their roots in psychology, and the bulk of academic output in areas such as psychology and management is from the United States. Michele Gelfand, quoting from Harry Triandis (1994) says, 'Indeed, there are estimates that more than 90 per cent of social and organizational theories have been developed and tested in largely Western contexts' (Gelfand, 1999, p. 249). Other American writers have also commented, 'Americans are also reluctant to acknowledge cultural differences in cognitive patterns. We are raised and educated to believe that, under the skin, all people are the same' (Klein et al., 2000, p. 3). Given this conjunction, it is hardly surprising that ideas based on a North American context might be assumed to be applicable to the whole human race.

Now, a little further along the business shelves in the bookshop, the executive might find some useful guides to international business etiquette, which will tell them where and how they should present their business card and whether or not they can blow their nose in public. These are important matters: blowing your nose in the wrong place could put that million-dollar deal in jeopardy. So we place great importance on what we might call the psychomotor aspects of cultural differences – the customs and social practices that we need to observe. However, what is apparently accorded less importance is how culture affects the other two domains – the affective and the cognitive, or the emotions attached to working practices and the associated learning processes.

For example, consider Maslow's hierarchy of needs. This idea has been around since the 1950s and has been so well accepted that anyone with any exposure to psychology will have heard about it and will know how it defines a human condition. Or does it? In fact, Maslow's observations were based on high-achieving European Americans of the 1950s, who subscribed to a culture in which self-actualization was arguably a duty. But does this mean that it can apply to every culture in the world? The publicity machine supporting Maslow's theory would have us believe so (although, in fairness, Maslow himself never made such claims for the hierarchy). However, as a result, management texts repeat time and time again that to get the most out of a worker you need to do things that will help them move towards self-actualization. This may possibly be wrong.

If the executive were to dig a little deeper they would find a significant body of knowledge filed under the heading 'cross-cultural psychology' that explores affective and cognitive differences between people across the globe. Within this realm of knowledge we explore questions such as:

- Why do people in some countries make decisions after discussions with others, while in other countries one person takes full responsibility?
- Why, when they are paid more, do people in some countries work harder, while in others they decide to take more time off?

This book aims to bring together these disciplines to provide some answers to the question of how cultural differences affect people's performance in the workplace. This alone would make for an interesting textbook. But, being a practical rather than an academic sort of person, I want this to be a book that a manager working in a global organization would find useful, so to this end it introduces a third dimension: a practical process you can follow to analyse perceived problems in the workplace and find some solutions. Again, there is a healthy body of literature on this subject, but this is almost exclusively Western in origin, and so the problems described and the solutions prescribed heavily reflect prevailing Western culture. This era of globalization seems to offer an appropriate opportunity to draw on this impressive resource in order to explore its implications in the wider world.

What Does This Book Contain?

So, this book attempts to bring together several strands of management-related knowledge and advice.

First, it looks at ways in which you can analyse what is going on in your workplace so that you can come up with some potential ways of improving performance. Second, it provides some explanation about how we can look at the workplace from different cultural perspectives. And, third, it gives you a methodology that you can use to work through a problem in order to find solutions. It therefore aims to be both a source of information and practical guidance, hence its division into two parts: Part 1, 'The Theory', and Part 2, 'The Practice'.

Part 1 looks at the ideas lying behind the cultural analysis of problems. It draws on the work of cross-cultural psychologists in classifying cultural differences, the thoughts of performance engineers who have examined what affects performance in the workplace and then systems thinkers, who have shown the value of adopting holistic approaches to looking at how organizations function.

In Part 2 we work through a seven-step process for solving problems. If you have read problem-solving books in the past, you may well recognize the process, as it is common to various different approaches that have been described in that literature. However, here we apply it specifically to workplace performance problems.

What about the individual chapters?

CHAPTER 1 – HOW DO CULTURES DIFFER?

In Chapter 1 we look at how the cross-cultural psychologists have picked cultural differences apart and classified them. This is a very academic chapter, as it examines the work done by many different people and synthesizes their individual contributions in order to provide a useful starting-point for the subsequent analysis of how culture and performance are related.

These cross-cultural psychologists have dissected the peoples of the world in many different ways, some of which are of more relevance to the workplace than others. As in so many disciplines of this kind there are strong and healthy disagreements between many of the leading lights in the subject as to the validity of particular ideas, and it is not my intention here to discuss these subjects in sufficient detail to be able to recommend one set of cultural indicators at the expense of another. What I have done instead is select those indicators that are of most interest and value and look at how they can be applied to finding solutions to performance problems.

One of the most important arguments within cross-cultural psychology relates to what is academically referred to as the 'ecological fallacy' or, in plain language, stereotyping. So, for example one of the leading writers in the field, Richard Lewis, states: 'At business meetings, the British are rather formal at first, using first names only after two or three encounters' (Lewis, 2006, p. 197). But, as Lewis himself stresses, this does not mean that every single British businessperson will behave in this way: it is simply a useful generalization. It is also important to remember that such behaviour is not cast in stone for all time. Customs change, and it is probably true to say, at least from my own experience, that British businesspeople are becoming more informal as the years go by.

It is also a personal disappointment that the great majority of cross-cultural studies have compared North American (and, to a lesser extent, Western European) cultures with those of the East, particularly China and Japan. There are obvious economic reasons why this has happened, but it has been to the detriment of looking at the cultural perspectives of people from other regions of the world, particularly those from Africa and Latin America. Discussions and examples in this book therefore tend to focus on the North America/China and Japan comparison, and, in the interests of trying to maintain some level of academic rigour, I have avoided adding too many of my own anecdotal experiences, which focus on African cultures. So, my apologies to anyone who feels ignored.

What is the significance of this as far as this book is concerned? Well, what it means is that I will not be providing exact prescriptions for how to solve workplace problems involving particular nationalities. What I will be aiming to do is to give you ideas about the questions you need to ask so that you can develop some understanding about how someone from another culture may view a particular situation.

CHAPTER 2 – ANALYSING PERFORMANCE

This chapter draws heavily on the work of Thomas Gilbert, Robert Mager and Peter Pipe. Gilbert put forward the idea that people's performance in the workplace was affected by three main factors:

1. the provision and their understanding of information related to their performance;
2. the suitability of the tools and equipment provided for doing the work and their capacity to use these;
3. the desire to do a good job, which relates to the connection between what motivates people and the incentives offered for doing the job properly.

Mager and Pipe developed a simple flowchart that allows us to step through the process of analysing information, equipment and desire in order to draw up a list of the root causes of a performance problem.

In this chapter we look at how the cultural differences are described in Chapter 1 relate to the different factors that can affect performance in a culturally diverse workplace.

CHAPTER 3 – CULTURE AND WORKPLACE ACTIVITIES

Chapter 3 builds on the ideas outlined in the first two chapters and sees how cultural differences can affect every day workplace activities such as negotiation, decision-making, team-working and leadership. It also considers the special case of the new expatriate – someone who arrives to start work in a different cultural environment – and touches on the implications of cultural diversity on performance management processes.

This chapter will help you identify the problems that can arise when different cultures work together, but also provides some suggestions for how managers can take steps to minimize such problems and use the strengths of cultural diversity to develop a more effective and stimulating working environment.

CHAPTER 4 – THE SYSTEMS APPROACH

In 1990 Peter Senge published his bestselling management text, *The Fifth Discipline*. In it he talked about four different activities that organizations needed to support in order to bring about the reality of 'the learning organization'. After describing the need to encourage personal mastery, expand mental models, develop shared visions and promote team learning, he then went on to say that the fifth discipline – the one that pulled these all together – was to think about organizations as if they were systems, entities which operated as a series of interconnected causal links that created feedback mechanisms.

Senge maintained that, by doing this, we could develop much deeper understandings about how organizations operated and what factors contributed to or prevented their growth.

Systems thinking makes use of various diagramming techniques in order to help us understand how the system operates, and these techniques are used extensively in Part 2 of the book where we see how to find solutions to performance problems.

CHAPTER 5
– SOLVING
WORKPLACE
PROBLEMS

Chapter 5 brings the theory part of the book to a close. It outlines the seven-step problem-solving methodology that will be used in Part 2. It also looks at why we often find solving problems so difficult. There are various obstacles that can prevent us finding really effective solutions to problems that occur. These include:

- *Environmental obstacles.* We do not have enough time or other resources to spend looking at the problem. As a result, we tend to implement partial solutions or solutions that do not deal with root causes, which consequently prove to be ineffectual in the longer term.
- *Intellectual obstacles.* Because problem-solving is seldom taught as an academic discipline in the educational system, many people simply do not have the mental tools for picking problems apart. The complexity of organizational problems can therefore seem far too difficult for us to comprehend, and we respond by picking off something around the edges that we think we can deal with – again, failing to deal with the root causes.
- *Physiological obstacles.* For good evolutionary reasons our brains like to give us emotionally-based solutions for solving problems in addition to those that we might identify through a rational thinking process. This means that our previous experiences of dealing with such problems can lead us to select the wrong solution for a particular problem.
- *Cultural obstacles.* Different cultural perspectives cause people to see problems in different ways. They may pick out different aspects of the problem and its context or they may have different attitudes to how and whether problems can be solved.

CHAPTER 6 –
STEP 1: DEFINE
THE PROBLEM

This is the first chapter in the 'practice' section of the book. It looks at what you need to do in order to define a problem and stresses the importance of developing a number of different problem statements – simple sentences that describe what the problem is. This is an essential part of the problem-solving process for a number of reasons:

- Forcing ourselves to define and redefine a problem in a number of different ways starts the process of opening up our understanding about what is happening.

- Different definitions of the problem tend to lead us towards different sets of solutions.
- Developing alternative problem statements makes it much easier for us to introduce different cultural perspectives into the problem-solving process.

CHAPTER 7 – STEP 2: COLLECT DATA

You cannot solve a problem without gathering information about what is happening, and this chapter looks at what kinds of information you need to collect. This information is based on three crucial questions:

- Who is involved?
- What is happening at the moment?
- What should be happening?

CHAPTER 8 – STEP 3: ANALYSE THE PROBLEM

In many ways this is the most important part of the problem-solving process, as this is where you need to think carefully about the potentially numerous different factors affecting the performance you are examining and identify which of these are having a negative effect. This step is sometimes described as root cause analysis, and in this chapter you will learn how to use various systems thinking tools to dissect a problem and identify its root causes.

CHAPTER 9 – STEP 4: GENERATE IDEAS

Having pulled the problem apart you should have a good understanding of the root causes. You can then turn your attention to thinking about what steps you can take to eliminate or counteract them.

A key action here is to consider as many ideas as possible, so this chapter explains how to use techniques such as brainstorming and the performance flowchart to generate long lists of potential solutions.

CHAPTER 10 – STEP 5: SELECT SOLUTIONS

Picking up your long list of solutions from Step 4, you now need to think about what implications each might have, so that you can compare them in terms of such things as cost–benefit, acceptability and effectiveness.

Because at this stage you may need to compare many various types of solution, it is important to follow some rational methods for making comparisons. This chapter looks at some useful techniques for choosing the most appropriate solution.

CHAPTER 11 – STEP 6: IMPLEMENT SOLUTIONS

Once you have decided what solutions you want to implement you have to decide how to do this. This chapter explains that you need to take into consideration:

- the organizational culture, so that you can think about what obstacles might present themselves as you try to change the way things are done
- national cultural differences, and how these can affect change management processes.

CHAPTER 12 –
STEP 7: EVALUATE
SOLUTIONS

In this, the final, chapter we look briefly at how to evaluate whether or not your solutions have been effective. The key to doing this is to look back to your initial analysis where you should have developed some estimates of the seriousness of the problem.

How to Use This Book

The best way to use this book depends on your particular needs and circumstances. If you want to develop your knowledge of both cross-cultural issues and performance engineering, I hope that reading through from beginning to end will prove logical. You will find out about differences between cultures, then look at how to analyse performance problems and go on to see how these two areas can be brought together. The remainder of the book moves on to consider the problem-solving process, which shows how to apply these areas of knowledge. However, if you are more interested in the problem-solving process, you might want to concentrate on Part 2 and dip back into Part 1 as and when you need to clarify some particular concept.

In Conclusion

This book is an attempt to weave together creative and systematic approaches to identifying and solving problems that involve culturally diverse teams. It has been my intention throughout to avoid giving prescriptive instructions on how to do this, but instead to offer different ideas that can be used to explore different perspectives on a problem.

If in the process it helps us all, as an international community, understand each other a little better, it will have achieved far more.

The Theory

1 *How Do Cultures Differ?*

KEY POINTS

- How an individual behaves is determined by the relationship between their personality, human nature and their culture.

- Culture is a pattern of behaviour shown by a particular group that is manifested by surface behaviour and values and driven by a particular perception of the world.

- Culture is not static and evolves over time.

- Cultures can be analysed and compared in a number of different ways.

What is Culture?

The starting-point in our journey to explore how cultural values and beliefs affect performance in the workplace is to look carefully at how cultures differ. A considerable amount of research has been done since the 1960s into this subject, and the purpose of this chapter is to consider some of the key ideas that have been put forward.

First, the word 'culture' itself. It can be defined in many different ways, but in this book we use it to mean a pattern of behaviour shown by a particular group. Other writers have defined it in different ways – for example, as 'collective programming of the mind that distinguishes the members of one group or category of people from others' (Hofstede, 2005, p. 4) or as a 'functional blueprint for a group's behaviour' (Klein, 2000, p. 4). This programming is the result of growing up within a society and learning that certain ways of behaving are accepted and so strengthen your position within that society, whereas other behaviours may be unacceptable and lead to exclusion. However we define it, it is a physical manifestation of a group's values, and so to understand the significance of culture within the workplace we will have to consider the values held by people in the group.

It is important to remember that culture has two dimensions: *space* and *time*. The space dimension is obvious. People associated with a particular geographical area tend to have their own culture – for example, the Belgian, the

British or the Brazilian. Of course, within these there will be many subcultures of regions, towns, districts within towns and a myriad other affiliations, such as gender, social class, religious, corporate and generational. Each of these may display its own cultural manifestations, although each will almost certainly be recognizable as part of the overall national culture. As far as cultural differences associated with gender are concerned, Nisbett asserts, '... females of both cultures [Western and Eastern] tend to be more holistic in their orientation than males, but we find this only about half the time, and the gender differences are always smaller than the cultural differences' (Nisbett, 2003, p. 100).

What is less obvious is that culture is dynamic; it changes with time. Although this may not be obvious at a single point in time, when we think back to our childhoods we can see that the past was indeed a different country – we did things differently then. Culture changes everywhere with time, but at a different rate. For example, the changes in Western European countries over the last 20 years are dwarfed by the cultural changes that are taking place within China as its economy opens up and rapidly grows. While this is an example of cultural change being driven by political pressures, social and environmental factors can also play a part, through, for example, such things as opening up education to more people or climate change leading to different agricultural patterns or mass migration.

THE PROBLEMS OF CULTURAL STEREOTYPING

Variations across space and time mean that we must be very careful to avoid inappropriate *stereotyping* – for example, believing that all Japanese eat raw fish or that all Russians drink vodka. To some extent, stereotyping is inevitable and helpful, as it allows us to reduce the complexities of different cultures to a simple set of ideas that we can manage. It also creates an *in-group* (to which we belong) and an *out-group* (to which the others belong). This increases our feelings of self-worth and creates a separate group that we can use for scapegoating purposes.

The big problem with stereotyping is that it tends to be self-reinforcing. When we meet someone who conforms to the cultural or racial stereotype that we hold of their group it strengthens that stereotyped image, whereas when we meet someone who contradicts their stereotype we often dismiss them as exceptions rather than using their existence to modify our stereotyped image of them. Dealing with our stereotyped images is an application of emotional intelligence: when we meet someone and label them with the qualities of a stereotype we hold, we need to be able to recognize exactly what we are doing and then review the assumptions we have made on the basis of that stereotype.

Adler (2008) suggests that there are five things we need to do in order to make sure that a stereotype is a help rather than a hindrance:

- Acknowledge to ourselves that we are thinking of a stereotype, so that we know we are holding in our minds an image of a group rather than of an individual.
- Make the stereotype descriptive rather than judgemental, so that the stereotype says something about what that group does, rather than that this characteristic is good or bad.
- Make the stereotype the first best guess about this group, based on limited, existing knowledge.
- Be prepared to modify our stereotype as we find out more about the group and its values and norms.
- Make the stereotype accurate and as good a description as possible of the group.

THE VALUE OF WEARING CULTURAL GLASSES

Given that there are great differences within all cultures, stereotyping is a simplification, and assuming that the Japanese person in your team will behave in the same way as all Japanese do would be a big mistake. For this reason, in this book I have tried to avoid, where possible, labelling people from certain countries as having particular characteristics.

Instead, reflect on the stereotype and consider how a person might view a situation, given that they might have a particular mental programming. This is the notion behind *Kulturbrille*, or 'cultural glasses' as described by Ichheiser (1970) when writing about how we, as individuals, perceive other people. What you need to do, as a manager grappling with performance problems involving culturally diverse teams, is to put on your own pair of cultural glasses and think about how the situation looks from a different cultural perspective. This is crucial because, as explained in Chapter 6, the first stage in defining a performance problem is writing the problem statement, and if you fail to define your problem correctly, you will find it very difficult to identify effective solutions. Chapter 6 explains how important it is to define a problem statement in different ways in an attempt to capture different perspectives. So when doing this, wear your cultural glasses.

Failing to wear cultural glasses makes it very easy to misunderstand situations. Some nationalities frequently fall into this trap. These are mainly the big economic powers, whose past influence has led them to assume that they do not really need to take much account of others' differences. So, for example, Great Britain and France still find it difficult to recognize that the age of Empire is over, and the United States and Japan can be sensitive to cultural differences because of their self-sufficient and island backgrounds respectively. Conversely, smaller countries that have long been used to having to take account of the big powers in their commercial dealings have always had a tradition of cultural adaptability.

> About ten people worked in an open plan office. They were all white British with the exception of Sanjay, whose family originally came from India. The white British members of the team developed a jokey team culture, with a lot of teasing and a certain amount of swearing. Sanjay did not join in with this. As a result, the rest of the team decided that he was unfriendly and aloof and excluded him from general conversations within the office.
>
> Two cultural systems were at work here, the white British culture where teasing, swearing and banter was an important way of establishing a group identity, and Sanjay's, which was quite different.
>
> As a result of his upbringing he felt uncomfortable with the type of behaviour that the rest of the team demonstrated. This had nothing to do with how friendly he was, but the limited cultural perspective of the other team members interpreted his behaviour as being just that.

Because we regard our own culture as completely normal and unremarkable and other people as different, we can find it easy to almost assume that we ourselves have no culture. I can certainly remember how shocked I felt at seeing, really for the first time, what British culture was like when I returned home after spending two years working in the Sudan. As that was the first time that I had spent any extended period of time in another culture, I had never previously had the chance to reflect on the fact that other people might have different beliefs and values. This is a major reason why people who have had multicultural experiences early in their lives, perhaps because they have parents from different cultures or because of travel opportunities, generally find it easier to operate in culturally diverse teams.

Certain cultures are more prone to this than others. Living on an island made it less likely in previous times that British people would meet people from other cultures, with the result that they were perceived by others as being 'insular'. The sheer size and diversity of the United States means that it can provide holiday destinations of all types, so many Americans have never travelled abroad: in 2002, according to *The Guardian* (Travel section, Saturday 24 August 2002) only 22 per cent of American citizens had a passport, implying that 78 per cent of its citizens probably had very limited experience of what it might be like to be something other than American.

A lack of cultural self-awareness can have various effects. It might make us feel that people from outside our in-group are completely different to us and so are inferior. Extreme examples of this are the dehumanization of African peoples during the heyday of the European-controlled triangular slave trade and the Nazi slaughter of Jewish people during the 1930s and 1940s.

A lack of awareness of their own culture also makes people more likely to project their own beliefs and values on to others. When we meet someone for the first time their life will be a complete blank to us, so, in order to develop some sort of understanding, we fill in the blanks with our own personality, beliefs and values. This leads us to assume that they have the same drives and interests as us. So, for example, when negotiating with someone about some aspect of work, we might assume that they want exactly the same as us, which could lead us to adopt a very competitive approach to the discussion or, conversely, be disappointed that they show little interest in getting to know us better as a person.

Culture, Personality and Emotion

Let us now take a closer look at what we mean by 'culture'. Any individual person's behaviour can be regarded as resulting from three contributory factors: human nature, personality and culture (see Figure 1.1).

Emotion includes the basic human emotions that everyone is genetically programmed to display, such as anger, happiness, sadness, surprise or fear. We sometimes call these 'human nature' to distinguish them as something fundamental to a person's existence. They are factors that ultimately enable us to function as human beings and play our part in furthering the species.

Personality covers those traits that are unique to any particular person, and are a mixture of genetic and learnt features. Many psychologists talk about personality as having five key dimensions (sometimes called the 'Big Five'). Often referred to using one of the mnemonics CANOE or OCEAN, they are:

- **O**penness, appreciation of new things, curiosity, and so on,
- **C**onscientiousness, self-discipline,
- **E**xtraversion, energy and seeking company,

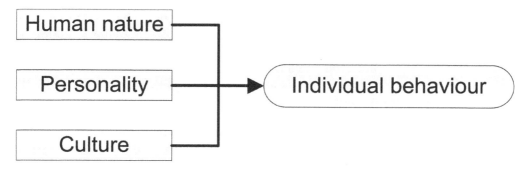

Figure 1.1   The three contributors to human behaviour

- **A**greeableness, being cooperative and compassionate,
- **N**euroticism, level of emotional stability.

The Big Five are reliably found when looked for in Western populations. However, Yang and Bond (1990) reported some differences in Chinese, Korean and Japanese populations. Testing showed that extraversion, neuroticism and conscientiousness were present, but they also identified a fourth factor that they translated into English as 'maintenance of interpersonal and inner harmony'. If Eastern cultures show personality differences, then what about African or Latin American cultures?

Culture, as we have defined it, is the pattern of behaviour shown by the group to which the individual belongs, and which the individual will, to a greater or lesser extent, also display. The group then accepts and protects individuals who conform to this pattern.

Clearly culture, personality and human nature are intimately connected, and where one ends and the other begins is unclear. A mistake made by much management theorizing is that every aspect of an individual's behaviour within an organization can be explained in terms of human nature. For example, motivation is often considered within Western management literature as a manifestation of human nature, implying that all human beings are motivated by the same factors, although, as we shall see in Chapter 3, this is not the case.

Looking more closely at culture itself, we can identify three constituents: surface behaviour, values and perception (see Figure 1.2).

Surface behaviour refers to the most obvious physical manifestations of culture: greetings exchanged, attitudes towards punctuality, expressions of emotion and so on – in other words, those aspects that both delight and frustrate the tourist. This is the level at which much acculturation training is delivered, and it has value in preventing, or at least reducing, the chances of the international businessperson committing a social faux pas. There is a considerable amount of information available about this level of culture, and I would certainly recommend Richard Lewis's excellent book, *When Cultures Collide: Leading Across Cultures* (2006), as a useful and often amusing summary of international behaviours.

But even a detailed understanding of this behaviour is of little value to the international manager trying to understand why their team is not functioning as it should. For example, Lewis advises that when working with people from Arab cultures, you should show an interest in Islam, show respect, come across as sincere and be personal, amongst other things. But if you are a European working on a project team with Arabs, and you find that important project communications are not being made, what do you do? Show more respect? Be more sincere? Be more personal?

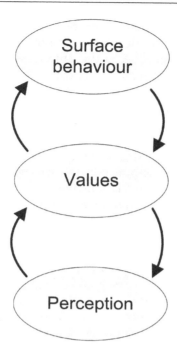

Figure 1.2   The constituents of culture

No, to do this we need to look deeper into the level of *values*, the principles, held by a group (and not wishing to give the wrong impression about Lewis's book, it does also do this). What is important? What is good? What is bad? A considerable amount of research has been done into this, and useful fruits of these studies are covered in subsequent chapters.

Now consider the mental process of *perception* – how individuals and the groups to which they belong to see the world around them. We might, on first reflection, think, 'Well eyes are eyes surely, and everyone must see the same thing when they look at a particular scene', In fact, what we are conscious of seeing is determined by processing within the brain, and what we are aware of depends on what is important to us as a human being. For example, Nisbett (2005) describes an experiment in which American and Japanese students were both shown the same animated sequences with distinctive, coloured fish moving through aquarium-like scenes containing pebbles, weed and smaller less distinctive fish. The students were then asked to describe what they remembered seeing. Both groups of students referred to the focal fish, but the Japanese students made much more reference to the background objects as well. In a second experiment individual fish and objects from the original scenes and completely new objects were shown to the two groups of students, sometimes with backgrounds from the original scenes and sometimes with new backgrounds. When asked if they had seen these objects before, the American students were able to decide whether or not they had seen them, irrespective of the background to the objects, whereas the Japanese students were much better at doing this if the objects were shown with the same background as before. What these experiments suggest is that the Japanese students paid much more attention to the context and environment of the focal fish than the Americans, who registered them separately.

Ultimately, this visual perception is the most important level because it underpins both values and surface behaviour. In fact, as in Figure 1.2, the relationships between these three elements can be represented as two feedback loops.

So how might these feedback mechanisms work? Well, in our early years we interact with the world around us and work out which behaviours are approved of and which are discouraged. This creates our value system, so that we perceive the world increasingly through a filter, paying more attention to those features that affirm these values. This is an example of *confirmation bias*, a term that we will return to several times in this book. It describes how we pay more attention to things that we accept, like or understand than to those things that we do not, and is an important concept that applies to how we interact with people from other cultures and decision-making, amongst other things.

There are many theories about how children develop psychologically, and one way of categorizing them is by how they treat a child's relationship with other people. Some (for example, Freudian theories) see child development as having an internal *intra*personal focus, where children are isolated individuals struggling against others to establish themselves. Other, such as 'symbolic-interactivist' and 'mediationist' theories, have a more *inter*personal focus, stressing the importance of a child's interactions with its environment, as it is only through these that the child can come to know itself. These contrasting ideas tie in closely with the distinctions discussed later between individualist and collectivist cultures.

Within the second feedback loop our values influence our behaviour. If we live in a society in which it is important to keep close contact with people and to know how they are and what they are doing, then our social rituals become elaborate and lengthy. For example, Arab culture has developed in a part of the world that is hot, dry and challenging to human life. To ensure people's survival, a rigid, collectively-oriented social code developed, with a mutual dependence within family groupings. Consequently, when meeting someone it is important to find out about not only their health, but also that of their close and extended family. Greetings between Arab people are therefore extensive, and the positive feedback generated by warm handshakes and discussions about family health confirms to each individual that this is the right thing to do, reinforcing the significance of these rituals in the value system.

How Cultural Values Have Been Categorized

Values are the standards held by a group of people that define what they consider to be good or bad, useful or not useful and important or insignificant, for example. Values directly influence behaviour, so an analysis of a society's set of values will give us a good indication of how individual members are likely to behave in any particular situation. But, mindful of the dangers of stereotyping, we must remember that not every individual will share the values of the society to which they belong: there will always be people who criticize, or even reject, their own society's values.

Cultural values are fundamental within a workplace because they define the terms of the psychological contracts that an employee holds with the organization. Unlike formal contracts of employment, psychological contracts are unwritten, often unarticulated and usually only exist as assumptions. In a culturally homogeneous setting, assumptions are generally understood and shared, so the psychological contracts in play may be relatively clear: rewards are dependent on how well you do, the employee expects to stay in the organization for many years or for just a few years, the corporate ethos reflects the ethos of that particular society, and so on. However, in a culturally diverse workforce people may have very different expectations of the psychological contract. For example, in some cultures an organization may reward people because of their family connections rather than on the basis of their performance, or, in the case of transnational corporations, the overall corporate ethos is very different to that of the host nation.

In recent times cross-cultural psychologists have extensively dissected and categorized aspects of culture. They have identified a wide range of indicators (or syndromes) that have varying degrees of usefulness to managers. Table 1.1 summarizes many of the key indicators identified, along with the name of the associated writer and a brief explanation of what the indicator means. These indicators are discussed in more detail below.

Before looking at any of these in more detail, we should acknowledge some practical and moral difficulties with these indicators.

First, there can be a significant overlap between indicators: for example, ascription is generally an important characteristic of collectivist cultures, whereas individualist cultures tend to place more value on achievement. There are also arguments within

Table 1.1   Key cultural indicators

Indicator	Characteristics	Writer
Value orientation	Varying degrees of importance attached to basic human concerns	Kluckhohn and Strodtbeck
Individualism–collectivism	Degree to which people within a culture see themselves as expecting to act independently of others or as being interdependent with other members of a group	Hofstede, Triandis
Power distance	Degree to which the less powerful in a culture accept the unequal distribution of power	Hofstede
Uncertainty avoidance	Relative level of anxiety induced by uncertainty	Hofstede
Work–life balance	Relative importance attached to career and material success or quality of life (originally labelled by Hofstede as masculinity–femininity)	Hofstede
Long-term orientation	Relative importance attached to the past, present and future	Hofstede
Universalism and particularism	Degree to which behaviour is based on universally accepted rules or determined by particular situations	Trompenaars
Affective and neutral	Acceptability of displaying emotions	Trompenaars
Specific and diffuse	Degree to which individuals within cultures compartmentalize different aspects of their lives	Trompenaars
Achievement versus ascription	Relative importance attached to individual achievement as opposed to that granted by their status or social or family connections	Trompenaars
Reactive, linear- and multi-active	Embracing a number of factors including time, personal relationships and organization	Lewis

the field of cross-cultural psychology about which indicators are independent: for example, if two different indicators are always found to be significant in the same cultures, are they independent or simply different ways of labelling the same value?

There are also arguments about the validity of the methodologies that have been used to develop the indicators, and whether or not the indicators themselves reflect a Western cultural bias. Casmir (1997) observes that they come from the academic disciplines of anthropology and sociology and tend towards 'academic museum construction', in which cultures are classified somewhat like exhibits, rather than as living, breathing and evolving entities. He also comments that they tend to suggest that this is what people within a culture 'are' rather than describing how they behave.

By labelling people in this 'how they are' way we run the risk of being seen as 'orientalists', as described in Edward Said's acclaimed *Orientalism*, where he wrote that '... the notion that there are geographical spaces with indigenous, radically "different" inhabitants who can be defined on the basis of some religion, culture or racial essence proper to that geographical space is equally a highly debatable idea' (Said, 2003, p. 322). Said's key idea was that Western cultures see 'the Orient' as a homogeneous object that can be dissected, examined and classified so that we can make confident predictions about how the 'oriental mind' operates. If readers do see that in this book, I will have truly failed in my objectives.

It is also important to realize that while researchers have studied many societies and have located them on their different value grids, current data focus very much on economically significant societies. So, for example, there is a huge amount of information comparing North America with China and, to a lesser extent, Japan but very little about sub-Saharan Africa. With the exception of South Africa, the rest of this vast continent is typically generalized as 'West' or 'East'. My own experiences of working in the Gambia earlier in my career made me aware that cultural differences between this former British colony and the neighbouring, and almost wholly enclosing, former French colony of Senegal are extremely significant and, in many aspects of life, transcend ethnic group affinities, even though people are from the same ethnic group. As in many former colonial countries, the colonial masters imparted cultural values that remained long after the European flags were lowered for the last time.

While this factor must inevitably limit the usefulness of this particular publication, it should be remembered that its principal aim is to give managers wrestling with performance issues in a culturally diverse organization a set of cultural glasses that allow them to ask questions about what is happening in their workforce. Being unable to place an individual on any particular scale because they come from a country for which there are no data should not mean that this book has limited value.

Nevertheless, despite these philosophical debates about their validity, we will use a number of these indicators to help in our analysis of workplace performance and leave these other discussions to the academic world.

Value Orientation or 'What's Important to You?'

One of the earliest attempts to distinguish between values within cultures was made by the anthropologist Florence Kluckhohn in the 1960s. Her work (Kluckhohn and Strodtbeck, 1961) identified a number of dimensions that cultures have with regard to four (later increased to five) dimensions of everyday life. Within each of these dimensions she identified a number of possible attitudes.

Table 1.2 summarizes these dimensions.

Table 1.2   Summary of Kluckhohn's dimensions and attitudes

Dimensions	Attitudes		
Relationship to nature	*Subordinate*: Life determined by external forces; people cannot change nature	*In harmony*: We should live in balance and recognize interconnections	*Dominant*: We should challenge and control nature
Orientation to time	*Past*: Learn from history; keep traditions going	*Present*: Make the most of today; don't worry about tomorrow	*Future*: Plan for the future; sacrifices made today will pay off
Nature of humanity	*Evil*: People are intrinsically bad and need to be controlled	*Mixed*: People can be good or evil and can be changed	*Good*: People are basically good at heart
Social relations	*Hierarchical*: There is a natural order; leaders make decisions	*Collateral*: Best to work as a group, sharing decisions	*Individual*: Control over one's own destiny; one person one vote
Mode of activity	*Being*: Existence is all that is necessary; accomplishment is not essential	*Becoming*: Inner development is what is needed	*Doing*: Working hard should be rewarded; accomplishment is a measure of an individual's value

Source: Gallagher (2001) and Maznevski and Peterson (1997).

Gallagher quotes research looking at cultures within the United States (Table 1.3).

What are the possible implications in the workplace of holding different cultural values such as these? Table 1.4 illustrates some

Table 1.3 **Comparison of Euro-American and Native American values**

Euro-American culture	Native American cultures
(future-oriented)	(past-oriented)
• focused on doing • individualistic • believes in dominance over nature • thinks that some people are good and some bad	• focused on being • emphasize collateral relationships • believe in harmony with nature • think that people are fundamentally good

Source: Gallagher (2001).

possibilities to consider if you are working with people holding particular sets of values.

Kluckhohn's work was one of the earliest in the field of cross-cultural psychology, and since then other writers have taken her ideas and used them to develop other categorizations. For example, the social relations dimension connects closely to Hofstede's power distance index and the orientation to time links with Hofstede's long-term orientation, Lewis's linear-active dimensions and Trompenaars' distinction between sequential and synchronic cultures.

Individualism and Collectivism or 'What's in it for Me/Us?'

Individualism and collectivism refers to the degree to which members of a society see themselves as:

- individuals, who act by themselves for the benefit of themselves or their immediate family because links between individuals are loose, or
- collectivists, who see their membership of a group as being the most important factor influencing their behaviour, as loyalty to the group brings protection.

It is important to point out here that collectivists value membership of a specific group. In sociological terms this is usually described as the in-group. So, while they may have collectivist feelings for their local community, region or country as a whole, their first loyalty will be to that small group of people who they see as being in their in-group, which might be based on family or a tightly defined ethnic grouping. Their feelings towards other groups might be somewhat distant, to the extent that separate collectivist in-groups might be regarded as behaving in rather individualistic ways

Table 1.4   Value orientation and workplace implications

Dimension	Attitudes	Workplace implications
Relationship to nature	Subordinate	Need to do your best; if things go wrong it is due to external factors.
	In harmony	Relationships are important; always work to restore the balance. Take decisions to balance the needs of people and nature.
	Dominant	Threats are opportunities; if something is not working, change the rules or procedures. If people need something, change nature.
Orientation to time	Past	What has happened in the past will work now; if we have done it before we can do it again. Use tradition to guide activity.
	Present	Carry on doing things as we are; if things go wrong, sort it out then.
	Future	Never make changes without considering the implications; investments in the future are always worthwhile. Plan for the future, innovate and be flexible.
Nature of humanity	Evil	People need to be controlled; provide clear rules and firm management. People will not change, so take care to select the right person for the job.
	Mixed	Make sure you understand people; be flexible with your management style. Training is important.
	Good	People can be trusted; delegate; manage in a low-key style.
Social relations	Hierarchical	Make sure the chain of command is clear; centralize decision-making; strong leadership is important.
	Collateral	Promote consensual decision-making; team-working is important.
	Individual	Encourage individual achievement and initiative; each person is entitled to their own opinion.
Mode of activity	Being	Difficulties in communicating any need for change; target-setting probably ineffectual. People do just enough work to meet their needs.
	Becoming	Provide opportunities for development; encourage ambition.
	Doing	Look for and reward hard work; offer incentive schemes. Work is an end in itself.

towards each other. In a workplace setting it is therefore important to remember that if there are a number of people who all come from the same country and that country has a collectivist culture, they may not necessarily behave in 'classically' collectivist ways towards each other. For example, although West African culture is regarded as collectivist, it would be a mistake for a manager to assume that all West Africans will feel a strong sense of solidarity with each other.

Hofstede's studies led him to classify countries according to the categorization shown in Table 1.5. Note that this table summarizes a continuous spectrum ranging from highly individualist to highly collectivist, and that there is no single point at which a culture really tips from being one to the other.

Table 1.5   Individualist–collectivist classification of different countries

Highly collectivist to less collectivist	Moderately collectivist to less collectivist	Less individualist to moderately individualist	Individualist to highly individualist
Ecuador	Hong Kong	Spain	Italy
Panama	Malaysia	Slovakia	New Zealand
Venezuela	East Africa	Israel	Canada
Colombia	Bulgaria	Austria	(English)
Pakistan	Mexico	Czech Republic	Netherlands
Costa Rica	Philippines	Poland	Belgium
South Korea	Greece	South Africa	(Flemish)
Peru	Turkey	Switzerland	Hungary
Taiwan	Brazil	Germany	Great Britain
Vietnam	Arab countries	Ireland	Australia
West Africa	Russia	Norway	United States
China	Argentina	Sweden	
Bangladesh	Japan	France	
Chile	Morocco	Belgium	
	India	(French)	
		Canada (French)	

Source: Hofstede (2005).

Some writers (see, in particular, Triandis, 1995) also distinguish between vertical and horizontal aspects. Table 1.6 summarizes these differences.

Of course, societies do not entirely conform to any of these: they contain a blend of the four possibilities. In Table 1.7 Triandis (1995) hypothesizes what these might be for a number of countries.

If you study these lists you will see certain patterns. Most significantly, the 'West' (Western Europe and North America) is predominantly individualist while the 'East' and Latin America is predominantly collectivist. There are many possible reasons for this, but a key factor seems to be that increasing affluence

Table 1.6   Examples of vertical and horizontal individualism and collectivism

Indicator	Shown by
Horizontal collectivists stress social cohesion and the importance of a feeling of oneness with the group.	Chinese (of a traditional, Confucian persuasion)
Vertical collectivists stress the importance of serving the group, doing one's duty and accepting inequality as important.	India, Chinese (sympathizing with Communist Party reforms), Japan
Horizontal individualists, valuing the importance of one's own interests, but with no desire to appear different.	Sweden, Australia
Vertical individualists, valuing the importance of one's own interests, with a need to be seen as individuals and distinctive.	United States

Source: Triandis (1995).

Table 1.7   Possible importance of individualism and collectivism modes in different countries

Country	Horizontal individualism	Vertical individualism	Horizontal collectivism	Vertical collectivism
United States	40%	30%	20%	10%
Sweden	50%	20%	20%	10%
Great Britain	20%	50%	10%	20%
Germany	20%	40%	10%	30%
Japan	20%	5%	25%	50%

Source: Triandis (1995).

encourages a move away from collectivism. In low-income and agriculturally-based societies, membership of a group means that limited resources are shared, providing security. As affluence increases, societies tend to become more urban, geographically more mobile and increasingly reliant on wage income, which means that maintaining relationships with an in-group becomes harder and the security advantages become less important. Exposure to mass media promoting individual consumption fuels the change.

Barack Obama, writing as the then senator for Illinois, described this in his 2006 book, *The Audacity of Hope*:

> *Even within my own family, Michelle saw how suffocating the demands of family ties and tribal loyalties could be, with distant*

cousins constantly asking for favors, uncles and aunts showing up unannounced. On the flight back to Chicago, Michelle admitted she was looking forward to getting home. 'I never realized just how American I was,' she said. She hadn't realized just how free she was – or how much she cherished that freedom.

Obama, 2006, p. 54

This extract illustrates at a personal level the journey taken by families in just a few generations: Obama's father was Kenyan and thus familiar with collectivist patterns of living, but his son, having moved away to grow up in the individualist United States has perhaps taken on a completely different set of values. It is also interesting to reflect on the use of the word 'freedom': Obama uses it to describe Michelle's sense of relief at escaping from the commitment of the complex network of in-group commitments that she had experienced while in Kenya, but a different cultural perspective might regard the security of the collectivist in-group as providing *more* freedom than is offered by living in an individualist society in which one has to rely on one's own wits and abilities to hold on to a source of income, with no family or governmental safety net to fall back on if things go wrong.

Triandis (1995) sees the relative position of a culture on the individualist–collectivist spectrum as being related to two factors in particular – the relative degrees of:

• cultural tightness or looseness, and
• cultural complexity or simplicity.

In culturally tight societies there is an agreement about what constitutes acceptable behaviour: people behave in this way and expect (and generally receive) punishment or criticism if they deviate from the norm. This is often influenced by climate: in extremely hot or cold climates it is important to behave in precise ways in order to survive, whereas in temperate climates this is not so important. Collectivist cultures are culturally tight, as they have a set of norms that the in-group follows, whereas individualist cultures are culturally loose, accepting a much wider set of behaviours. This is brought into sharp focus by, for example, the difficulties experienced by minority ethnic groups in the United Kingdom persisting with their practice of arranged marriages when this conflicts with the culturally determined law of the land if such a marriage is non-consensual.

Triandis discusses the various ways in which cultural tightness and looseness is measured and comments that, in his opinion, the most reliable measure is the percentage of people in the population who are left-handed. In virtually all cultures left-handedness is the least desirable of the two possibilities, and culturally tight societies usually suppress it. He quotes a range of figures varying from 0.28 per cent in particularly tight societies ranging to 14 per cent where there is no pressure applied on handedness. Fellow left-handers reading this paragraph will, I am sure, remember this observation.

Cultural complexity is relatively simple to explain in that it correlates closely with gross national product: the more affluent the culture, the more complex it is. For example, within the United Kingdom there are tens of thousands of different job descriptions, whereas in a culture dominated by subsistence agriculture there would be merely tens of different occupations.

Collectivist cultures are, therefore, characterized by cultural tightness and simplicity, whereas individualist cultures are culturally loose and complex.

Collectivist cultures are what Hall described as 'high-context' cultures (Hall, 1976), meaning that much of what happens and matters is not made explicit. Because relationships are close, people have shared understandings about how things work and so do not need to discuss them. They also make more use of Bernstein's 'restricted code' communication (Bernstein, 1971), in which much of the information exchanged in everyday life is conveyed through non-verbal means, such as body language, reliance on assumptions and so on. People know what other people mean without anyone having to say very much. By contrast, individualist cultures are low-context, in which everything is much more explicit. In these cultures people use an 'elaborated code', in which language is clearer and more direct.

To illustrate the difference between restricted and elaborated code communications, consider these two ways in which a supervisor might give instructions to one of their team:

- In restricted code the supervisor says, 'Make sure you check that letter before it goes out', raising their eyebrows and looking directly at the team member until they make eye contact.
- In elaborated code the supervisor says, 'You will need to check through that document to make sure that everything is correct and that there are no spelling mistakes in it. Use the spellchecker', and immediately leaves.

In the restricted code communication, the manager and team member share the assumption about what is important within the document, and the non-verbal communication is used to convey the importance of doing it. The elaborated code version, on the other hand, contains much more explicit instructions about what needs to be done. Neither is essentially any better than the other: the key point concerns shared assumptions leading to different communication patterns. Problems only arise if people do not understand the same elements of the restricted code.

In practice every society employs both restricted and elaborated code communication, but in collectivist cultures restricted code predominates and vice versa. Difficulties may arise, however, when, say, someone from an individualist culture tries to operate in a group where much of the communication is done non-verbally, making the potential for misunderstandings and mistakes relatively high. For example, in British culture if someone says, 'Yes', they generally mean yes. However, in other cultures the meaning of the response is also determined from their tone of voice, how quickly they respond, body language, eye contact and so on. So it is quite possible for someone to say 'Yes' when they mean 'No', with the non-verbal parts of the communication relating that information.

Related to the distinction between individualism and collectivism is the idea that different cultures also vary as to whether they are oriented towards tasks or relationships (Laurent, 1983), which can perhaps be seen as the relative importance attached to form or function. In task-oriented cultures the emphasis is very much on function, on achieving work-related objectives, and the form must follow this. So, given a particular project, a task-oriented team will decide what needs to be achieved and will then decide what staff are needed and how they will be organized. If certain people are not needed, they are surplus to requirements and will be 'disposed of appropriately'. However, in relationship-oriented cultures form drives function. In such a culture a project would not be contemplated without considering the people who would be working on it and the roles they would all play. It can therefore be seen that there are strong parallels between individualism and task-orientation and collectivism and relationship-orientation.

A British local authority appointed a woman to be head of a particular department, with the remit to reorganize it so that it operated more efficiently. As part of the process, she had job descriptions rewritten and required everyone in the department to reapply for the now reduced number of jobs available. She then personally took part in the selection interviews.

One of the men in the department was married to someone who was in a women's group with the new head. He applied for one of the new positions but failed the interview and consequently lost his job. His wife felt that she had no alternative but to leave the women's group, and the tensions created by what had happened led to the group folding, even though it had been meeting for many years.

The new head's task-orientation had been so strong that she felt it to be essential that she personally conducted the interview that led to the redundancy, even though she could have declared a personal interest and stepped aside in this instance. This ultimately caused serious damage to her relationships.

It is also interesting to reflect on the possible connection between increasing individualism and rising mental ill-health. This is discussed at length in Oliver James's book *Affluenza*, in which he points out that the United States, the world's most individualist society, is also on the top of the league for mental disorders (as recorded by the World Health Organization's World Mental Health Survey, (Demyttenaere et al., 2004)). Several other countries that rate highly on individualism also figure highly in this league table. Comparing just 14 countries, including New Zealand (2nd), France (4th) and the Netherlands (7th), James (2007, p. xiii) defines 'affluenza' as 'the placing of a high value on money, possessions, appearances (physical and social) and fame', and he attributes to this to what he calls 'selfish capitalism' (ibid., p. xviii). The contrast between what motivates people in individualist and collectivist societies is discussed in more detail in Chapter 2, but it could certainly be argued that the relative importance attached to materialistic factors related to self-esteem are particularly important in cultures where 'selfish capitalism' is strong.

Gardner, in his groundbreaking thesis about multiple intelligences, discusses the distinction between individualism and collectivism at the level of the individual (Gardner, 1983). Within individualist cultures, mature adults reflect on what it is to be an individual human being, striving towards self-actualization. People are autonomous and focus on *intra*personal development – for example, in exploring their own identity and managing their personal 'emotional intelligence'. However, in collectivist cultures, people become more skilled in adapting to the environment within which they live. The 'sense of self' is more oriented towards recognizing those aspects of the self that contribute towards that environment, so *inter*personal intelligence and the skills needed to adapt to, and integrate with, others are more important.

So, according to Gardner, individualist cultures promote a different set of intelligences than do collectivist cultures. Individualist cultures encourage its members to 'know themselves better' by developing their intrapersonal intelligence. The low-context nature of individualist cultures means that explicit communication is more important so linguistic intelligence is promoted, and the importance of technology means that logical–mathematical intelligence is prized. In contrast, collectivist cultures encourage the development of interpersonal intelligence.

Eastern collectivism is strongly influenced by Confucianism, a set of rules for daily life developed by Kong Zi (Confucius) around 500 BC. Central to Confucian philosophy is the importance of preserving strong relationships between different parts of society. Confucius identified the key relationships as those between ruler and subject, father and son, husband and wife, elder and younger brother, and friend and friend. These relationships do show the importance of a hierarchy, but Confucius did not see this as being one of one-way dominance. In order to maintain the stability of the relationship there needed to be a recognition of mutual obligations, so, for example, as long as a subject showed loyalty to the ruler, the ruler would protect the subject, and so on.

IMPLICATIONS OF INDIVIDUALISM– COLLECTIVISM IN THE WORKPLACE

Attitudes to individualism and collectivism can have profound implications in a workplace setting. Collectivism, particularly when influenced by Confucianism, implies the need to respect older members of society, which inhibits the possibility of junior employees questioning the judgement of older members of staff in any way. Promotion criteria focus on age and loyalty rather than on individual ability. Decision-making is centralized and based on consensus rather than on debate (which would be seen as potentially threatening). Self-advancement is unacceptable, and a manager praising someone directly would make that person feel very uncomfortable as it would be seen as 'singling them out'. Instead, the manager should tell other people about someone's good work so that it passes on indirectly (Triandis, 1995). Western management theories encourage managers to praise good performance, but in a Confucian setting negative criticism is more effective as those receiving it feel that they are letting their group down and will work harder (Nisbett, 2003).

The tightness of collectivist cultures means that there is a greater reliance on rules and standards of behaviour, whereas people from an individualist background will be much more accepting of different behaviours. This phenomenon is explored in more detail later in this chapter under the heading 'Uncertainty Avoidance'.

Organizations operating within a collectivist culture tend to train their staff more thoroughly than they do in individualist cultures. This is all part of the exchange of mutual obligations: training increases levels of skill, but also increases loyalty to the organization. Training also transmits the organization's culture, strengthening the feeling of being part of the organizational in-group. By contrast, the lower level of employee loyalty in individualist cultures deters organizations from training, because of the fear that they will take their new skills to another employer that offers more incentives or inducements.

One important point to note about collectivist cultures is the definition of the group to which people owe their loyalty. While people will be closely committed to their own in-group they may display no commitment at all to other groups (who are, by definition, out-groups) and may act in distinctly individualist ways towards them. This was, of course, a phenomenon exploited by 'divide and rule' colonialist strategies, whereby the colonial power favoured one in-group and relied on them to exert control over the other groups in the society. It is therefore important to remember that, in a culturally diverse team, the fact that many members of the team come from collectivist cultures does not necessarily mean that they will operate together in a collectivist way. Of course, they might be more likely to embrace closer team-working relationships, but, on the other hand, they might display greater hostility, particularly if team members come from competing in-groups. This might particularly apply where team members are from cultures with a history of ethnic group rivalry, for example. Gabrenya's and Barba's work comparing how white English-speaking and Hispanic Americans approached group decision-making is interesting here (Gabrenya and Barba, 1987). Although the Hispanics were from a more collectivist-oriented culture the groups within which they were operating in the study consisted of strangers, and the processes they followed in order to come to a group decision were much less cooperative and harmonious than were those of the white English-speakers. The importance attached to harmonious relationships within the in-group did not extend to those from without it.

Power Distance or 'Who's in Charge Here?'

Power distance is a measure of a society's tolerance of its inequalities. Hofstede defines it as 'the extent to which the less powerful members of institutions and organizations within a country expect and accept that power is distributed unequally' (Hofstede, 2005, p. 46).

Hofstede's research indicates the ranking shown in Table 1.8. Countries are listed in descending order of Power Distance Index, where a high value shows a high acceptance of inequality. Note that this table indicates that the highest power distance is found in Malaysia and the lowest in Austria.

IMPLICATIONS OF POWER DISTANCE IN THE WORKPLACE

People from cultures that accept a high power distance find it much easier to accept rigid power structures and hierarchies, and organizations growing from such cultures tend to centralize power. Supervisors are highly respected and can inspire great loyalty. Hofstede describes the ideal manager as a 'benevolent autocrat', but it would be wrong to see this as akin to dictatorship. In most cases, the loyalty accorded to the boss is rewarded by a paternalistic, caring approach to employees. Trompenaars and Hampden-Turner (2004) describe this as 'servant leadership' in the East Asian context, where the employer gives employees more than they can repay so that they become indebted and compliant. High power distance cultures encourage more controlled, disciplined approaches to team-working. In high power distance cultures decision-making

Table 1.8   Relative power distance ratings for different countries

Low to lowest power distance	Moderately low power distance	Higher power distance	Highest power distance to lower
Hungary	Chile	Singapore	Malaysia
Jamaica	Belgium (Flemish)	Croatia	Slovakia
United States	Greece	Morocco	Philippines
Canada (all)	South Korea	Switzerland	Russia
Netherlands	Taiwan	(French)	Romania
Australia	Czech Republic	Brazil	Mexico
Germany	Spain	France	Venezuela
Great Britain	Pakistan	Poland	Arab countries
Norway	Canada (French)	Belgium	Bangladesh
Sweden	Japan	(French)	China
Ireland	Italy	Colombia	Indonesia
Switzerland	Argentina	Turkey	India
(German)	South Africa	East Africa	West Africa
New Zealand		Peru	
Denmark		Thailand	
Austria			

chains are very clearly defined, so if someone has a problem or a query, they will refer it to their immediate manager: approaching a different manager in another chain of command would be seen as tantamount to insubordination, and certainly as showing a complete lack of respect. The concept of matrix management would clearly be regarded with great suspicion in such cultures.

In low power distance cultures organizations tend to be more decentralized and have flatter management structures. Decision-making is more consultative, even though ultimately a supervisor will make the final decision. These are the cultures in which Western management concepts such as performance management, matrix and participative management can flourish. Individuals in low power distance organizations are encouraged to innovate and show initiative.

These differences suggest that organizations based in high and low power distance cultures may have their own particular competitive advantages. Nisbett (2003) has observed that low power distance cultures, such as the United States and Northern Europe, are good innovators (for example, in developing electronic technology) whereas Asian cultures, with high power distance beliefs, are very good at mass-producing electronic technologies to become household items.

There are clear parallels between the individualist–collectivist and power distance indicators, and the two do correlate strongly. Clearly, collectivist structures are more resilient because people accept their particular place in the hierarchy unquestioningly.

Uncertainty Avoidance or 'I Don't Like the Look of This'

Hofstede's next indicator is uncertainty avoidance, or how much a culture dislikes uncertainty. In cultures with a high uncertainty avoidance index there is a strong preference for predictability in everything. Table 1.9 shows Hofstede's evaluations of uncertainty avoidance for different countries. Uncertainty avoidance is the lowest in Singapore and highest in Greece.

IMPLICATIONS OF UNCERTAINTY AVOIDANCE IN THE WORKPLACE

People in high uncertainty avoidance cultures like rules and clarity. So, for example, in France lunch is served between 12 and 2 pm and not earlier or later; you know where you are with that. British tourists, with their happy tolerance of uncertainty, find such rules perplexing and frustrating. While such rules can help society function in normal circumstances, they can cause problems when the unexpected happens and the rules to be followed are inappropriate for dealing with the unexpected event. People with such values will also wait before taking action, hoping that more information will become available, reducing the uncertainty to a level at which they feel able to make the decision. These factors can create serious problems in military settings, particularly in multi-country deployments (Klein et al., 2000).

Senior managers in high- and low-rated cultures tend to focus on different things. In organizations comprising high uncertainty avoidance people, managers like to concentrate on operational aspects, which are comparatively well defined, whereas in low

Table 1.9   Relative uncertainty avoidance ratings for different countries

Lowest uncertainty avoidance to higher	Moderately low uncertainty avoidance to higher	Moderately high uncertainty avoidance to higher	High uncertainty avoidance to highest
Singapore	Australia	Switzerland	Chile
Denmark	East Africa	(French)	Argentina
Sweden	Netherlands	Pakistan	Peru
Vietnam	West Africa	Czech Republic	Romania
China	Switzerland	Italy	Serbia
Ireland	(German)	Venezuela	Japan
Great Britain	Finland	Brazil	Poland
India	Canada (French)	Columbia	Belgium (French)
United States	Bangladesh	Mexico	Russia
Canada (all)	Thailand	Hungary	Belgium (Flemish)
South Africa	Germany	Turkey	Uruguay
New Zealand	Morocco	South Korea	Guatemala
Norway	Arab countries	Spain	Portugal
	Taiwan	Panama	Greece
		France	

Source: Hofstede (2005).

uncertainty avoidance cultures senior managers enjoy strategic thinking, revelling in the uncertainty of it all. Similarly, high uncertainty avoidance organizations like to have lots of experts and specialists available, whereas low uncertainty avoidance culture organizations opt for generalists. With the French preference for high uncertainty avoidance, managers in French organizations are expected to have detailed, expert knowledge of the area for which they are responsible and would lose credibility if they were unable to answer task-related questions. By contrast, British organizations prefer to see managers as problem-solvers, using their generalist skills to organize other people's activities and seek out specialist help as needed.

It has also been suggested that high uncertainty avoidance cultures may feel less comfortable dealing with IT systems and automated processes, as the lack of other people around to provide reassurance or validation can create anxieties (Zakour, 2004).

Work–Life Balance or 'What's Important to Me?'

Hofstede's fourth indicator looks at the relative importance accorded within the society to such factors as assertiveness and importance of material wealth.

Hofstede labelled this indicator as masculinity–femininity, where masculinity is associated with being assertive and focusing on material success, and femininity with quality of life issues, such as relationships with other people and general social concern. However, some writers (for example, Adler 2008) have described the masculinity–femininity labelling as perhaps contentious, and possibly getting in the way of using the indicator as an analysis tool. Therefore, in this book we shall refer to Hofstede's masculinity as a preference for 'work success' and his femininity as one for 'quality of life'.

There are obvious similarities between this indicator and the individualist–collectivist dimension, but the work success–quality of life balance indicator is not connected with any particular in-group interdependence.

Hofstede's index ranks countries as shown in Table 1.10. The table summarizes a spectrum moving from Japan with the highest work success (masculinity) evaluation along to Sweden with the highest quality of life (femininity) evaluation.

IMPLICATIONS OF WORK–LIFE BALANCE PREFERENCES IN THE WORKPLACE

People in work success cultures feel more of a need to be the best and to compete. In business, disagreements are resolved by discussions leading to a winner and a loser, and meetings can be places where people use their power or abilities to get what they need. People like to be rewarded by more pay or more power, and jobs can be improved by making them more complex or challenging.

Table 1.10   Relative work success–quality of life ratings for different countries

High quality of life preference to highest	Moderate quality of life preference to higher	Moderate work success preference to lower	Highest work success preference to lower
Vietnam	Indonesia	Australia	Japan
South Korea	West Africa	Belgium	Hungary
Uruguay	Canada	(French)	Austria
Russia	(French)	New Zealand	Venezuela
Thailand	Taiwan	Switzerland	Switzerland
Portugal	Turkey	(French)	(German)
Chile	Belgium	Czech Republic	Italy
Costa Rica	(Flemish)	Greece	Ireland
Denmark	France	Argentina	China
Netherlands	Iran	India	Germany
Norway	Peru	Bangladesh	Great Britain
Sweden	Romania	Arab countries	Columbia
	Spain	Canada (all)	Poland
	East Africa	Luxembourg	South Africa
	Bulgaria	Pakistan	United States
	Croatia	Brazil	

Source: Hofstede (2005).

In quality of life cultures competitiveness is much lower, and conflicts are resolved by discussions leading to consensus or compromise. People work in order to survive and want to be rewarded by such things as more holidays and shorter working hours, rather than by more pay or power. Improving a job means providing more social contact and collaboration.

Long-term Orientation or 'How Long are We Prepared to Wait?'

Hofstede defines long-term orientation as 'the fostering of virtues oriented towards future rewards' (Hofstede, 2005, p. 210). In other words, people with a long-term orientation place more importance on things that will help them in the future than on those that will provide short-term gains.

Patience and perseverance are therefore important, as is being economical because you will not see the returns for some time. Collaboration with other people is important, so a long-term orientation is often associated with collectivism.

Table 1.11 shows Hofstede's long-term orientation ratings for a number of different countries. The table shows that Chinese culture has the highest long-term orientation and Pakistan the lowest.

Table 1.11 Relative long-term orientation ratings for different countries

Low long-term orientation to lowest	Moderately low long-term orientation to lower	Moderately high long-term orientation to lower	Highest long-term orientation to lower
New Zealand	France	Hungary	China
Portugal	Belgium	Denmark	Taiwan
United States	Italy	Netherlands	Japan
Great Britain	Sweden	Norway	Brazil
Canada	Australia	Ireland	India
Spain	Germany	Switzerland	Thailand
Nigeria	Canada (French)		
Pakistan			

Source: Hofstede (2005).

IMPLICATIONS OF LONG-TERM ORIENTATION IN THE WORKPLACE

Cultures with a low long-term orientation look for quick results, and social status issues are often important. Management styles focus on small isolated actions that can achieve easy results in the short term: the reductionist approach that this fosters can be seen in the style of popular management books that promote being a 'one-minute manager', adopting 'seven habits' or embracing '12 elements'.

Trompenaars (1993) links a culture's long- or short-term orientation to its overall attitude to time, as described by Kluckhohn's orientation to time dimension (Trompenaars 1993). He suggests that the culture of the United States is not very interested in what has happened in the past, but is keenly interested in the short-term future, with the long term being discounted as being subject to too many unforeseeable influences. The emphasis in management is therefore on short-term incentives, such as receiving immediate rewards for what you do. So, for example, if an investment banker pulls off a deal that brings in a multi-million dollar profit they immediately receive a bonus. However, as the economic crisis of 2008 has shown, the failure to think carefully about the 'unforeseeable influences' can lead to disaster in that the longer-term future does inevitably arrive.

That the future does always materialize sooner or later is recognized by the *scenario planning* approach to planning adopted nowadays by many organizations. Traditionally, organizations have planned by deciding what they want to achieve by some point in the future and to then work out the sequence of actions that are needed in order to achieve this. The weakness with this method is that it implicitly assumes that the organization will exist in the future, unaffected by the world around it. By contrast, an organization using the scenario planning approach develops a picture of what the world it operates in will look like at some point in the future and then decides how it would be most successful within that. Based on that picture it then develops a plan of action. Because the future is unknown, the organization would typically develop a number of scenarios and develop a plan that is hopefully robust enough to deal with whatever the future brings. Scenario planning therefore represents a technique that is more long-term-oriented and recognizes the causal connections between the past, present and future.

Universalism and Particularism or 'Rules are Rules, aren't They?'

The universalism–particularism indicator has been proposed by Trompenaars (1993). In universalist cultures behaviour is defined by rules accepted by everyone within society, whereas in particularist cultures behaviour in any situation is dictated by obligations.

Table 1.12 shows a classification of countries based on information provided in Trompenaars' *Riding the Waves of Culture* (1993). The table represents a continuous spectrum of countries ranging from Canada as the most universalist to Venezuela as the most particularist.

Table 1.12   Universalism and particularism for various countries

Moderately particularist to strongly so	Moderately particularist to more so	Moderately universalist to less so	Most universalist to less so
Singapore	United	Germany	Canada
Spain	Kingdom	Sweden	United States
China	Mexico	France	Australia
Russia	Thailand	Netherlands	Japan
Venezuela	Bulgaria		

The table shows that universalism is stronger in more developed societies, probably because their increased complexity makes it more important to have rules governing behaviour. Trompenaars observes that universalism is also more prevalent in Protestant societies.

IMPLICATIONS OF UNIVERSALISM AND PARTICULARISM IN THE WORKPLACE

The business world in universalist cultures is characterized by rules and contracts, which, from a particularist perspective, indicates a lack of trust within the society.

In the particularist business world, decisions take into account relationships with other people. So whereas decisions on awarding a contract in a universalist culture will be based on clearly defined rules about such things as cost or acceptability, and the name of the tendering organization would be kept secret from decision-makers, in a particularist culture the organization that is tendering will be vitally important. Universalists see this as potentially corrupt, but from the particularist perspective it means that the contract is awarded to someone who is trusted and known to be able to deliver, rather than to a stranger who may be cheap and able to write a good proposal but be completely unreliable.

The implication of this is that relationships are vitally important, and it can therefore take time to build these up and to acquire trust.

Affective and Neutralist or 'Public Displays of Emotion'

Trompenaars proposed an indicator rating the affective and neutral qualities of a culture. In an affective culture emotions are displayed openly, whereas in neutral cultures emotions are a private matter, not to be expressed publicly (although, of course, they may still be felt).

Table 1.13 shows how Trompenaars ranks a small number of countries on an affective–neutral scale, based on how people are prepared to show in the workplace that they are feeling upset.

Table 1.13   Ranking of countries on an affective–neutral scale

Affective	Italy
	France
	United States
	Singapore
	Hong Kong
Neutral	Netherlands
	Norway
	United Kingdom
	Indonesia
	Germany
	Japan

IMPLICATIONS OF AFFECTIVISM IN THE WORKPLACE

The most significant implications of such differences in the workplace are in how interpersonal understanding is affected. Neutral people can find it difficult to understand why an affective person is displaying such strong feelings about something, whereas affective people see neutralists as cold or reserved, or as having something to hide. These misunderstandings do not help effective team-working.

Specific and Diffuse or 'How Many Boxes in Your Life?'

Trompenaars' indicator of specific or diffuse refers to the degree to which cultures divide and protect different areas of their lives (Trompenaars, 1993). In specific cultures, people separate their working and personal lives: in the workplace they associate with colleagues and concentrate on work; when they go home they have a different set of friends. Privacy is also important, and people protect their personal space carefully.

In diffuse cultures, work and social lives overlap. Friends come into the workplace, and taking time out from work to deal with personal matters is perfectly acceptable. Personal space is less important. Good relationships are vital, both between supervisors and subordinates and with peers. Management tolerates this because they do it themselves and they know that it strengthens loyalty.

IMPLICATIONS OF SPECIFIC AND DIFFUSE IN THE WORKPLACE

Communication in diffuse cultures is high-context, with much information being exchanged through non-verbal signals and shared understandings. This can make life very difficult for someone from a specific culture, who is used to low-context communication where much more is made explicit. The ambiguity of high-context communication, while frustrating to someone from a specific culture, is welcomed in a diffuse workplace culture because it is seen as allowing people to use their judgement and initiative, rather than expecting them to simply follow orders. For example, consider the instructions given by a supervisor to their team member earlier in this chapter. Telling the team member to use the spellchecker could be seen as patronizing and insulting their intelligence in some cultures, while, in others, it would be a sensible thing to do.

Western concepts such as performance management or performance-related pay are unacceptable in diffuse cultures, because they relegate the importance of workplace relationships.

Elements of the specific–diffuse indicator relate to an indicator proposed by Lewis (2006): linear- or multi-active. Lewis bridges the specific–diffuse concept with that of orientation to time by pointing out that cultures differ in how they operate in time. Linear-active cultures are strong on planning and timetables and work sequentially, going from one task to the next (for example, work–home–work–home and so on) whereas in multi-active cultures work and personal life are inseparable and take place synchronously.

Achievement versus Ascription or 'What You Know or Who You Know'

Trompenaars (1993) says that in achievement-oriented societies people are rewarded for what they have done, whereas in ascription-oriented societies people are rewarded because of who they are, in terms of age, gender, social status, family relationship, ethnic group connection, for example.

Table 1.14 shows a ranking for achievement–ascription based on Trompenaars' information.

Table 1.14   Achievement and ascription for various countries

Strongly ascriptive (Strong to strongest)	Moderately ascriptive (Less strong to stronger)	Moderately achievement-oriented (Strong to less strong)	Strongly achievement-oriented (Strongest to less strong)
Russia	France	Sweden	United States
Argentina	Italy	Germany	Denmark
Egypt	Hong Kong	Mexico	Canada
Austria	China	Switzerland	Norway
Philippines	Spain	Finland	Australia
Bulgaria	Uruguay	Netherlands	United Kingdom
Thailand			

To a large extent, achievement-oriented societies have individualistic cultures and are also predominantly Protestant. Ascriptive societies are more collectivist in nature and many of them are Catholic, Buddhist or Hindu. Achievement and ascription can live happily together: low social mobility in Britain is in no small part due to high-achieving people who send their children through the private education system in the belief that having gone to the 'right school' accords useful status within British society, irrespective of ultimate educational achievement.

IMPLICATIONS OF ACHIEVEMENT AND ASCRIPTION IN THE WORKPLACE

David was a male manager in an Australian company and was transferred to his company's regional office in a Latin American country. His wife had worked as a personal assistant in the company in the past, but now worked as a housewife, looking after their small children.

When he arrived in his new office he decided to get together with his administrative and secretarial team to tell them about how he expected things to work. He spent five or ten minutes talking about how excited he was to be working in the new environment and how he wanted to develop a good team-working atmosphere. The talk went well, although he felt that there was a certain tension in the air.

When he had finished talking he asked if there were any questions. Silence. David asked again if there were any questions. Finally, one of the female secretaries nervously put her hand up and asked, 'Will your wife be coming to work here?'

It turned out that the office staff were expecting that a male manager would create a job for his wife, and that would threaten the position of the existing secretaries. Before David had arrived, the secretarial team had done the necessary detective work to find out about his wife, and so had added two and two together. However, Australian and Latin American mathematics were different.

From the achievement-oriented perspective ascription is hard to understand, but rewarding people on the basis of their status is a recognition of what they can do for the organization, rather than what they have achieved. So appointing someone because they are male or from the right social class simply reflects the realities in that culture.

This is difficult to accept for people with beliefs in equality of opportunity and individual human rights, but these are not necessarily understood globally in the same way. The current Western perception of human rights derives largely from the 1948 Universal Declaration of Human Rights, which can trace its ancestry through a largely Christian tradition, taking in Magna Carta, John Locke and the American Declaration of Independence (Freeman, 2005). However, other cultures with different religious traditions have alternative perspectives. Islam stresses the need for individuals to submit to Allah, and freedom is seen as surrendering oneself to divine will, so that only Allah has rights, not individual people (Dalacoura, 2005). The sanctity of the Koran as the word of Allah means that what it says cannot be challenged, which brings it into conflict with some precepts of the Universal Declaration – for example, in the case of the position of women. In the case of Confucianism, a central tenet is to reflect carefully about one's respect and concern for other people, so it has been argued that this notion of duty to others means that individual rights is not a necessary concept (Chan, 2005). It can also be argued that the liberality implied by the Western concept of human rights tolerates the existence of attitudes and lifestyles that would not be conducive to the practice of Confucian ethics. A final perspective comes from *ubuntu*, a code of ethics practised in varying forms through many parts of east, central and southern Africa. This criticizes Western human rights concepts as promoting individualism and neglecting the importance of the obligations that people owe to each other within a society (Murithi, 2005). Condemning ascription on the basis that it restricts human rights is therefore not as universally applicable as the Universal Declaration might suggest.

Ascription can also be criticized as a way of giving jobs to completely unsuitable people who just happen to be relatives or friends. However, in most cases, being appointed for what you can do because of your status does bring obligations, and people will work hard to maintain their status. Ascription does not necessarily equate to the creation of sinecures. For example, international organizations with offices in some countries sometimes find that their secretarial staff comprises a high percentage of wives of government officials. This is not necessarily because they are the best qualified at secretarial functions but because the country's internal networks help them to get appointed to what are seen as high-status jobs. From some perspectives this might be seen as poor management practice (and perhaps even corrupt), but a significant benefit to the organizations employing these wives is that it provides strong communications links to the host government, and so makes some aspects of their work easier to carry out than might otherwise be the case.

Different perspectives on achievement and description within teams can create problems. For example, a young person from an achievement-oriented culture can find it very difficult working with an older ascription-oriented person, and there is great potential for frustration and insult. On the other hand, if the culture within the team is ascriptive, it can be very difficult for someone of a lower status and hierarchical position to be involved in discussions about subjects on which they have technical expertise but not the appropriate status.

Also, because status in ascriptive cultures is so important, how a supervisor displays their status has an effect on how their subordinates can display their status. For example, imagine that a new manager from a country where status symbols are less important, or who personally is not interested in them, arrives to take charge of a team largely comprising people for whom displays of status are important. This manager decides, for environmental reasons, to have a small compact car as their company car. That would mean that the subordinates would have to make sure that their cars were even smaller, and if they were used to expensive German makes which made them look important, they could become extremely unhappy, which could have a significant impact on performance.

Achievement-oriented societies accord a great deal of importance to what a person has done in the past, and this creates a more open atmosphere for people of different levels in the hierarchy to express opinions and propose solutions. However, we should not have too rosy a view of this openness. It can still be difficult, and perhaps risky, for a junior employee to express an opinion that may be contrary to received wisdom – groupthink[1] strikes. The greater occupational mobility within individualist societies also means that people are more dispensable and anyone who is seen as a 'potential troublemaker' or 'dissident' may be unwanted.

Linear-active or Multi-active or 'How Many Things can I Do at Once?'

The distinction between linear-active and multi-active has been proposed by Lewis (2006). We looked at this idea earlier when considering Trompenaars' distinction between specific and diffuse

---

1   Groupthink: 'a mode of thinking that people engage in when they are deeply involved in a cohesive in-group, when the members' strivings for unanimity override their motivation to realistically appraise alternative courses of action' (Janis, 1972, p. 9).

cultures. However, while that categorization focuses on the social aspects of life, Lewis's idea approaches it from a time-oriented perspective. It therefore relates closely to what Trompenaars has described as the difference between sequential and synchronic approaches to time.

Lewis sees linear-active (sequential) cultures as those that concentrate on doing one thing at a time, whereas multi-active (synchronic) cultures carry on several different activities at the same time. Of course, each thinks that theirs is the most efficient.

Lewis's proposed ranking for linear-activity and multi-activity is shown in Table 1.15.

Table 1.15   Degrees of linear- or multi-activity for various countries

Strongly multi-active (Strong to strongest)	Moderately multi-active (Less strong to stronger)	Moderately linear-active (Strong to less strong)	Strongly linear-active (Strongest to less strong)
Spain	Slovenia	South Africa	Germany
Southern Italy	Croatia	Japan	Switzerland
Mediterranean	Hungary	Netherlands	Americans
countries	Northern Italy	Belgium	(European)
India	Chile	(Flemish)	Scandinavian
Pakistan	Russia and other	American	countries
Latin America	Slavic countries	subcultures	Austria
Arab world	Portugal	(Italian, Polish)	Britain
African countries	Pacific Islands	France	Canada
		Belgium	New Zealand
		(Walloon)	Australia
		Czech Republic	

IMPLICATIONS OF LINEAR- OR MULTI-ACTIVITY IN THE WORKPLACE

Linear-active people see time as sequential and as a commodity ('I can give you 30 minutes tomorrow'), whereas multi-active people are happy integrating different parts of their lives into the same periods of time. They can frustrate each other considerably: linear-active people may feel that multi-active people are not prioritizing or are not giving them enough respect, whereas multi-active people think that linear-active people are inflexible and one-dimensional.

Linear-active people are keenly interested in planning and in the detail of what is going to happen and when, whereas multi-active people take a more relaxed approach to planning, so that they are often more flexible at dealing with the unexpected.

These different ways of looking at how current time unfolds are also related to how people consider the relationship between the past, present and future. Cultures where the past is important will want to take this into consideration in developing plans for the future. Germans and Americans, for example, might take a very different approach to planning. Although both nationalities are linear-active, the Americans are much less interested in historical precedent and will be more interested in the short-term aspects of what the plan delivers than the Germans will be. An example of this, related to global security, occurred when, just a few days after the terrorist attacks of 11 September 2001, President Bush referred to 'This crusade, this war on terrorism ...' (reported by Jonathan Lyons, Reuters, 21 September, 2001). From the perspective of an American with little attachment to the past, planning for a crusade might seem perfectly reasonable, but the Islamic world with its very strong interest in the past, immediately interpreted the retaliatory action taken, starting with the invasion of Afghanistan in 2001 and continuing with that of Iraq in 2003, as yet another crusade by Christians against Muslims.

Reactivity

To complete this look at cultural categories, we shall briefly mention Lewis's description of reactive cultures – cultures in which people prefer to listen and react rather than initiate. As examples he cites China, Taiwan, Singapore, Korea, Turkey and Finland.

These cultures are generally introverted, patient, interested in general principles and the big picture, amongst other qualities. Their communication is high-context: whatever they say is surrounded by a considerable amount of perspective that may not be explicit.

Lewis suggests other ways in which reactive cultures manifest themselves, and these often echo other ways in which we have described cultural differences. For example, reactive cultures are:

- people-oriented, as in cultures that prefer quality of life to material wealth;
- holistic, interested in the big picture, as with people from collectivist cultures;
- happy to connect the personal and the professional, as with diffuse cultures.

Summary

In this chapter we have looked at how cross-cultural psychologists have picked apart and classified how people around the world view different aspects of their lives. We have only briefly touched on the implications of these different perspectives in the workplace, as these are addressed in more detail in the subsequent chapters, in particular:

- Chapter 2, which looks at the factors affecting workplace performance and relates these to our cultural indicators;

- Chapter 4, which suggests a process you can follow for analysing workplace problems and finding solutions, and explores the possible effects of cultural differences during each stage of this process.

Having read and reflected on these cultural differences, you may wonder just how relevant they are in present-day organizations, with their emphasis on organizational culture transcending cultural and national boundaries. Indeed, there are many management textbooks devoted solely to the subject of developing organizational culture with the aim of ensuring that everyone is working towards the same goals. However, if we draw an analogy with general international travel, the huge increase in this in recent years has not led to a general homogenization of international culture and sense of oneness. Rather, any positive effect that it might have had has been dwarfed by the increase in nationalist tendencies worldwide (evidenced, for example, in the tensions created by the break-up of the former Yugoslavia and the Soviet Union). Similarly, at the corporate level, people within organizations are not all turning into corporate clones.

According to research quoted by Adler (2008), we need to consider two levels within organizations. At the higher level of organizational structure and technology there is indeed global convergence. Businesses are adopting similar structures to run their businesses and are implementing the same sorts of technology. In fact, this is really what 'organizational culture' is generally taken to mean; how the organization operates, rather than what it believes in. However, at the lower levels of the organization, individuals continue to operate in ways that reflect their wider world cultural characteristics, with the result that they use various structures and technology differently.

In fact, according to Laurent (1983), working in a transnational organization can make people behave in even more culturally distinct ways, so that the British become even more British, the Germans more German and so on. His research did not offer any real explanation as to why this might be the case, but it is not unreasonable to imagine that people working in an organization where they are under subtle or not-so-subtle pressure to conform to a perhaps alien culture might react against this by more precisely defining their own cultural individuality. Another possibility might be that the discomfort people experience when working with others who have different values might lead them to cling on to values that they understand more than otherwise would have been the case. It is also important to remember that by the time people enter the workforce they are fairly well formed as culturally determined entities, so the organization has only a limited ability to change values, beliefs and norms.

We conclude with a mind map summarizing what this chapter has looked at (Figure 1.3).

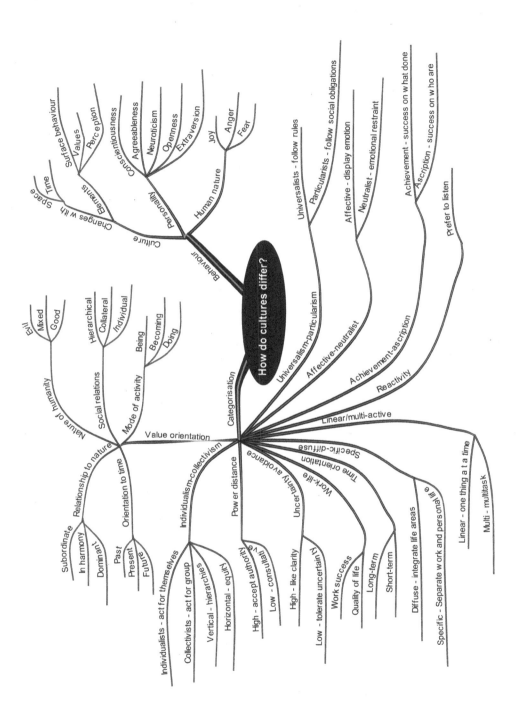

Figure 1.3 Mindmap of Chapter 1 contents

2 *Analysing Performance*

KEY POINTS

- Good performance relies on the provision of information, suitability and capacity to use equipment and the desire to do the job well.

- Perception of information is, to some extent, culturally determined.

- Suitability and capacity to use equipment depends on the culture within which the equipment was designed and may not be universal.

- All cultures are motivated in different ways, and the offering of incentives needs to take this into consideration.

- The Mager and Pipe performance flowchart provides a useful way of systematically examining reasons for inadequate performance.

To Analyse or Not to Analyse?

Nasruddin is an important character in Sufi traditions. Stories about his both wise and foolish ways are told and retold in many countries, and one of the most popular is about someone who found Nasruddin one night on his hands and knees underneath a lamppost.

'What are you doing?' they asked.

'I'm looking for my keys,' Nasruddin replied.

The person got down on their hands and knees and helped in the search, but after a while, thinking there was nothing to be found, they asked Nasruddin, 'So where exactly did you drop your keys?'

'Oh, it was just there down the street.'

'Then why are you looking here?' the puzzled helper asked.

'Because the light is over here and I can see better,' the eminently logical Nasruddin retorted.

It is a story that tends to make us both wince and smile at the same time, as we immediately recognize something foolish from our past flashing before our eyes. And it also applies in performance improvement: the problem is in one place, but we look somewhere else for a solution. Why?

Well, apart from in the United States, where it exists as a distinct academic discipline, the field of 'performance improvement' often seems to be something of a Cinderella subject. All too often, when faced with problems of poor performance, managers rush to implement solutions that they feel are appropriate or have tried before. A very common immediate reaction to a perceived performance problem is to prescribe training: send people on a course or commission an e-learning programme. There is often a failure to analyse, in any systematic way, why performance is suffering, which is what the field of performance improvement or, to give it another name, performance engineering, is all about. The reasons why this happens are discussed in more detail in Chapter 5, but they often stem from an immediate emotional response to the problem. This might include fear about what a thorough performance analysis might uncover, coupled with a lack of knowledge about systematic problem-solving techniques.

The language of management shows that this is true: most of us will be familiar with the acronym TNA, or training needs analysis. What do we do in a training needs analysis? We look at a problem, interview people, sift through piles of performance data, reflect carefully, drink lots of tea or coffee and then decide that training is the answer. Why? Because the name of the activity tells us that this is what we must find. Just like in those infuriating lateral thinking puzzles, as soon as we are given a basic description of a situation our minds create all sorts of limitations. So, just like Nasruddin, although we suspect that the key is somewhere else, we want to look inside a solution box that we understand.

Chapter 1 may have left you feeling somewhat perplexed. We looked at a number of different ways in which people interpret and judge the world around them, and reflected on what implications that can have in a workplace. In that respect it raised many more questions than answers, so in this chapter we will look at how we can analyse performance problems systematically to discover how typical issues are affected by cultural issues. Then, when we come to look at problem-solving approaches later, we will have a clear idea of how to pull the problem apart and where to look.

A Framework for Analysing Performance

As a framework for this process I shall draw on the ideas of Thomas Gilbert (2007). When looking at the root causes of performance problems, Gilbert proposes that a person's behaviour in the workplace resulted from the combination of the following:

- a *repertory of behaviour* – the person's ability to process information, their capacity to use necessary equipment and instrumentation, and their motivation for the task.
- a *supporting environment* – the information a person is given about the task, the equipment they have to carry it out and the incentives they are given for completing it.

Gilbert calls this the Behaviour Engineering Model, and it is illustrated in Figure 2.1.

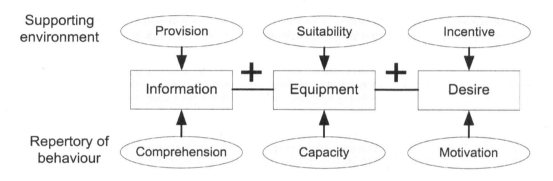

Figure 2.1   Gilbert's Behaviour Engineering Model

The model shows that we need to consider three separate areas – information, equipment and desire – when analysing performance and that, for each of these, there are two dimensions, one emanating the person themselves and the other from the actual workplace.

Of the three areas, arguably the most important is information: indeed, Gilbert claims that more than half the performance problems encountered in the workplace can be traced back to inadequate information. It is always therefore a very important aspect to consider. However, all six elements are potentially important and they are interrelated, so that a change to one element can have an impact on one of the others. For example, if a piece of equipment is designed well, we do not need to give the operator as much information about how to use it. If the operator has high levels of ability and is well motivated, they also need less information about how to operate the equipment. But if we fail to consider any one of these six, we could find ourselves drawing the wrong conclusions about what the solution to the problem might be.

Let's take a closer look at each of these elements.

Information

Information must be both provided and understood. Let us look at what each of these means, and then consider cross-cultural implications.

PROVISION OF
INFORMATION

Gilbert suggests that the working environment needs to provide a person with information about three things:

1. feedback on their performance,
2. statements of the desired performance, and
3. guidance on how to carry out the task at hand.

Give feedback
about how well
they are doing

People need to know how well they are carrying out their job, this feedback needs to be relevant to the performance and it must be provided frequently. So if I am operating a machine making widgets, I need to know that my widgets are being made within the specified manufacturing tolerances and that I am producing them at the desired rate. If, for some reason, the machine starts to produce widgets that are too big, and I am not told about this, then my performance will be perceived to be suffering, even though in practice I may not have done anything to make this happen. If I am managing a project, I need to receive frequent feedback about whether or not the project is within budget and whether it is on time.

Provide clear
statements of
the desired
performance

People need to be given a clear description of what they are supposed to be achieving, what the desired standards of performance are and how this will be measured. What is the 'acceptable' widget? What are the manufacturing tolerances for the widgets? How many widgets need to be produced each hour? What is the deadline for each stage of the project? What budget is available for each stage of the project? What are their specific responsibilities? What are they not expected to do?

The idea of what is to be achieved is very important, and is one that is often misunderstood. A good test for a statement of achievement is to ask what will exist once the person or people responsible have gone away. So, for example, we might state the technical specifications for the widget or the list of requirements for the paperwork that would confirm that a project is on plan and within budget.

Provide clear guides
to performance

There needs to be clearly written, unambiguous and comprehensive descriptions of each aspect of the task in hand, as standard work instructions or operating procedures. They should describe:

*   procedures to be followed;
*   suggestions for best practice;

- explanations about how procedures fit into the larger operation;
- why doing things this way is important, so that people can develop mental models about their work and its significance.

And, of course, these need to be kept up-to-date and be easily accessible.

If possible, people should be pointed towards others who are exemplars of the desired performance. Provide information that will help people to troubleshoot problems that they may encounter, or that they can use to help other people.

COMPREHENSION OF INFORMATION

The person needs to have the skills and knowledge necessary to complete the task to the desired standard. Have they been trained to do this? Has the training been carefully designed so that it provides people with exactly what they need in order to complete the task satisfactorily?

INFORMATION AND CULTURE

How people perceive information varies from culture to culture. And, of course, how we perceive information influences how we choose to present information to other people. This means that when a manager or other process designer wants to explain to a workforce how a particular task is carried out, the communication style they choose will depend on their own preferences. Designing information is therefore a three-stage process. The manager must:

- identify their own perceptual preferences (how they themselves prefer to receive information)
- consider perceptual preferences in their workforce
- design information appropriately.

In order to understand what information is telling us we need to first perceive it and then interpret it. Consider this graphic description of perceptual differences.

> *... six different kinds of being meet by the banks of a river. The human being in the group sees the river as water, a substance to watch in awe to quench his thirst; for an animal such as a fish, the river is its home; the God sees it as nectar that brings bliss; the demigod as a weapon; the hungry ghost as pus and putrid blood; and the being from the hell realm as molten lava. The water is the same, but it is perceived in totally different, even contradictory ways.*
>
> Sogyal Rinpoche, 1992

Studies have shown how perception and values are closely linked. Researchers (Kitayama et al., 2003) took two groups of volunteers, one North American and the other Japanese, and asked them to perform some simple manual tasks requiring them to manipulate a wire frame that had a movable central feature set within a framework. The experiments showed that the North Americans found it easier to manipulate the central feature without regard to the orientation of the surrounding framework than did the Japanese. Conversely, the Japanese subjects paid much more attention to the orientation of the framework when manipulating the central feature.

Other researchers (Imai and Gentner, 1994) took groups of American and Japanese volunteers and showed them an object – for example, a pyramid made of cork – to which they gave some neutral name, saying something like, 'Look at this dax'. They then showed them two other objects, perhaps a pyramid made of white plastic and a flat block of cork, and asked them to point to the 'dax'. The Americans generally pointed to the pyramid, showing that they had coded the dax as an object, whereas the Japanese generally pointed to the block, indicating that they had coded it as a material.

What these studies suggest is that people from Western cultures tend to be interested in objects and detail whereas those from Eastern cultures are generally more interested in the context or broader significance. These different ways of perceiving the world have been described as field dependence and independence (Witkin and Goodenough, 1977):

- Field-dependent observers take into account the background or environment of an object.
- Field-independent observers focus on the object and take less account of its environment.

People from different cultures can also perceive images showing three-dimensional scenes in different ways. Wyndham (1975) describes studies done in the South African mining industry, in which representatives from several of the country's different ethnic groups were shown perspective drawings depicting an antelope and a hunter in the foreground with an elephant on a hill in the background. White South Africans interpreted the picture as the artist had intended, recognizing the three-dimensional depth and perspective. However, the black South Africans interpreted the line showing the hill upon which the elephants stood as a path or river rather than as an indication of elevation. Many also found it difficult to comment on the perspective of the drawing because they objected to the hunting practices being shown. Europeans are familiar with the use of perspective in two-dimensional art, but we must remember that this familiarity is comparatively recent, having been a development of the Renaissance.

In another test, people were asked to draw a profile of a cow. White South Africans drew the profile as a straight two-dimensional image, but the black participants drew the side of the cow in profile and its head looking out of the paper. Wyndham interpreted this as the white participants drawing what they could see and the black participants drawing what they knew the object to be. It is interesting to reflect that this two-dimensional representation from multiple perspectives characterizes much of Pablo Picasso's best-known works. Apparently, after viewing an exhibition of Dogon masks from Mali in Paris in 1907, Picasso was inspired to develop a new approach to his work that led to such masterpieces as *Les Demoiselles d'Avignon*.

Having appreciated how different cultures interpret the world around them at this macro-level of values, it is fascinating to realize that there are also differences operating at the micro-level of brain activity. New medical technologies are showing this by letting us see (literally) how different cultures view the world. Denise Park and Angela Gutchess (2006) placed North Americans and Singaporeans inside functional magnetic resonance imaging (MRI) machines and observed what happened in their brains when presented with visual stimuli. These studies showed more activity taking place in those areas of the brain dealing with object processing within the North American brains than in the Singaporean brains. Conversely, the Singaporean brains were much busier in those areas dealing with background processing, showing that they were more interested in the context of objects than the objects themselves.

These cultural differences in perception have important implications for how information should be provided. Think about the use of symbols to convey information. These are increasingly being used in global settings, on the assumption that because everyone in the world will understand a picture there is no need to provide translations in many different languages. However, as anyone who has spent a weekend wrestling with the pictorial instructions provided with flat-pack self-assembly furniture or storage systems will confirm, a picture can tell a thousand different stories about how something needs to be put together.

A number of different studies confirm this. Huer worked with a range of people from different ethnic backgrounds (such as Euro-American, African-American, Chinese and Mexican), but who all lived in Los Angeles, testing how well they understood different symbols. She showed that their culture did have an effect on the 'translucency' of the symbols: 'consumers … from some cultural backgrounds may not perceive symbols in the same way as they are perceived in the dominant European-American culture' (Huer, 2000, p. 183). Nakamura et al. (1998) suggested that the way in which symbols were perceived could be influenced by the syntax of a person's first language, so that someone whose first language used a subject–verb–object construction might perceive the meaning of a symbol differently from someone more comfortable with a subject–object–verb construction. Piamonte et al. (2001) compared how American and Swedish subjects interpreted the symbols used in technical illustrations and showed that there were significant differences in interpretation. Studies carried out in India to see how well local people understood road signs imported from Britain during the colonial period showed that many were poorly understood. For example, a sign that prohibited blowing a horn was interpreted by most people as an instruction to blow it (Daftuar, 1975). We can therefore see that, when designing graphical information, the cultural backgrounds of the people whom the information is aimed at must be carefully considered, and that a consistent, universal understanding of pictorial explanations cannot be guaranteed.

TRAINING AS INFORMATION

The provision of clear information about how to carry out a task includes the delivery of appropriate training. Gilbert describes this as the need to be given 'scientifically designed training that matches the requirements of exemplary performance' (Gilbert, 2007, p. 88). Anyone familiar with the training needs analysis process will know that it is vital to be able to describe the target group for the training. In culturally homogeneous settings this is generally limited to factors such as job roles, experience, age and gender balance, for example, but cultural diversity introduces a new set of issues.

This issue of making sure that training is culturally appropriate is covered in more detail in Chapter 11.

Equipment

Equipment must be provided for the task at hand, and a person needs to be able to use the equipment. Let us look at these two dimensions.

SUITABILITY OF EQUIPMENT

The equipment provided for the task needs to be suitable. Producing widgets to tight manufacturing tolerances requires high-quality machinery that can be adjusted and maintained to give consistent and reliable performance. The project manager may need some suitable software that will allow them to construct Gantt charts, and enterprise software that gives them instant access to current project expenditure will help them to keep budgets under control.

But what is suitable for one person may not be suitable for someone else, so equipment needs to be designed or provided with the needs of the worker in mind. Providing unsuitable equipment will have implications for other elements in the Behaviour Engineering Model: for example, more training may be needed and motivation may be reduced.

| CAPACITY TO USE EQUIPMENT | People carrying out the task need to have the physical capability to do it to the standards required. |

Work scheduling

Working conditions need to be designed so that people can operate at the desired standards of performance. This can be affected by environmental conditions, such as:

- *shift-working* – the human body functions least efficiently in the early hours of the morning, so it may be unreasonable to expect consistent, high-quality performance from a night shift.
- *high performance targets* – targets that are too high may cause people to pay less attention to quality in order to meet them (and this may also have an effect on safety and motivation issues).

Physical abilities

People need to be physically matched to the work. People who are not strong will be unable to satisfactorily complete jobs that require physical strength unless they are given equipment that can overcome this problem.

Desks need to be positioned and set up so that they allow people to work efficiently, effectively and safely. 'Hot-desking' may make sense for organizations operating flexible and mobile workforces, but may well lead to reduced individual efficiencies as people spend more time than normal finding things and adjusting the positions of computer screens, for example.

Performance aids

It is always a good idea to make sure that people are provided with performance (or job) aids that can help make specific parts of the task easier. For example, the widget manufacturer could have a simple gauge that it could use to see if its widgets were too big or too small without the need for careful measurement. The project manager's financial system could generate automatic warnings if expenditures reach a predetermined percentage of the budget.

Figure 2.2 is an interesting example of a checklist that would be of particular value in a situation where there are opportunities for things to go wrong.

A potential problem with culturally diverse surgical teams is that power distance considerations can discourage junior members of the team from pointing out errors or omissions made by team leaders, even though there might be an espoused team ethos. The checklist standardizes performance and reduces the chance of mistakes not being pointed out due to culturally-driven emotional issues (see Helmreich and Merritt, 1998).

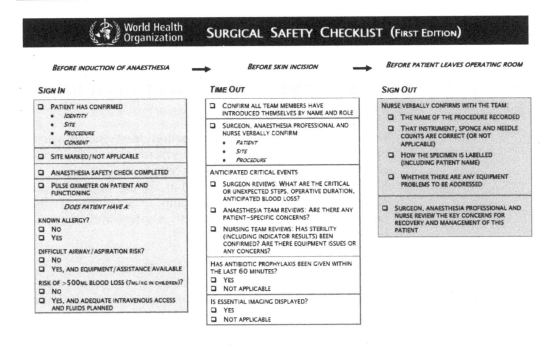

Figure 2.2   World Health Organization surgical checklist

© WHO 2008, reproduced with permission.

EQUIPMENT AND CULTURE

It might be thought that, out of equipment, desire and information, the former would have the least complications as regards cultural differences. That may be true, but it is certainly not the case that equipment, tools and other technology used in the workplace are culturally neutral. That said, this topic of what is sometimes known as 'cultural ergonomics' is one that is little studied, certainly when compared to the amount of research that has been done into other aspects of culture in the workplace.

According to the *Oxford English Dictionary*, ergonomics is 'the study of the efficiency of persons in their working environment'. When applied to the use of workplace technology this essentially means making sure that the equipment can be used effectively and safely. However, as a discipline coming out of Western technology, it has tended to fall into the same trap as occupational psychology in making assumptions about just who the 'persons in the working environment' are. As discussed below, popular ideas about motivation have tended to assume that motivational needs operate at a deeply human level – below the level at which culture operates

– but this is not in fact the case. A similar issue applies with the use of workplace technology.

How do people accept (or not accept) foreign methods?

Most of the research that has been done into cultural aspects of ergonomics has focused on the issue of technology transfer, a term used to describe the process of introducing new technologies into low-income or newly industrializing countries. One way of conceptualizing how technology transfer can work is through the Technology Acceptance Model (TAM) (Davis, 1989). This suggests that the two parameters that need to be considered as far as technology users are concerned are:

- *how useful* they think the technology will be;
- *how easy* they think it will be to use the technology.

These perceptions are shaped by external factors. Perceptions of both usefulness and ease of use influence the person's attitude towards using the technology, and the perceived ease of use also influences how useful they think the technology will be: if they think it is easy to use, they will be more likely to see potential uses. A positive attitude towards using the technology will then create the intention to use and make actual use more likely. This is summarized in Figure 2.3.

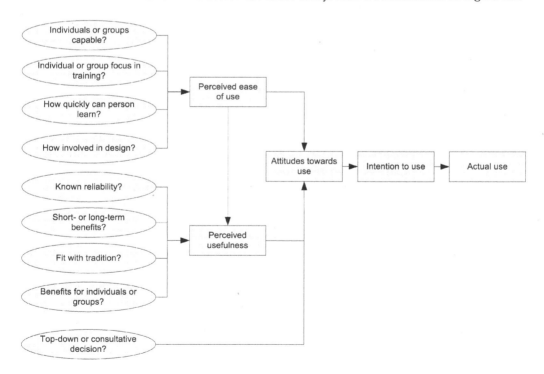

Figure 2.3   Cultural indicators and the Technology Acceptance Model

Source: Adapted from Veiga, Floyd and Dechant, 2001.

Veiga, Floyd and Dechant (2001) considered how the TAM might combine with Hofstede's cultural indicators in the context of introducing new information technology systems, although many of their findings can be generalized to cover any sort of technology implementation.

Looking at how cultural factors fit into Figure 2.3, the first indicator to consider is that for individualism and collectivism. In individualist cultures people are always interested in developments that can help them to achieve, so it is generally true that individualist cultures are more receptive to new technologies as they will more readily see potential uses. If people with a collectivist orientation are to embrace new technologies they must be able to see some benefit to their in-group rather than to themselves as individuals. Veiga, Floyd and Dechant refer to studies done in Japan where strawberry farmers embraced the use of computer technology when they were shown how they could use it to get better market information so that, as a group, they could sell their produce for a higher price. However, Japanese computer users are much less interested in technologies such as e-mail which they see as minimizing interpersonal contacts.

Nevertheless, some Eastern cultures do seem to have been very enthusiastic in adopting new electronic technologies. Shahnavaz (n.d.) suggests that one factor behind this is that many of these enthusiastic adopters are influenced by Confucianism, which places great importance on learning, and Buddhism, which teaches the importance of harmony and respect for other people. These factors have contributed to an environment that is very receptive to the use of advanced technologies, particularly those related to communication such as mobile telephony, which can certainly be used to increase the frequency with which members of an in-group can communicate with each other. Kedia and Bhagat (1988) have taken this further, singling out Hong Kong, Singapore, Taiwan and Japan as countries that have seriously embraced new technology. They argue that while these cultures may be essentially collectivist, they also have strong preferences for work success and a long-term orientation. So, when industrializing, they recognized that high technology was the path they needed to follow for long-term success. Thinking about Singapore in particular, the desire for economic success and the largely collectivist nature of the local cultures meant that people were prepared to accept quite a high degree of social control in order to develop an affluent society.

Other implications of individualism or collectivism shape the perception of ease of use. In an individualist culture people will feel more confident about using the technology if they themselves have done something similar before, whereas in a collectivist culture people will think about whether the relevant skill or knowledge exists anywhere within their in-group.

Training in using the new technology should also take into account individualism and collectivism. In individualist cultures new technologies are often 'championed' by enthusiasts, and they then encourage other people to embrace the technology either by their encouragement or the perception created of the additional rewards that they receive for their higher levels of performance. Veiga, Floyd and Dechant (2001) recommended that the emphasis on training should be on encouraging high levels of individual skill and encouraging competition to achieve this. However, this strategy would probably not be very effective in collectivist cultures, where people avoid displaying high levels of individual performance that would set them apart from other people. The strategy most likely to be effective in this case would be to design training that helps the group as a whole to perform more effectively, focusing on those people who find the technology the hardest to understand.

The study then considered uncertainty avoidance. In cultures that display high levels of uncertainty avoidance anything new or unknown is likely to cause anxiety and is therefore seen as difficult to use. In such cultures it would therefore be important to present the technology as, indeed, easy to learn, and to make sure that it is supported by information and training that makes this true. Such support would be less important in low uncertainty avoidance cultures.

Involving users in the design and development of technologies helps them understand how they work, so it would be a good strategy in a high uncertainty avoidance culture to try to make sure that users are involved at this early stage. Although this seems eminently sensible, it can be difficult to persuade people in such cultures to participate in something as open-ended as product development, even though it would provide substantial benefits.

Veiga's, Floyd's and Dechant's further analysis considered how cultural factors might affect the perceived usefulness of a technology. From the uncertainty avoidance perspective they suggested that it was important that the technology was proven. Managers should therefore work hard in high uncertainty avoidance situations to reassure staff that the technology is completely reliable. This can be difficult when considering the implementation of IT systems, which (justifiably) have reputations for problematic introductions.

Perceived usefulness is also affected by several issues concerned with a person's time orientation. People in a short-term-oriented culture need to know that the technology will provide them with quick wins, unlike long-term-oriented people, who will be interested in how the technology can help over a much longer timeframe. The initial selection of the technology may well have taken this orientation into account, but it is important to make sure that the relative benefits are made clear to the technology user.

Another significant aspect of time is the relative importance attached to the past or the future in the technology user's culture. In a past-oriented culture people will feel more comfortable if the technology resembles something that they have used before, whereas in a future-oriented culture users will feel quite happy if the technology is innovative.

Veiga, Floyd and Dechant finally considered power distance. In high power distance cultures people prefer a clear hierarchical command structure, so the implementation of technology would normally be a top-down initiative. If, for example, the new technology were an IT system, it would be necessary for senior managers to be seen to be using the system. In a low power distance culture a bottom-up implementation could be effective.

When Kenya's Ministry of Agriculture introduced computers into its offices, the first users were secretaries because they were the only ones who could use a keyboard. Of course, the secretaries were virtually all women.

At first the male managers thought that the computers were no more than sophisticated typewriters, but when they started to realise that they were far more powerful than that and that the female secretaries were acquiring new skills that threatened the existing power structure they introduced a regulation that no-one could use a computer unless they had a degree in computer science. Of course, only men had computer science degrees.

The introduction of this technology had failed to take into consideration the high power distance culture operating in the country.

(Ren, 1998, reported in Veiga, Floyd and Dechant (2001).

The Kenyan example above can also be seen as an example of what has been called 'knowledge disavowal' (Kedia and Bhagat, 1988). This is something that can occur in high power distance cultures when the introduction of technology also introduces some aspect of knowledge that is threatening to the existing power structure, so that gatekeepers within the society selectively ignore or suppress it. In the Kenyan case, the male, senior management introduced an arbitrary educational requirement that prevented the women from acquiring any more knowledge about how to use the new technology.

Hill et al. (1998) took a close look at attitudes towards the introduction of computer technologies in the Arab world. While acknowledging that there was a counterculture that was challenging many traditional values, they characterized Arab culture as being oriented to the past and as having a strong collective spirit, with people who are generally obedient and respectful to those with a higher status and having a fatalistic outlook on the world. Consequently, they concluded that there was a degree of reluctance to fully embrace what computer technologies had to offer. A major reason for this was that Arab culture places a great deal of importance on tradition, social contact and face-to-face relationships, and computer technology was seen as presenting a threat to these values.

MACRO AND MICRO-ERGONOMICS

Having looked at the Technology Acceptance Model to see how people can react to new technologies from a cultural perspective, we can now approach this subject from a more conventional ergonomics direction. When considering some of the typical ergonomic aspects of workplace performance, how can cultural issues appear? To this end it is useful to distinguish between:

- macro-ergonomics, which looks at the overall setting of workplace technology and systems within a society, and
- micro-ergonomics, which focuses on the detailed design of the workplace and the usability of equipment.

Sadly, there has been little research in either area into cross-cultural aspects, so what there is seems rather patchy.

Building participation in to ergonomic design

At the macro-ergonomics level the need to take different cultural preferences into consideration would suggest that a participatory approach to ergonomic design could be very valuable. This is normally done by a small team of ergonomists working with a number of people who are expert in the workplace performance. These people need to be trained in basic ergonomic principles, and sufficient time needs to be set aside for experimentation and development. The exact details of how a participatory ergonomics programme should be run must take into account the specific details of the organizational setting. It might be expected that a participatory ergonomics programme might be difficult to run in a setting with high power distance values, as more junior staff involved in workplace performance might not feel confident enough about collaborating on something that might appear to go against the desires of senior management. Short-term-oriented cultures might also feel frustrated by the potentially slow nature of the improvements generated.

The importance of mental models of what is happening

One particularly important aspect of ergonomics at the higher level is that of recognizing that people at work need to have a picture in their minds, a mental model, of what is actually going on around them and how they fit into this. This does not need to be a detailed understanding of how the entire organization works, but, as a minimum, people should know what happens before and after their particular part of the organizational process. This can be particularly important in industrial settings where there are health and safety implications. For example, a study of what happened in the Union Carbide factory in Bhopal in 1984 concluded that one contributory factor was that members of the local workforce had very little understanding about how the plant operated (Meshkati, 1991). They were therefore completely unable to see how anything that they might do could possibly lead to an industrial accident, and certainly not of the scale of that particular incident.

The importance of mental models is one of Peter Senge's five disciplines. He writes that 'new insights failed to get put into practice because they conflict with deeply held internal images of how the world works, images that limit us to familiar ways of thinking and acting' (Senge, 1993, p. 174). Here, Senge is writing about how organizations can develop, but this insight also applies to how different cultures can operate alien technologies. If we carry in the back of our minds a notion that something works in a particular way, we will make all sorts of assumptions about what we can or should do with that technology. I remember that in the late 1980s, when desktop computers were first appearing in British workplaces, people would often say they were afraid to use them 'in case they blew up'. Up until then, screen-based computer technology had been associated with industrial machinery and science fiction, so newcomers to computers may have held mental models that said that there were likely to be certain keystroke combinations that would lead to a self-destruct sequence being initiated.

Cultural perspectives will clearly shape how people interpret a technology that they are expected to use, and clearly, as the Bhopal tragedy shows, the assumption that Indian workers will instinctively adopt the same attitudes to working practices as would American or Western European workers is fundamentally flawed.

Attitudes to maintenance

Another area of interest at this level is maintenance. Inadequate maintenance, leading to reductions in output or breakdowns, is a common cause of unacceptable performance in industry. It can become even more of an issue when a technology is introduced into a different culture, particularly one that does not have a strong industrial tradition. It is a common lament of engineers working on industrial plant in newly industrializing countries that the local people do not pay enough attention to regular, preventative maintenance.

Western engineers can find this very hard to understand, but in societies where agriculture is still predominant, local people may be much more familiar with the slower pace of nature's maintenance: the rain washes unwanted materials away, the land recovers during the winter or dry season and so on. When viewed from this perspective, it is perhaps not so surprising that they may not readily appreciate the need for daily inspections or weekly oil changes. This also creates implications for manuals and training programmes: what works in a culture that is familiar with technological concepts and its underlying assumptions will almost certainly not be suitable in a country where such concepts are relatively new.

Attitudes to maintenance may also be influenced by a culture's orientation to time. Referring to some of the concepts covered in Chapter 1:

- a past oriented culture might be interested in maintenance if it was something that was done in the past, but not otherwise;
- a present–oriented culture might not see preventative maintenance as being important, being instead happy to wait until problems happened;
- a short-term–oriented culture would be keen to avoid taking time out from productive activity now in order to 'repair something that wasn't broken';
- a future- or long-term–oriented culture might really see the importance of keeping operating equipment in good condition.

Work scheduling and local circumstances

The working practices required by Western technology may also not fit in well with the practical circumstances of everyday life in a different country. For example, shift-working takes as an implicit assumption that the process continues while, at regular intervals, the workers supervising it change over.

However, in many countries everyday transport may be difficult or unavailable or roads may be impassable following an overnight storm. People's living conditions may be poor, so that, for example, they cannot easily wash themselves thoroughly every day after work, and their perceived inability to do this might mean that they were unable to perform certain workplace tasks in the way assumed. Cultures may have deeply ingrained or obligatory social rituals, such as an after-lunch nap or the need to take prayer breaks at certain times during the day. In Muslim societies people observe a sunrise to sunset fast during the month of Ramadan, which will clearly have an effect on performance. Female workers may have special problems, because, as well as holding down a job in order to earn money, they may have responsibilities for childcare or looking after elderly relatives.

Cultural perceptions of work

Workplace analysis needs to take into consideration how the work required is viewed in the setting of the local culture. For example, the nature of the work, particularly if it means getting hands dirty, or the technology used might mean that the job is seen as low-status or undesirable in some way. That in turn might mean that it can only be performed by members of a particular caste in the society, or only by men and not women, or vice versa. The work may be unacceptable because it has connotations of a previous colonial relationship. In many traditional societies agricultural work was carried out by women, but during the colonial era European farm managers often recruited men to work in their fields, as this was the cultural norm in their own homeland. So for a man to do certain types of work may be linked within the culture to perceived colonial oppression. Similarly, it may be completely unacceptable for a woman to have supervisory responsibilities over any men.

The macro-ergonomist considering performance problems in a setting that is alien to the origin of the workplace technology must certainly learn to look holistically at the cultural setting, in order to take into consideration those aspects of everyday life that can largely be taken for granted in the technology's homeland.

> Lillrank and Kano (1989) describe how the 'seven tools' method used for quality assurance in Japan was originally developed. Starting with an initial nine recommendations, the originators of the method looked to Japanese traditions and the idea of the seven weapons that were regarded as the minimum number that a samurai warrior needed to carry with him whenever he went out to fight.
>
> (Reported in Shahnavaz, n.d.).

Micro-ergonomics

Micro-ergonomics focuses on the detailed design of the workplace. Again the research in this area is limited and throws up a variety of issues which have cultural implications. For example, what cultural assumptions are attached to spatial movements? This is important because different cultures may have their own ideas about what response they expect after a particular stimulus. Consider, for example, something as ubiquitous and simple as the light switch: in most countries you flick the switch down to turn a light on, but in the United States you flick it up and in Japan you may even have to flick it sideways. Inconsistent stimulus–response connections can mean:

- it takes longer for someone to learn how to do a job;
- they make more mistakes because long-established habits mean that they operate a switch incorrectly from time to time;
- particularly importantly, in a crisis they may take the wrong action.

> In August 2005 Helios Airways flight ZU522 left Larnaca in Cyprus, heading for Athens. Before take-off a standard procedure was to make sure that the cabin pressurization controls were switched to 'auto' mode, which meant that as the aircraft climbed, cabin pressure would be maintained automatically. Instead, the switch was left in the 'manual'

position. The crew misinterpreted warning horns and cancelled them as they sounded.

Slowly the cabin pressure fell, the crew and passengers became starved of oxygen and all fell unconscious. By this time Athens air traffic control knew that there was a problem, and two Hellenic Air Force aircraft were scrambled to investigate, but they could only watch helplessly as the commercial plane flew on and on until its fuel ran out and it crashed, killing all 121 people on board.

The accident had been caused by the simple failure of staff to recognize the incorrect positioning of a switch.

Comprehension of controls and information

Visual representations and control panels may seem relatively straightforward to us if they have been developed in our own culture, but how might other people use them? Researchers Hsu and Peng asked a selection of Chinese and American volunteers to look at the positioning of knobs controlling four burners on a cooking stove and found that they made consistently different assumptions about the relationship between the knobs and the burners (Shahnavaz, n.d.).

Equipment produced in the safety-obsessed West will usually have switches and indicators that indicate an unacceptable or unsafe condition. Emergency or unacceptable states are generally signified by the colour red, because in Western cultures red is almost always associated with danger. However, in Chinese cultures, red is the colour of joy and happiness, while in India it is associated with good luck and in Egypt with death. One wonders how many pieces of machinery have been accidentally switched off by Indian or Chinese operators who were looking for good luck or happiness...

Globalization and the need to avoid producing labels and documentation in a variety of local languages means that organizations are increasingly using graphics to convey information and instructions. For example, think about a computer's graphical user interface and its reliance on icons and the instruction sheet that comes with flat-pack furniture from a well-known Swedish retailer. A picture may still be worth a thousand words, but if those thousand words were in a foreign language the picture may also be incomprehensible (Huer, 2000; Nakamura et al., 1998; Piamonte et al., 2001). Simple symbols and pictures can mean different things to different people: a picture of an owl suggests shrewdness to someone in Taiwan, wisdom in Britain, but bad luck in India; a dragon is auspicious in Chinese culture, but is a monster in many other societies (Lim and DeVries, 2003). The sequencing of graphics-only instructions developed by someone who normally writes using a script that goes from left to right may mean something different to people familiar with writing scripts that go from right to left or top to bottom.

Wyndham (1975) describes attempts made in the South African mining industry to use graphics to explain health and safety issues to illiterate workforces. Two sequences of graphics were used to show good and bad practice in wearing goggles when using grinding equipment. In one sequence a drawing showed a worker not using goggles, and the sequence ended with an image of a beggar, whereas in the other the worker was using goggles and ended up being paid. When questioned, workers failed to see any connection or causality in the sequences. Interestingly, in the drawing showing the worker receiving pay they were shown holding one hand out to the paymaster, but, when local people were consulted about the design of this drawing, they said that in their culture people gave things with one hand but held out two hands when receiving something. As far as they were concerned, therefore, the 'good' sequence showed that if they wore goggles they would end up paying money to the company. Not what was intended!

Physical operation of equipment

Positioning and size of equipment can create problems if it is designed for a particular type of average person, as people may not be able to reach controls properly or provide enough leverage if manual force is needed. One of the most comprehensive studies into this aspect of cultural ergonomics was done by the US Air Force during the Vietnam War (Kennedy, 1975). Fighter aircraft perhaps represent an ultimate application of ergonomic design, as the complex control and display systems are essentially built around a pilot operating in a very confined space. Of course, American aircraft are designed for average American people, who are perhaps among the largest on the planet, and certainly much bigger than the average Vietnamese person. Kennedy estimated that the aircraft would have to be about 13 per cent smaller if a Vietnamese pilot were to be able to operate it as efficiently as an American one. Pilots' individual muscular strengths were also quite different: the 75th percentile strength of Vietnamese pilots was the same as the 25th percentile of the American group. When people have to operate equipment that is designed for someone taller or smaller they have to use more energy, and so will tire more quickly and will not be able to apply as much force. Obvious in situ adaptations, such as providing platforms, can simply mean that while one control becomes easier to operate, another is moved out of reach.

Many pieces of equipment are designed to be operated by someone who is sitting in a chair, with the controls set at a height that allow the operator to rest their elbows. However, in many countries people do not sit in chairs in their social lives and actually feel more physically comfortable squatting or sitting cross-legged on the floor. Sometimes they continue to do this even when a chair is provided! If they do not occupy the assumed position for operating the machinery, they may be unable to operate it correctly, and there could also be health and safety implications of not being able to see warning indicators, operate emergency switches or even of sitting in a position that is not adequately protected.

Difficulties with occupational clothing

Again, safety concerns may well dictate a requirement that certain workers must wear personal protective equipment (PPE). In some cultures this may present difficulties. Heavy industrial gloves or high-visibility jackets may be seen as denoting someone who does manual labour, which may be unacceptable. Hard hats may be unacceptable for Sikhs who must wear a turban, and other clothing requirements may present problems for women in Islamic countries where female dress codes are particularly rigid. Personal protective equipment may be imported and designed for use in another country where people are quite different in size. Surveys in the South African mining industry showed that African workers were often reluctant to use goggles and gloves because they were just too big. Wearing the goggles made it much harder for them to see what they were doing, so they left them off, considerably increasing the chances of serious eye injuries, and the looseness of the gloves made it very difficult to manipulate controls and use hand tools (Wyndham, 1975).

A checklist of macro- and micro-ergonomic issues

This section has looked at a large number of practical issues that might affect the way in which people physically carry out a task. Before continuing, it is useful to summarize what these issues have been.

- Do people have accurate mental models about how their workplace technology operates?
- Do people appreciate the importance of maintenance?
- Does work scheduling take into consideration local circumstances?
- What are cultural attitudes to this particular task?
- Does equipment work in a way that local people are familiar with?
- Is information designed in a way that everyone can easily understand?
- Can everyone use the necessary equipment easily, comfortably and safely?
- Is all personal protective equipment easy to wear and culturally acceptable?

Desire

Unrequited love is a tragedy in anyone's life. Unrequited desires in the workplace may not make such good films, but they are probably more important for the manager trying to solve a performance problem. As with love, desire needs to work in two directions: satisfactory completion needs to provide a reward, such as through a separate reward or because of intrinsic satisfaction in the task; and the reward available must be seen as attractive by the workforce. Without this nexus, desire is dead.

- *Incentives for the task.* Satisfactory completion of the task must be rewarded by an appropriate incentive. This might be financial, additional time off or some physical acknowledgement of good performance, or a combination of different types of incentive. The key point is that it must be closely allied with what motivates the individual, which implies that what is a suitable incentive in one location may be ineffectual, or even a disincentive, in another.
- *Motivation for the task.* A person needs to be motivated to complete the task to the desired standard. Motivation needs to match incentives, so either the sort of people that are motivated by the incentives on offer must be recruited or the incentives must be changed to match what motivates the workforce.

DESIRE AND CULTURE

Most management texts assume that all workers are motivated by the same factors and so propose the same solutions for incentivizing. This is because most ideas about motivation have come from the same cultural perspective and are strongly linked to individualist values. Consider three of the main theories associated with motivation:

1. Maslow's hierarchy of needs.
2. Herzberg's two factor theory.
3. McClelland's needs theory.

Three theories with one thing in common: all were proposed by white American males. So perhaps it is not surprising that their proposals on motivation reflect the motivators for middle-class, late twentieth-century white American males, perhaps not necessarily universal.

Maslow's hierarchy of needs

Consider Maslow. He proposed that an individual's motivation is related to the desire to move up a hierarchy of needs, with them needing to have each step satisfied before they could concentrate on the next (see Figure 2.4).

This theory has become so pervasive that many people assume that it is a basic human desire, but this is not necessarily the case.

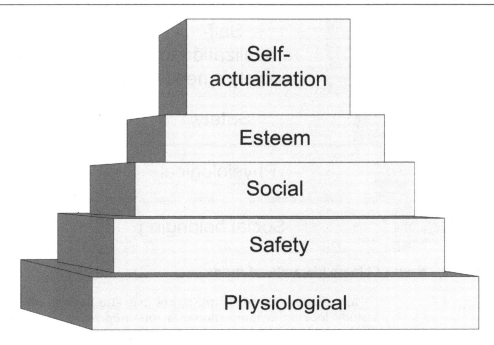

Figure 2.4   Maslow's hierarchy of needs

Nevis's studies in the collectivist culture of the People's Republic of China led him to conclude that a Chinese hierarchy of needs (Figure 2.5) starts with belonging, as, until someone is a member of a group, physiological and safety needs cannot be met (Nevis, 1983).

He concluded that the highest desire, self-actualization existed in the Chinese context as being the best one could be for meeting one's society's needs rather than the Western concept of realizing one's individual potential.

Nevis also observed that self-esteem did not exist as there was no concept of 'self'. The Chinese concept of 'face', which is very important in Chinese society, is often understood in the West to be a manifestation of self-esteem, but losing face more accurately corresponds to damaging the sense of belonging within the relevant in-group (Jackson, 1998).

Also, in cultures where uncertainty avoidance is high, security is seen as crucially important. A safe job is more desirable than one that is fulfilling.

Maslow's hierarchy also has problems in dealing with realities such as suicidal martyrs. It can be argued that killing oneself for a political or religious cause represents self-actualization (or, perhaps more accurately, the 'self-transcendence' that Maslow described as existing above the level of self-actualization in his later writings). However, how does this equate with the need to ensure physiological security and safety?

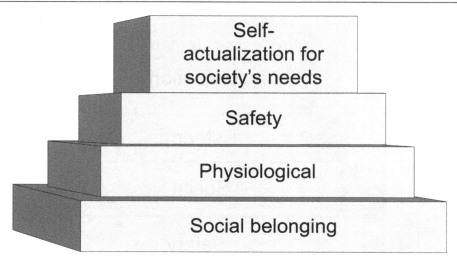

Figure 2.5   Nevis's Chinese hierarchy of needs

Immediate political circumstances may also have an influence. A study looking at motivational factors influencing managers in Liberia in 1975, a time of increasing political tensions, showed an extremely high need for security (Howell et al., 1975). Given that Hofstede assesses West Africa as being an area with moderately low uncertainty avoidance, we might expect Liberians to be relatively tolerant of political uncertainty, but clearly immediate physical danger seems to outweigh this relaxed approach to life.

Herzberg's two factor theory

Herzberg's two factor theory identifies hygiene (or maintenance) factors and motivators, where the former make us unhappy and the latter make us happy.

Looked at from a cross-cultural perspective, this classification can seem far too simplistic, and many studies have shown that different cultures value these factors quite differently. For example:

- The model relegates the importance of interpersonal relationships to being something that can only cause dissatisfaction, whereas in a collectivist culture strong relationships can bring a positive feeling of fulfilment.
- Herzberg's view of supervision seems to be as a one-way street of command and control, whereas supervision in a high power distance culture that leads to the appropriate exchange of obligations can inspire great loyalty on the part of subordinates.
- Individual recognition and advancement in a collectivist society can cause great distress to those being given them if not handled appropriately.
- Acknowledging an individual's achievement may push individualists on to do even more, but collectivists may be more

Table 2.1   Herzberg's two factor theory of motivation

Hygiene (maintenance) factors	Motivators
Policies and administration	Achievement
Supervision	Recognition
Salary	Intrinsic nature of work
Interpersonal relations	Responsibility
Physical conditions	Advancement

motivated by being told about low achievement. Studies have shown that while Canadians perform better after doing well and receiving positive feedback, Japanese people do better after first failing and receiving negative feedback (Ide, 1999). Ide ascribed this to the Japanese desire for self-improvement (a 'becoming' mode of activity in Kluckhohn's terms).

- In cultures with a more quality-of-life culture, improving physical conditions to improve social contact is a motivator (such as using small teams, rather than production lines, to build cars in Swedish car factories).

McClelland's three needs

McClelland proposed that motivation is driven by three needs – to achieve, to affiliate and to have power – although he did also recognize that their importance to an individual was driven by their socialization and so might vary both within and between cultures. Again we need to examine this more carefully:

- Individuals within collectivist cultures may not show a high need to achieve.
- Cultures where uncertainty avoidance is high often have low achievement needs (why take the risk?).
- The need to affiliate will be much greater in collectivist cultures than in individualist ones.
- The need for power will be different in low and high power distance cultures. If you live in a high power distance culture and are low down in the hierarchy, will you want power?

An alternative: Vroom's expectancy theory

A more useful idea to consider is Victor Vroom's expectancy theory. This proposes that an individual is motivated if they:

- see a positive correlation between effort and achievement, and
- good achievement will result in a desired reward, and
- the reward satisfies an important need, and
- the desire to satisfy the need makes the effort worthwhile.

This is summarized in Figure 2.6.

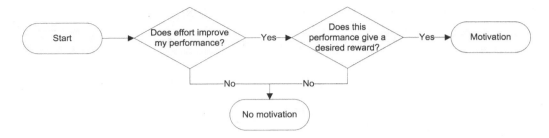

Figure 2.6   Vroom's expectancy theory

Expectancy theory is an improvement because it makes fewer assumptions about what individuals look for. However, let us look at these questions from a cultural perspective:

1. Does effort improve my performance?
    *   Is the individual actually interested in the level of their performance? They would be in an individualist or work success culture, but for someone from a collectivist culture or where the quality of life is more important than work, interpersonal relationships within the team or workgroup may be the motivator. In Confucian terms the motivation may be to reciprocate the faith shown by the employer in giving the person their job through their loyalty.
    *   Do people think they are dominant over or subordinate to nature? Euro-Americans and Europeans may think that they are dominant, whereas Muslims will see it as being in the hands of Allah, and other cultures may see it as down to luck or being predestined by their social class
2. Does this performance give a desired reward?
    *   Here needs-based theories are useful: does the performance give security, self-esteem or self-actualization, for example? And is this reward what is wanted in this culture?
    *   Can the job be changed to make it more rewarding? If so, how? Making the work more complex and challenging may be effective in a work success society, whereas increasing its sociability may help in a quality-of-life society.

To summarize, while the older theories of motivation do have validity in purely Western contexts, their simplistic analyses and lack of consideration about the impact of culture mean that managers seeking to understand the motivation of diverse workforces should only use them to ask questions rather than to find answers. However, expectancy theory can provide a useful tool for considering whether or not the right conditions are in place to encourage motivation for a particular cultural group.

Troubleshooting Performance Problems

Having looked at the different factors that can influence performance, we now need to think about how we would go about looking at a performance problem, taking each one into consideration. Gilbert's Behaviour Engineering Model gives us an excellent breakdown of the different factors affecting performance, and closely related to his ideas are those of Robert Mager and Peter Pipe, who developed a flowchart-based systematic way of analysing a performance problem in order to identify root causes and hence draw up a list of potential solutions. Figure 2.7 is based on the flowchart they presented in their book, *Analysing Performance Problems*.

Flowcharts can be very useful tools for showing how a process works or for providing a procedure to follow, but their simplicity can hide subtleties in the decision-making process and they also suggest that there is a tightly defined sequential process that must be followed. So it is important to point out, before looking at Figure 2.7 in more detail, that the performance flowchart is only supposed to be used as a guide to the analysis process, and should not necessarily be followed rigidly. For each question I have given some examples of how this might manifest itself in the real world. Sometimes you may feel that the example given relates equally as well to another question: that is quite possibly true, but remember that you should only use the flowchart to aid your thinking, not to provide a neatly classified set of problems.

IS THE PROBLEM SERIOUS?

It takes time and energy to poke around in the corners of a workplace to find out the root causes of a problem and to come up with potential solutions, so the first question to ask is 'Is the analysis worth it?', which of course, depends on whether or not the problem is serious. There are perhaps three basic criteria we can use to evaluate the seriousness of a problem:

1. *financial* – the cost to the organization, in hard money terms, of what is going wrong.
2. *regulatory* – where the workplace problem is infringing some legislation.
3. *ethical* – where what is happening in the workplace is regarded within the local culture as unacceptable in some way (which may, of course, lead to financial costs as well, if the ethical breach damages the organization's reputation, for example).

Figure 2.7   The Mager and Pipe performance flowchart

Source: Adapted from Mager and Pipe (1990).

Of course, a workplace problem may fail all three of these tests. For example, workplace practices can discriminate in some way against people with disabilities, where there are:

- financial costs, due to factors such as people not being able to perform efficiently or being more likely to injure themselves, which will have many costs associated with it.

- regulatory implications, where the discriminatory practice may be in contravention of various pieces of legislation.
- ethical issues, because making working life difficult for people who have other challenges to deal with on an everyday basis just feels wrong to most people in the society.

Ethical considerations

Evaluating against these criteria is not always straightforward. The ethical issue is particularly complex, and a decision will ultimately depend on the values held by that particular organization, which will come, at least in part, from values within the society. In an individualist, work success-oriented culture we might therefore expect that the ethical dimension might carry less weight than it would in a culture that placed more importance on collectivist relationships and quality of life.

Ethical issues may also be seen to have financial costs. Consider, for example, the issue of clothing manufacturers using factories in countries such as Vietnam because the cost of labour there is much lower. From a Western ethical perspective, these are often pejoratively described as 'sweatshops', because of the low pay and poor working conditions. However, from the perspective of someone looking for employment in Vietnam, such a job might be very attractive.

Irrespective of this ethical dilemma, many manufacturers have tried to present a more positive image of their employment practices in low-income countries because they recognize the bad effect that this issue can have on their reputation, and hence sales in Western countries. Ethicality therefore ends up having a financial value.

Legal considerations

Regulatory issues are perhaps simpler. Essentially, a working practice is legal or not legal, but there will, of course, be many instances where the distinction between what is legal and what is illegal is not very clear, and, employers may be less than willing to make any necessary investment in putting a working practice clearly on to the safe side of the distinction. Sometimes employers may persist in illegal working practices because they know that the sanctions in place to punish these will cost less than what it would cost to make the changes needed to legalize them. And, of course, in some countries corruption may mean that legislation is an irrelevance. Again, as with ethicality, regulation can be reduced to money.

Financial considerations

This leaves us with filthy lucre. As both ethicality and regulatory compliance may end up having some financial dimension, it is important to try to decide what the monetary cost of a problem might be. This might be in the form of direct costs, such as damage, wastage or the need to employ extra labour, or less tangible costs, such as lost sales, increased sickness or a negative effect on the organization's or team's reputation. Mager and Pipe (1990) suggest a number of sources of performance-related costs:

- *Money and products*: is actual money being lost in transactions within the business or are finished products disappearing for some reason?
- *Time*: is time being wasted, meaning that production is affected, or that other people are having to spend more time (perhaps on overtime rates) trying to compensate?
- *Waste materials*: is the process generating more waste or scrap than is necessary?
- *Damage to equipment*: does the problem in the workplace cause damage and, if so, how much does it cost to replace or repair equipment?
- Production loss; is the process not producing as much, or is the team not achieving as much as they could or should do? If so, what is the difference between the actual and theoretical outputs in financial terms?
- *Accuracy of output*: how good is the final product? Is reworking necessary, and how much does this cost? What effect does this have on the organization's reputation, and how much might that cost?
- *Insurance premiums*: if poor performance causes accidents or damage, insurance premiums might be higher than necessary. If so, by how much?
- *Accidents*: as well as affecting insurance premiums, accidents will have a cost in terms of working hours lost, possible recruitment costs and, of course, the costs of legal action being taken against the organization.
- *Duplication of effort*: are two people doing what one person could, perhaps as a result of inefficiencies or quality issues?
- *Extra supervision*: are extra people needed to monitor the work carried out? If so, how much does this cost?
- *Lost business*: this might be due to some of the other factors, such as public perception of poor quality or a reputation for poor workplace safety or unethical practices (such as, for example, using 'sweatshops'). What might sales be if these were not happening?

The cost of doing nothing

After reviewing all of these possible costs, you should be in a position to decide whether or not the problem is serious enough to warrant further attention. If it is not, and you do not think it is worth investigating any further, leave it for now but do not forget it completely. Sadly, few problems get better naturally: usually things get worse if we do not attend to them, so monitor the situation from time to time.

This is the cost of doing nothing. It is surprising how quickly the less obvious costs resulting from poor workplace performance can add up to significant sums. If you do decide to carry on and find solutions to the problems, you can also estimate how much it would cost to implement these solutions and look back at this total cost, to make a decision as to whether making changes is worth the investment.

IS THERE A LACK OF KNOWLEDGE OR SKILL?

Finding out if the performance problem is due to a lack of knowledge or skill is crucial, because it determines whether or not we need to ask a number of questions related to providing knowledge or skill. Thinking back to the beginning of the chapter and our story about Nasruddin, we can see that this is the question that is almost never asked because it is generally assumed that the answer will be 'yes'.

You can see that if you follow the flowchart carefully, answering 'yes' will not necessarily preclude considering other problems, but in reality deciding that there is a lack of knowledge or skill means that the buck will stop with training. This happens partly because most people who are trying to solve a performance problem will not be aware of the other questions that they should be asking, but also because they practise satisficing – in other words, they find one solution, training, and then stop looking for anything else.

There is a simple question to ask to find out if knowledge or skill is a root cause: could the person do the task if their life depended on it? If the answer to this question is 'yes', then you do not need to worry about the expense of designing and delivering training. Instead, the problem lies within the organizational setting.

CAN THE TASK BE SIMPLIFIED?

When I was first old enough to drive a car, back in the early 1970s, my father had carefully shown me how to check the level of oil in the engine using a dipstick and had said how important it was to check this every week. Of course, as the years rolled by, the level of my performance dropped considerably, and many was the time that I set off on a long journey only to uncomfortably remember that I had not checked the oil level for several months.

Now, when I bought a new car back in 1997 the first thing I noticed when I switched the engine on was that for the first ten seconds the odometer LED display was replaced by a line of dashes showing me the level of oil in the engine. So now that I had an automatic electronic indication of the oil level every time I started the engine I could set off every time feeling reasonably comfortable that at least the oil level in the engine was okay.

What those clever engineers at Renault had done was to simplify the task of checking the oil level: they had created a *performance aid*. LED displays are, of course, not the only type of performance aid. Other examples are flowcharts, decision tables, checklists, user guides and directories.

Therefore, the first questions to ask when considering issues related to knowledge and skill are:

- Is it possible to simplify the task?
- Can the person be supported in some way?

If the task can be simplified, then this should be done; otherwise you may find yourself having to design training to help someone carry out an unnecessarily complicated job. Ways of simplifying a task include:

- breaking a large and complex task down into a number of smaller, simpler tasks;
- providing performance aids that people can refer to, rather than having to remember a lot of information;
- arranging for someone to receive extra support to carry out the job through such things as coaching or supervision.

There are certain circumstances in which performance aids are particularly useful (Harless, 1986) – for example, where:

- tasks are performed relatively infrequently, perhaps less than once or twice a month;
- the overall task is complex because it is composed of many different steps or because some of the steps involved require highly developed discriminatory skills;
- there is criticality in completion of the task, so that making a mistake could be dangerous (for example, pilots work through a manual checklist before every flight rather than relying on their memory because the consequences of even a single fault could be catastrophic);
- there are likely to be changes in the task (which would make investment in such things as training poor value for money).

The WHO surgical checklist (Figure 2.2, p. 64) is a good example:

- The task is complex, in that there are a relatively large number of small steps.
- There is criticality in that failure to complete all of the procedures listed could potentially result in a death.

On the other hand, performance aids would not be suitable in situations where, for example:

- the task must be performed quickly, which would make it impossible to refer to the performance aid;

- the task is performed so frequently that formal training may be more cost-effective;
- people would not use the aid because, for example, it would have a negative effect on their self-esteem or it would be visible to customers.

When simplifying a task you need to take into account the nature of the workforce and its culture. Simplifying a task may be seen as deskilling and consequently cause dissatisfaction or unrest. Breaking a task down might have an effect on working relationships and so be unpopular in a collectivist or quality-of-life culture. Removing challenges may make the job less appealing to people in work success cultures, where achieving something difficult is a sign of 'occupational virility'. Status-oriented people may view the simplification of a job as an insult, and may feel that the new task is inappropriate for someone of their gender, age, social standing or with their educational qualifications.

Conversely, simplifying a task may be well received in high uncertainty avoidance cultures. Developing performance aids may also be seen as a good idea in particularist cultures, where people are keen to abide by rules.

DID THEY USED TO BE ABLE TO DO IT?

When I was at school I used to enjoy woodwork, and in my bedroom I still have a large wooden chest that I made when I was 17 years old. It contains a number of mortise and tenon joints which, for readers who have never practised any form of do-it-yourself, are joints made from a rectangular hole (the mortise) into which slides a tightly fitting rectangular projection (the tenon). To make the finished joint look better, the tenon has a shoulder, which involves trimming the end of the piece of timber down so that when the tenon slides into the mortise, the hole is covered. Now, doing this requires a certain amount of skill, particularly in cutting the rectangular mortise, and while a professional joiner might not be impressed with the quality of my joints, I do look at it from time to time with a certain pride that once upon a time I was able to do it reasonably well.

However, if I decided to make a chest using shouldered mortise and tenon joints now I would find it very difficult, because I have not practised doing this during the last 35 years. But, there are certain aspects of the job that I could do reasonably well, and I feel fairly confident that, with appropriate help, I could pick things up again relatively quickly, and certainly do not think that I would need to go to a beginner's woodwork class.

Nevertheless, this is what people are often required to do on training courses: regardless of their existing levels of skill they have to go through the same training course. The problem is, of course, that if you don't use it, you lose it – your levels of skill in anything will fade away if you do not have the chance to practise.

The first question to ask is therefore:

• Did the person used to be able to carry out the task correctly?

If the answer to this question is 'yes', the next question to ask is:

• Do they carry out the task frequently?

If the answer to this question is 'no', then we are looking at a case of skill fade: the person does not practise the skill enough to keep their level of performance up to that required. There are two solutions needed in this case: practice and feedback.

The person needs to be given regular opportunities to practise the skill. This is something that the military recognizes during peacetime: armed forces personnel are constantly rehearsing military procedures, so that when they actually have to carry out the real performance they can do it perfectly.

In some cases practice might be supplemented by refresher training, but this must be designed so that the person can move quickly through topics with which they have some familiarity. A 'one size fits all' training course, designed for novices and experienced members of staff would lead to previously skilled people becoming extremely frustrated, and would possibly not be very effective.

If you find that the person does indeed carry out the task frequently, but is still not doing the job correctly, then the problem lies in the feedback they are receiving about how well they are doing the job. After all, if their levels of performance have slipped but nobody has told them, as far as they are concerned they are still performing adequately.

CAN PEOPLE BE TRAINED TO DO THE JOB?

Sometimes people underperform in a task because they are simply not suited for it. There are various reasons why this might be the case:

• They might not be qualified intellectually. The task might require more intellectual abilities than they have, and training would not be able to bring them up to the required level.
• They might be overqualified for the task. People who are, or feel that they are, overqualified for a particular job can quickly become bored and dissatisfied, which can lead to them 'rebelling' by not doing the job properly. Conversely, they might try to make the task more complicated than it actually is in order to make it interesting, ending up taking more time or creating problems for other people.

- The task might not provide the right motivation. The discussion of cultural ergonomics earlier in this chapter identified various examples of how some cultures may view certain tasks as unacceptable. If the task falls into this category for the workforce's culture, no amount of training is going to achieve anything.
- The task might require certain physical actions that the current workforce is unable to carry out. Again, micro-ergonomics can suggest how this might occur: equipment designed for Westerners who are, on average, taller than people from the East might prove difficult for a Chinese or Indian worker to operate properly, for example.
- If you can find no reason to conclude that people are untrainable, then training is an answer. You then need to embark on a training needs analysis in order to identify the most appropriate blend of training solutions. To do this, you would need to take into consideration factors discussed earlier in this chapter.

ARE PEOPLE PUNISHED FOR DOING THE JOB WELL?

Having worked your way down the left-hand side of the flowchart depicted in Figure 2.7, you have considered all of the knowledge- or skill-related factors affecting performance. You can now move over to the right-hand side which takes you through a series of questions which explore organizational factors that may be affecting performance. Many of these relate to motivation, which has been discussed earlier in this chapter.

The first question to consider is:

- What happens when people perform as required?
- Are there any negative consequences to performing as required?

We enter here into some quite subtle matters. The best way to understand these is to think about delivering a training course. If you are delivering a course that has a high knowledge content, you may have decided to send out, along with the instructions, some pre-reading materials that the participants are required to read through carefully, in addition to completing exercises, doing some research in their workplace and so on, before attending the workshop. However, from previous experience you know that the great majority of people will not do this preparatory work, and so you start the workshop by going over all of the content anyway.

So what is going on here? Well, most of the participants will know quite well from their own previous experience that the trainer will go through all of the pre-reading material anyway, so spending some of their valuable time going through this material would be pointless. Doing the job well – that is, completing the pre-work – will be punished; they will lose spare time or be put under more pressure at work.

In what other ways might effort be punished? Here are a few examples:

- An enthusiastic worker learns how to carry out a new task very well. She finds that everyone else keeps asking her questions about the task so that she can no longer do it properly.
- A Chinese member of staff who does a particularly good piece of work is singled out for praise in a team meeting. This makes them very embarrassed, as they feel that their performance is due to the effectiveness of the team as a whole. They decide not to make this 'mistake' again and so lower the standard of their performance.
- An American company operating in Russia encourages its employees to show initiative. One member of staff does this and upsets his Russian line manager, who, with his strong attachment to power distance, feels that this initiative is not appropriate in a subordinate. They make their feelings clear to the unfortunate subordinate.
- A project to improve the efficiency of poultry farming in India failed because the group that it was designed to help were low-caste members of society, and they perceived that if their improved rearing techniques made them more successful it would jeopardize their position within society (reported in Daftuar, 1975).

You can therefore see that cultural differences can make it very easy to punish someone for doing well. The mismatch will often be caused by failing to judge the connection between incentives and motivation correctly: a manager will do something that they think is incentivizing (which it might well be in their own culture), but which is actually a demotivator to the group that they are managing.

ARE PEOPLE REWARDED FOR DOING THE JOB POORLY?

The opposite to punishing people for doing a job well is to reward them for doing the job badly. Consider team-working. A number of people work together to achieve a particular objective and, in doing so, develop a good and supportive team spirit, so that people who struggle in some way are helped, perhaps to the extent that other people do their work for them. Nevertheless, at the end of the project the whole team is rewarded.

Now, this is all fine and dandy as long as everyone is committed to the task. However, teams often have people who free ride, which is where they decide to do less than is expected of them because they know that the rest of the team will carry them along. So, although our team may be behaving supportively, less committed members may be taking advantage of this and basking in the reflected glory when the team as a whole is praised for its performance: they are being rewarded for doing their job poorly.

An individualist culture solution to this might be to abandon team rewards and offer individual rewards instead. However, if the task requires team-working in order to be completed satisfactorily, this strategy will increase competition at the expense of collaboration, affecting overall performance negatively. For example, a consultancy firm instigated a sales bonus scheme that paid individual commission for making sales. However, selling in this marketplace was complex, and it took several meetings to convince a customer of the overall proficiency of the consultancy. This was best done by a team-based approach, but the desire to capture the commission led to individuals interfering with the selling process in order to increase their bonuses. The reward system therefore led to the sales task being performed poorly.

What are some other examples?

Workers in the cutting department of a glass factory – all men – had to cut large sheets of glass into predetermined shapes and then throw the cullet, or waste slivers, into a skip. They placed the skip as far away as possible so that they could demonstrate to workers in the adjoining area, who were predominantly female, their skill in throwing the glass. This dangerous behaviour was rewarded by an increase in their machismo ratings.

Adler (2008) reports that an American company operating in Mexico decided to incentivize its employees by increasing their wages. The Mexicans, who valued their quality of life more highly than career success or income, responded by working fewer hours – happy to earn the same amount of money for a shorter working week – but the company found that less was achieved.

A French person working in a team largely comprising Chinese people found that his passionate reactions to events in the workplace were met by uncomfortable silences. Interpreting this as disapproval, he decided to contribute less to team activities and then realized that the lack of enthusiasm he then displayed seemed to fit better with his colleagues' apparent attitudes. A lack of awareness of the difference between affective and neutralist cultures had led to his reduction in performance being rewarded by his feeling more comfortable.

Goleman describes a situation in a restaurant chain in the United States where senior management seemed to tacitly condone discrimination against black customers. He quotes an attorney involved in a legal action against the chain as saying, '... management closed their eyes to what the field staff was doing. There must have been some message ... which freed up the inhibitions of local managers to act on their racist impulses' (Goleman, 1995, p. 157). In our context, the poor performance of discrimination was rewarded by senior management's tacit acceptance.

What are the questions to ask in order to identify the rewarding of poor performance?

- What rewards does the person get for doing the job the way they do it at the moment?
- Are these rewards increased if they do the job inadequately?

IS DOING THE JOB WELL IMPORTANT?

Sometimes people just think that there is no point to doing a job. For example, for many years I have been trying to improve my ability in French and so have regularly signed up for evening classes in conversational French. There was no pressure, no homework, no examinations, just a pleasant few hours once a week chatting away. After a while I realized that my French was not getting any better, and this was because I was not putting in the extra work I needed to develop my vocabulary and improve my understanding of irregular verbs. Although I enjoyed the lessons, studying the language just wasn't important enough.

As a result, I decided to sign up for an A-level French class. I had to do homework each week and had the pressure of an examination the following summer. My daughter had achieved a Grade A in A-level French, and I couldn't let her beat me, could I? Consequently, I started to work much harder, doing homework, studying the dictionary and even buying occasional copies of *Le Monde*. There were now consequences to not performing, so studying had become important.

It can be like this in the workplace.

- An administrator regularly fills in returns about stock levels in his department. One month he forgets to do it because of the pressure of other work and then he realizes that nobody has asked for it. So the next month he deliberately fails to do it. Still no consequences. Doing the job well is not important.
- A British company with a subsidiary in a country with an ascriptive culture decides to offer some training to its local staff. In Britain, staff are told that it will help with promotion prospects, and it is well received. However, there is little interest in the subsidiary when it is advertised with the same message, as there is an assumption that promotion is determined by who you know rather than what you know, and the training will not help in any way.
- Shopfloor workers in a country where there is a strong power distance culture are given a suggestion box, where they can post any ideas they have about how to improve performance. Hardly any ideas are ever suggested. In a high power distance culture, decisions are made by senior management, and shopfloor workers 'know their place'. Suggestion boxes are therefore an irrelevance.

To find out if people think that doing a job well is important ask:

- Does doing the task well bring any favourable outcomes?

- Does doing the task inadequately bring any negative outcomes?
- Do people get any satisfaction out of completing the task?

ARE THERE ANY PROBLEMS IN THE WORKING ENVIRONMENT?

The final question to ask when identifying organizational issues that affect performance is about factors surrounding the task itself, either in the immediate vicinity or in the contextual setting of the work. For example:

- Workers in an African sugar-cane factory are having more small industrial accidents than would seem normal. They have been adequately trained, and the machinery is in good working order. However, the workers have to travel a long distance each day to get to the factory, and, particularly in the humid rainy season, the factory can be very hot. So they often feel sleepy and are more prone to making mistakes.
- A French company installs some machinery in one of its local factories in Pakistan. Realizing that there will be a language problem, it fits to the side of the equipment plates that use graphics to show how to stop and start the machine. Unfortunately, because the local operators' first language is Urdu, which is written from right to left, they misinterpret the meaning of the symbols and find it impossible to start the machinery without a supervisor's help.
- A Dutch company operating in Romania decides to set up a cross-functional team with responsibility for delivering a specific objective. The team leader is Romanian, as are the line managers for most of the team members. Because Romanians have a strong respect for authority, they find it difficult to identify their boss and who is responsible for making decisions about their day-to-day activities.
- Someone at the top end of a middle management grade in a government organization is seconded to a specific project for a 12-month period, during which they will be operating on a senior management grade. Halfway through the secondment they discover that they have not been invited to a series of meetings discussing this particular project, because the meetings are only open to senior management and because of their substantive grade they are not considered to be sufficiently senior.
- Triandis (1995) quotes research by Earley looking at how well individualists and collectivists judge their own effectiveness. These studies showed that individualists felt that they performed better when working independently, while collectivists thought that they performed better when their working environment was populated by members of their in-group.

Clearly, the whole area of 'problems in the working environment' is something of a catch-all, which means that there is no single question that you can ask to identify these problems. However, here are some suggestions:

- What might be stopping this person from performing their task?
- Does the person know what they are supposed to be achieving?
- Are there any conflicting demands on this person's time?
- Does the person have the authority to do the task?
- Are there any ergonomic factors that make doing the task difficult?

Select the Best Solutions

If you have done a thorough analysis of the situation, you will probably have developed quite a list of potential solutions. You now need to decide which ones to implement. First ask yourself the questions:

- Have I found all possible solutions?
- Is each solution at all realistic? If not, put it to one side. Ask this question from three different perspectives:
  - Practically?
  - Legally? Solutions may contravene legislation in other countries.
  - Ethically? An ideal solution may be acceptable in one culture but potentially unethical in another.
- How much would each solution cost to implement?
- Will this solution have any negative implications for other areas?
- How do these solutions rank in order of cost, effectiveness and attractiveness to stakeholders?

Financial costs do not end with the investment needed to implement the solution. They can have a wide range of effects, ranging from a temporary reduction in output while people learn new procedures through to long-term unrest due to perceived deskilling or other slight.

Think back to the costs calculated in the first stage of the analysis process – the cost of doing nothing. How do the costs of your solutions compare to this?

You will find more discussion about techniques you can use to help you select solutions to problems in Chapter 10.

Summary

This chapter has unpicked and analysed the factors that affect how well people carry out their work. It has enabled us to see how both ideas and physical objects that have originated in one culture may not be immediately applicable in another. However, a systematic approach, such as the performance flowchart depicted in Figure 2.7, allows us to reflect on what problems might exist in the different areas impact in on an individual's or team's performance.

Figure 2.8 summarizes what we have looked at in this chapter.

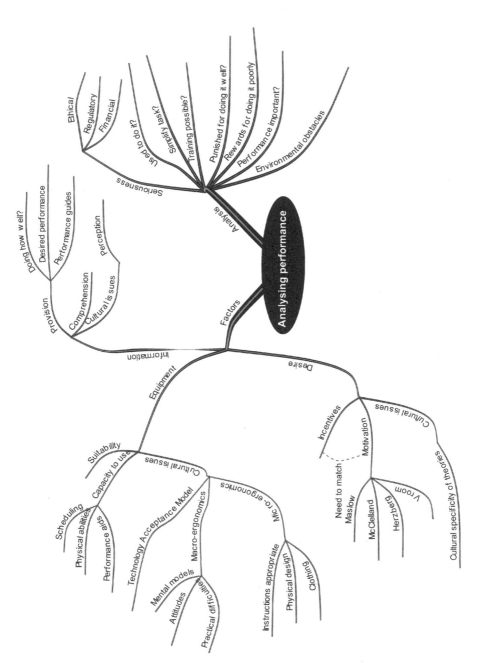

Figure 2.8   Mindmap summary of Chapter 2

3 *Culture and Workplace Activities*

Introduction

Chapter 1 looked at how cultures around the world vary in their views about how things operate and Chapter 2 looked at performance in the workplace, focusing particularly on how factors that affect performance can have cultural dimensions.

In this chapter we will look at the importance of culture in a number of common workplace activities. First, we will consider how different cultures approach negotiation and then see how this can affect decision-making processes. These are both activities that people perform constantly in the workplace, often when working together as part of a team. We will therefore move on after these to consider what the implications of cultural differences are for team development and performance. Finally, we will look at a specific instance of cultural dislocation, that of the new arrival in a foreign culture and the implications of cultural diversity on performance management systems.

Culture and Negotiation

Negotiation is a key skill in the working environment. We not only negotiate financial deals, but also hold discussions on a wide range of everyday issues, such as processes to follow, targets to meet and appointments to make – all issues on which a decision needs to be made. In extreme situations negotiations can literally be about life or death: international humanitarian organizations often have to negotiate with border officials or military personnel about carrying essential medicines through potentially dangerous areas.

Negotiation skills are also important in conflict resolution, which is a topic discussed later in the chapter when looking at effective team-working.

The exact nature of the negotiation progress will depend on the significance and complexity of the topic under discussion, but in general it consists of a three-stage process:

1. pre-negotiation, where the actual negotiation process and tasks that must be completed are discussed and agreed;
2. negotiation, where the interested parties meet, discuss and attempt to persuade each other in some particular way;
3. post-negotiation, where final concessions and compromises are agreed and formalized.

These stages may be completed over a period of time or all within one session.

As the purpose of negotiation is to agree a mutually acceptable outcome, it is pertinent to consider what different cultures regard as acceptable outcomes of a negotiation process. Usunier (1996) suggests that there are five potential outcomes of any negotiation process:

*   *Partnership*: the negotiation results in a relationship between the parties that will be both ongoing and mutually beneficial.
*   *Contract*: the negotiation results in a clearly defined agreement relating to an exchange of services or money or both.
*   *Profit*: each side will emerge from the negotiation better off than when they started.
*   *Winning*: a party will feel that the negotiation has been successful if they have defeated the other party in some way, perhaps on money, quality or power relationships.
*   *Time*: the negotiation will be completed in a finite and appropriate length of time.

Cultural expectations define the relative significance of these outcomes. For example, when I, as a British person, go shopping in a British marketplace I do not expect to spend very much time on agreeing a price, as each stallholder will have identified the price of each and every item that they have for sale. This makes contractual issues very clear. However, if I were to repeat my shopping trip in, for example, a North African marketplace my cultural expectations could be severely shaken. Stallholders would expect us to enter into some sort of relationship while we discuss price, and that this could take a certain length of time, perhaps several minutes or longer. If stallholders felt that my custom was important, the negotiations over price would be conducted in such a way that we entered into a partnership, so that when I needed similar goods in the future, I would always go back to that particular person. Both of us would be looking to make some sort of profit, but winning (and hence losing) would be undesirable, as this would affect our partnership.

So, cross-cultural negotiations need to take into consideration each party's desired outcomes.

PARTNERSHIPS AS AN OUTCOME

People from cultures that place importance on relationships are much more likely to see a partnership as a desirable outcome of a negotiation. So this would apply to quality of life and collectivist cultures, and means that negotiation and decision-making are extremely serious matters to, say, a Chinese or Japanese person. While negotiation for someone with an individualist or short-term perspective is simply to close a deal for a small short-term gain or in order to move on to the next item on that person's agenda, for a collectivist the decision-making is about choosing a long-term partner. To give it a personal analogy, it is the difference between deciding whether to accept an invitation to go for dinner with someone and deciding if you are going to marry that person.

Historical factors can also come into play. If the cultures involved in the negotiation come from a tradition of dominance–submission – in the case of previous colonial relationships, for example – someone from the historically dominated culture may see an equal relationship in the final decision as a key outcome.

CONTRACTS AS AN OUTCOME

Contracts are perhaps potentially one of the most contentious outcomes of a negotiation. To a North European or American mind, what could be simpler than a simple written document that clearly defines what is agreed during the negotiation process? But, from a different perspective, writing down and requiring people to put their signature to the contract to show that they have read and agreed what it says demonstrates distrust: 'We have discussed this and agreed it, so why should I sign this? Do you not trust me?' So from certain cultural perspectives, contracting may have a negative effect on partnership development.

Different cultures also view the purpose of a written contract in different ways. As Lewis (2006) says:

- Japanese see a contract as a 'statement of intent', a starting-point in defining the relationship which reflects the situation at the time of the negotiation, and as such it should be flexible should conditions change.
- Italians see a contract as a description of what should happen in the ideal world, but if things do not turn out as expected, that's the way it goes.
- Americans think that contracts should be written so that they cover all possible eventualities, with clearly defined consequences should contract terms be infringed.

> A much quoted story that illustrates the different ways in which two cultures can view the idea of a contract is that of the Japanese–Australian sugar contract case of the 1970s.
>
> Japanese sugar refiners negotiated a five-year agreement with Australian suppliers to buy sugar at $160 a ton. However, because of the vagaries of the commodities markets, the price of sugar dropped considerably soon after delivery started.
>
> The Japanese refineries said to the Australians that the contract should be cancelled because the conditions under which it had been negotiated had changed. After all, a contract is just a statement of intent.
>
> However, the Australians said the contract was a legally binding agreement and they refused to renegotiate its terms in any way.
>
> (Quoted in Nisbett, 2003).

The importance attached to contractual relationships is mirrored in the respective job markets: according to Lewis, the United States has 300,000 lawyers to a population of over 300 million (one lawyer to 1000 people), whereas Japan has just 10,000 lawyers to a population of 128 million (one lawyer to 12,800 people). In systems terms it would be interesting to consider what is driving the feedback loop: the numbers of lawyers promoting litigation to encourage work for themselves or the litigious culture demanding the lawyers.

At the workplace level, therefore, a manager therefore needs to give careful attention to how they define expectations with employees. For example, cultural diversity makes it possible for the 'sanctity' of objectives in performance agreements, developed as part of a performance management system, to be interpreted in different ways.

TIME AS AN OUTCOME

The relative importance attached to achieving a satisfactory outcome on time is connected to other outcomes. For example, if a partnership is a desired outcome, as would be the case for collectivist-oriented negotiators, there would be more willingness to spend time in the negotiation process in order to develop trust and understanding and, ideally, reach a consensus.

People with a long-term orientation would also be more prepared to spend time in the negotiation process, because this would be seen as helping to develop relationships and therefore trust, as well as making it more possible to have an extensive discussion about the subject at hand, which would all contribute to a negotiated outcome with long-term benefits.

Negotiators from a linear-active culture, who divide their lives up into parcels of time that can be bought and sold, can find extended negotiations very frustrating. They prefer to allocate a specific amount of time to the process, expecting to work through the three stages of the negotiation during this period. Experienced negotiators who know that they are in discussions with a linear-active person can use this to their advantage, as they will make sure that discussions move slowly, knowing that the pressure the linear-active person is putting on themselves can lead to them making concessions they would otherwise not make.

WINNING AS AN OUTCOME

Negotiations can end as win–win, win–lose or lose–lose. To competitive individualists, winning so that someone else loses may be very important, although in the long term this could turn out to be a lose–lose result, if the process and other outcomes are unsatisfactory to the other party.

The win–win situation is a consensus that is equally acceptable to all parties. Achieving consensus can be difficult and time-consuming, but it is often something that collectivists expect to do during a negotiation as the benefits gained can be significant. Often, building a consensus is not something that can be done in a single room or a single session: it may require separate, behind-the-scenes conversations, which can be frustrating to individualists and linear-active types who are keen to make a decision so that things can move on. However, from the perspective of the collectivist, investing time in achieving a consensual decision means that relationships are strengthened and trust is built, so that when the decision is put into practice everyone is in agreement and things are much more likely to work smoothly.

Winning can mean different things. To the American executive it would probably mean agreeing a deal at the price wanted, whereas to someone from a country with a strong sense of national pride winning might mean having their national honour vindicated, particularly if the negotiations are with people seen to be representing countries that have historically had dominant colonial or similar relationships with their own country.

THE
NEGOTIATION
STAGE

The negotiation stage is where the parties come together to discuss and agree the outcomes. Approaches to negotiation vary across cultures. Gelfand and Christakopoulou describe negotiation as 'a cognitive decision-making task in which individuals construct mental representations of the conflict situation, the issues, and their opponents' (Gelfand and Christakopoulou, 1999, p. 250). So, when two people are each constructing mental representations of the other, we need to consider what those representations look like.

From an individualist–collectivist perspective, two concepts are useful here. The first is what is known as the 'fixed pie error': an assumption made that the other party in the negotiation wants exactly the same slice of the pie as you do, implying that your interests are diametrically opposed. With this as a perspective, negotiation is, from the outset, competition. Gelfand's and Christakopoulou's research showed that individualists start with a strong belief in the fixed pie and, wanting to maximize their own needs and interests, use negotiation tactics that fail to develop any more accurate understanding of what the other party wanted. They therefore end the negotiation with no challenge made to their fixed-pie belief. Collectivists, on the other hand, attempt to find out what their counterparts want and so amend their perceived share of the pie. At the end of negotiations between individualists and collectivists, even when both parties have expressed satisfaction at the details agreed, collectivists can feel unhappy about the process because they think that the individualists have still not understood what they wanted.

The second useful perspective is that of the 'fundamental attribution error' (Ross, 1977). This describes the assumption made that another person's behaviour is due to their personality traits rather than features of their current situation. Barack Obama describes this when writing about people working in Washington's political circles (Obama 2006):

> ... most people who serve in Washington have been trained either as lawyers or as political operatives – professions that tend to place a premium on winning arguments rather than solving problems. I can see how, after a certain amount of time in the capital, it becomes tempting to assume that those who disagree with you have fundamentally different values – indeed, that they are motivated by bad faith, and perhaps are bad people.

Obama, 2006, p. 48.

Curiously, or perhaps not, people rarely apply the fundamental attribution error to themselves!

We might see the fundamental attribution error as a manifestation of the field dependence/independence dichotomy, and, as such, it is an assumption that people from individualist cultures make more readily than those from collectivist cultures. When applied to negotiation, it explains why individualist negotiators assume that their counterpart's position is personally held and is therefore difficult to explore, rather than deriving from some aspect of their situation.

Collectivist negotiators are also reluctant to operate on their own, as what they are really looking for is a consensus rather than a win–lose result. Working with at least one other kindred spirit makes it much more likely that they will be able to achieve this. Nisbett (2003) argues that, as far as Eastern cultures are concerned, this is due to the lack of a concept of 'agency', the idea that we have control over the world around us and that we can therefore, with a suitable argument, make it do what we want. This has therefore stifled any tradition of debate, as people from these cultures are simply not trained in the art of taking a position and arguing for it: from their perspective that would mean the disruption of vital harmony.

Attitudes to power distance will affect behaviour during negotiations. Strong beliefs in, and acceptance of, hierarchies will make it difficult for people who see themselves as of a lower status to express themselves fully during the negotiation process. People from work success cultures will adopt competitive attitudes, whereas those from quality-of-life cultures will, like collectivists, be more interested in developing relationships and looking for mutual benefits as outcomes.

Uncertainty avoidance may also play its part. People from cultures where uncertainty is to be avoided will be keen to have rules to follow (protocols) during the negotiation process, and they may want to ask for help from other sources if things happen that are beyond their comfort zone.

Here are some key things to remember about cross-cultural negotiating:

- There are several different potential outcomes from a negotiation, including partnerships, contracts, time and winning.
- Parties in a negotiation do not always necessarily want the same outcome, so it is important to establish what each party's needs are.
- Negotiating strategies reflect cultural perspectives and do not necessarily indicate personal characteristics.

Culture and Decision-making

Cultures approach decision-making in different ways. For example, studies comparing British expatriates and Chinese staff in Hong

Kong-based businesses (Crookes and Thomas, 1998) showed clearly that the two groups approached decision-making in very different ways, with the two approaches being very much derived from their different cultural backgrounds, particularly with regard to power distance and individualist–collectivist factors.

In high power distance cultures decision-making is the preserve of the person highest in the hierarchy. Empowering people in subordinate positions to make decisions is likely to be ineffectual and to cause considerable stress. People from low power distance cultures may find a lack of consultation and the inability to influence a decision frustrating.

Cultures with a strong attachment to the past or who see time as cyclical will place a greater weight on historical factors in making their decisions than will people who are more future-oriented. Future-oriented people may see thinking about the past as being a drag on moving forward, whereas cyclical people may see not thinking about the past as being wilfully reckless.

Decision-making in high uncertainty avoidance cultures will be based very much on rules rather than on innovation, even if the rules are ineffectual in that particular situation. If they do not have enough information to be able to comfortably make a decision, people from such cultures will delay making a decision until enough information is available.

People of a universalist persuasion will also be relying on rules for making decisions, which they will see as ensuring such things as fairness and consistency, for example. In particularist cultures rules will be much less important, and people will consider a wider variety of factors and possibly display rather more inconsistency in making a decision. They may also have a looser idea about what a decision actually is. A decision is a rule that has been agreed, so universalists will see that, once the decision has been taken, it is legally binding and a matter of honour that it must be seen through. However, particularists may see a decision as being nothing more than a general statement of intent which can be renegotiated if circumstances change.

Decision-making is a much quicker process in cultures in which people draw a clear distinction between working and personal lives than in those that are diffuse. In both diffuse and collectivist cultures decisions cannot be taken until you can see the 'big picture' of the other people involved and the implications for them and interpersonal relationships. The process will involve a considerable amount of informal discussions, so that everyone's opinions are explored and the possibilities for consensus are identified. So, although the actual decision-making process will take longer, implementation should be quicker and easier because everyone has bought into the decision.

A good example of this is the Japanese process of *ringi-sho*. In this an idea that originates at a lower level of management is presented to a group of managers at a similar level to discuss and refine the idea to a point at which everyone is fully in agreement and signs the document to show that this is the case. The document then moves up to the next level of management where it is again discussed and refined, and complete consensus is sought. This continues until the idea reaches the head of the company. The process can take a considerable time, but does mean that the document has been very carefully thought through and that everyone involved in its implementation has been consulted and agrees with what it says. This tradition for decision-making is why Japanese people in discussion with Westerners dislike making immediate decisions about new ideas brought up around a negotiation table. If Westerners involved are not aware of what is happening, it can be a source of great frustration.

People with a long-term orientation will weigh factors differently from those whose time horizons are shorter. They are more likely to choose small, incremental actions and do things to enhance relationship networks.

Decision-making is closely connected with risk-taking – for example, where the decision is about some sort of financial investment. We might expect that a preparedness to take risks would be higher in strongly individualistic cultures, but in fact there is evidence to suggest that people from collectivist cultures may be prepared to take more risks when it comes to such things as making investments.

Various ideas have been put forward as to why this is the case. It may be that the collectivist society surrounding an individual provides a cushion, because they know that if they make the wrong decision that the consequences are less severe than if they were in an individualist 'you're on your own' culture (Weber and Hsee, 1998). It has also been suggested that, at least in the case of Chinese cultures, people are more confident about their decision-making skills (Yates, 1998). Yates suggested various reasons for this:

- It could be because education is more rule-based, which tends to suggest to people that everything is more straightforward.
- Chinese culture also places less emphasis on logical analysis, which means that people are less likely to consider obstacles or contradictions to a course of action.
- The culture is also more past-oriented, and people take historical precedent into more consideration, so that if they feel that a current decision is similar to one which has been taken in the past, they will choose the course of action that was selected previously, in full confidence that it will work again.

To summarize, when looking to make decisions with culturally diverse teams:

- Consider who might be expected to make the decision and what role other people involved might play.
- Allow more time for decision-making in diffuse or collectivist cultures, as maintaining relationships is important and consensus needs to be achieved.
- Be prepared to be flexible about the extent to which rules are applied in the decision-making process.
- Accept that different cultures will take into consideration different factors and weigh them differently.

Culture and Team-working

Most activities in the workplace revolve around team performances, whether process- or project-oriented. So what is a team? One working definition is that it is a relatively small identifiable group of people working together with a shared objective and more or less well-defined roles, who interact to achieve the objective (West, 1996). The presence of a shared objective is what distinguishes a team from a group, and is what introduces the possibility of cross-cultural challenges.

The effect that culture might have on a team depends to a large extent on how culturally diverse a team is. Adler (2008) identifies four different ways to classify a team from a cultural perspective.

Homogeneous teams contain people drawn from just one culture. The cross-cultural issues described within this book may not be expected to affect its performance as there will be a shared understanding about values, beliefs and norms. But, of course, that does not mean that the team will operate effectively!

Token diversity means that the team contains just one or two members of a different cultural group. The word 'token' can be somewhat pejorative, in that it suggests that these lonely individuals have been included for perhaps cynical organizational reasons (which, of course, may be true). However, there will be many cases where this has happened simply because of the cultural composition of the community from which the team is drawn.

Depending on the behaviour of the majority, these minority representatives might feel anything from comfortable to discriminated against or even ostracized, overtly or otherwise. However, it is extremely likely that they will have to make significant cultural concessions in order to fit in with the team, and it is also quite likely that the majority members will pay little attention to cross-cultural issues.

Bicultural diversity describes a team consisting of just two cultures, and each is significantly represented. This type of team is often found in overseas branches of transnational corporations. The cross-cultural dynamic in this case will often be shaped by the external power relationship determined by the national culture of the parent company.

Multicultural teams are made up from small numbers of many different cultures. The classic example of this is the United Nations. Quite how cross-cultural dynamics work themselves out in teams such as this will depend very much on the personal qualities of individual team members and on the overall organizational ethos. So, for example, everyone working within the United Nations agrees to abide by the rules of its Code of Conduct which provides a frame of reference within which team cultures should evolve.

From an overall performance perspective, the most potentially problematic type of team is one in which there are several representatives from a small number of different cultures. Such a team may perform less effectively than other types because it can tend to fragment into a small number of sub-teams, each of which is made up from a different culture.

How effective a team is depends to a large extent on how well its members work together, and cultural diversity can have a significant effect on this. Adler (2008) suggests a number of potential advantages and disadvantages to cultural diversity in the workplace.

Advantages:

- Diversity opens people's minds to new ideas, opening up new perspectives on challenges the team might face. The chance of groupthink developing is substantially reduced.
- Diversity can make a team more creative in its approach to solving problems, so that it can see a different range of solutions.
- The team may be able to operate more flexibly.
- Representatives from different cultures may make it possible to see, and take action on, business opportunities in different locations.
- Practical knowledge about different cultures can increase the team's understanding about political or legal aspects of work in that culture.
- Cultural diversity can provide a more stimulating working environment.

Disadvantages:

- Diversity makes ambiguity or misunderstanding more likely.

- Communication may be more difficult, due to language difficulties and different approaches to negotiation and decision-making. This may slow things down and lead to misunderstandings and difficulties in deciding when, where and how to act.
- Different cultures may view the relative importance of the team's goals differently.
- Inefficiencies in team functioning may make the team cost more to run.
- It will be harder for the team to develop the mutual trust that it needs in order to operate effectively.
- Teams may fragment into cultural cliques.

As a generalization, it seems that cultural diversity is particularly valuable when a team is operating in a divergent direction – in other words, when it is trying to create something new or better – whereas it can be a disadvantage where activity is convergent, and the organization needs people to all behave in a similar way.

The United Nations Department of Peacekeeping Operations operates around the world to help countries recover from wars and other conflicts. Planning these operations must take into consideration the perspectives of the host country, the political demands of other countries in the United Nations organization and the practical requirements of countries providing military personnel.

The cultural diversity of the organization is therefore a great advantage in the planning stage, in that it provides a multitude of different perspectives that can help in implementing the peacekeeping intervention.

However, once the operation is under way, it is vitally important that all military personnel operate in the same way, regardless of their country of origin, however difficult or dangerous an immediate situation might be. Cultural differences that might lead to different interpretations of an order could cost lives, and so diversity becomes a potential disadvantage.

Adair et al. (2006) provide a useful way of looking at how cross-cultural issues can impact on team performance, and this is summarized in Figure 3.1.

What the team does is affected by ideas that team members have about both task and team. Task ideas relate to how people understand the team's goals, what equipment it works with and the process that it needs to follow. Team ideas relate to understandings of what skills team members have, what roles they play and responsibilities they each have. However, because the team is made up of individuals, they will all be bringing their cultural expectations – their values, beliefs and norms – to the party. As far as team performance is concerned, these will impact mainly on the roles and responsibilities within the

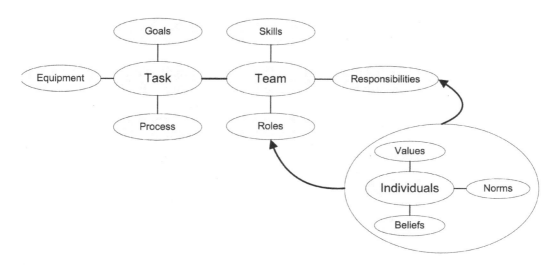

Figure 3.1   Elements in team performance

team (although, as we have seen elsewhere in this chapter, culture has an impact on all aspects of performance).

CULTURE
AND TEAM
DEVELOPMENT

Various models have been proposed over the years to describe how teams come together and develop (or not) into effective units. One of the best known, if perhaps for its catchy naming, is Tuckman's four-stage forming, storming, norming and performing model (Tuckman, 1965).

Stage 1: Forming

In the forming stage individuals come together for the first time. In a multicultural setting people are less likely to know each other than in a monocultural setting, so the issues of getting to know each other will be more problematic. When meeting a stranger from our own culture we can rely on a shared understanding about such things as appropriate greetings and topics of initial conversation, what physical gestures are acceptable and what silence means, to name but a few, but when meeting strangers from a strange land there are so many more unknowns. Everyone will pull out their stereotypes of the other team members and make all sorts of possibly unwarranted assumptions about what type of person they are.

Quite what will happen during the forming stage largely depends on the cultural consciousness of the team members. Halversen and Cuellar (2001) suggest that people can be regarded as occupying one of three different stages of cultural awareness – dependent, counterdependent or independent.

Dependent people are unaware of issues of racism or sexism and see problems that they have with other people as resulting from that individual's personal characteristics (the fundamental attribution error). People in this stage of consciousness are usually from cultures that have traditionally been either dominant or subordinate.

Counterdependent people are aware of cultural differences and the power relationships that these have brought, but use this awareness in negative ways. For example, people from the dominant culture will feel guilt and shame about the situation and may find it difficult to engage openly with representatives of the subordinate culture. Counterdependent people from a subordinate culture will, on the other hand, express anger and resentment at the situation.

Independent people recognize the cultural differences and associated power structures, but work actively to eliminate them. They have constructive dialogues with people from different cultures and collaborate effectively.

From this perspective, the forming stage may be characterized by a range of emotional reactions, ranging from ignorance about cultural differences to guilt and awkwardness about traditional power relationships through to a genuine interest and commitment to develop a strong working relationship.

How comfortable people feel, about getting to know people from different cultures therefore depends on both attitudinal factors and knowledge. Knowing about, and being able to cope with, cultural differences has been described as 'cultural intelligence', sometimes abbreviated to CQ. This was an concept put forward by Earley and Mosakowski (2004) and is clearly related to Goleman's emotional intelligence and Gardner's ideas about multiple intelligences. Earley and Mosakowski propose that cultural intelligence derives from three areas:

1. *cognitive* – the ability to identify and take account of differences in another person's cultural values.
2. *physical* – the ability to adapt to physical practices, such as greeting rituals and the use of personal space.
3. *emotional and motivational* – the level of confidence and desire to get along with people from a different culture.

Cultural intelligence is crucial to making first meetings easier: knowing that things will be different, even if you do not know what those differences will be, is at least a step forward, and people who are culturally intelligent can look forward to a period of getting to know each other's different ways of approaching life. However, these uncertainties may mean that the group spends an abnormal amount of time being overly polite to each other.

Much will depend on historic relationships between the different cultures. If they have been in some sort of colonial master–subject relationship or if there has been some recent history of war or other political tension, people may approach being part of a team in different ways.

A team working on a construction project comprised two British people, a Kenyan, two Indians and three Chinese.

For one of the British people it was their first experience of working in an international team, and their education meant that they had little understanding about how a Kenyan might feel about the historical colonial relationship between Britain and Kenya. He therefore found the Kenyan's slightly frosty attitude difficult to understand. However, he called on some old negative stereotypes and applied the fundamental attribution error to assume that this person was 'difficult' and perhaps 'aggressive'.

Conversely, the other British individual had been born in East Africa and so was very conscious about the colonial history, to the extent that he felt awkward and guilty, which initially made team-working difficult.

However, both the British people felt confused by the Chinese, who seemed very polite but were apparently unwilling to get involved in any 'meaningful' dialogue about the team's objectives. Here the British people's task orientation made them feel that it was important to get on with the task at hand, but the more collectivist-oriented members of the team wanted to spend more time getting to know each other better, in order to strengthen interpersonal relationships.

One of the two Indians was of a higher caste than the other, but both felt that their superior–inferior relationship was natural and found it difficult to understand that one of the British team members felt strongly that this was not the natural order of things.

Master–subject patterns may begin to be replicated within the team. The connection between economic power and individualism means that 'master cultures' tend to be individualist in nature, and individualists, being more used to operating in settings in which they do not have the strength of an in-group around them, will often take leading roles in the early stages of a team's development. Assertive members of a team may find it difficult to understand the lack of direct communication from other team members, attributing it perhaps to a lack of interest or simple shyness. They might then try to deal with this by putting pressure on the others to speak more or take more action, possibly further alienating them.

The issue of leadership and the establishment of power relationships may occur earlier if people within the team dislike uncertainty. Any domination–subordination relationships that exist at a national cultural level may start to be replicated within the team, particularly if team members are operating in the dependent mode.

Dominant personalities may start to take over, and pressures to conform and to not do anything to disrupt the process of team-building may lead to difficult issues being buried and not dealt with. This might be less likely to happen if some team members are from affective cultures, as they would be more likely to express frustration or anger, perhaps acting as the team's safety valve.

Individualist, task-oriented team members may well find this a frustrating stage as they want to get on with the task at hand and find spending time developing relationships difficult. Collectivists in the team will be much more interested in finding out about other people in order to start the relationship-building process.

However, regardless of the nature of the intercultural mix in a team, the forming stage is characterized by the lack of any real progress, and any achievements made are often later seen to be perhaps lacking in quality. So, irrespective of cultural differences, the most important thing in the early days of a team's existence is for people to get to know more about each other's norms, values and beliefs.

Stage 2: Storming

At the end of the forming stage people will have come to understand the team's objectives and will know a little more about other members. In this next storming stage they start to work out decision-making processes and establish hierarchies of respect and control. This is probably the most difficult stage in the life of any team.

Patterns of dominance that started to develop in the forming stage come to maturity here. Those people who are dominant often effectively form a clique that can exclude the members who have become subordinate. Should someone from a subordinate culture start to appear to be a potential leader within the team, they may be ignored or suffer something akin to a coup.

Communication between the dominant and subordinate members of the team can become difficult, and this is often made worse by different methods of communication within cultures. Views are expressed strongly but are often not listened to actively, so that there may be little collaboration but a lot of competition.

Team members from high power distance cultures will probably look to hierarchies to sort things out. These might be dependent on any number of variables such as organizational status, social status, gender or even nationality. Representatives from work success cultures will probably relish the competitiveness of this stage as this provides the best moment for them to show themselves as winners. Again, people with a preference for avoiding uncertainty will probably push very hard for the roles, responsibilities and relationships within the team to be agreed quickly, so that the acute discomfort of this stage ends as soon as possible.

The absence of any real group identity during this stage means that people will often try to opt out of team membership and will be negative about the value of the team. Individualists, in particular, may, as in the forming stage, be tempted to feel that they could do things better on their own.

Storming is a crucial period in any team's life. It is a make-or-break stage, and many teams fall apart at this juncture. However, the opportunity that it presents for a perhaps open and frank discussion of attitudes can provide members with a clearer understanding of what drives their colleagues. In a multicultural team it can therefore provide a lot of the information necessary to develop the culture required for the team to be able to develop its norms in Stage 3.

Stage 3: Norming

During the norming stage the team will be developing its norms – the standards for the processes it will follow to make decisions, resolve conflicts, conduct meetings and communicate information.

Competition is replaced by collaboration; people are starting to actively listen to each other and develop agreed ways of working. Disagreements within the team are viewed as opportunities for learning and improvement rather than as battles that must be won in order to confirm one's status. Trust is developing, and people are revealing more about themselves and about how they see the team and the world around them.

Norming is likely to be a harder stage to work through in culturally heterogeneous teams, as different cultures will probably want to define team processes in different ways. For example, earlier in this chapter we have seen how people from different cultures approach decision-making and negotiation in quite different ways. The only way in which a team can achieve a true consensus about team processes is by developing the process of self-disclosure that will have started during the storming stage. How this can be done is covered in more detail later in this chapter in the section 'Getting culturally diverse teams to work together'.

Stage 4: Performing

At last, the sunlit uplands of performing. The team is now a close-knit group of people, working effectively together to achieve the team's objectives. It will be characterized by flexibility, trust and strong relationships. The leadership style will have evolved to suit the culture developed by the group, and so may vary considerably from one team to another.

However, even when a team has reached the performing stage it cannot sit back and think that no further development is needed. As time goes by, the environment within which the team operates will change and this will create a need for change within the team, and, if the team does not respond appropriately, its performance will deteriorate.

Senge (1990) analyses this deterioration in terms of the 'defensive routines' that teams (and individuals) switch on whenever faced by the need to change. These might be simple denial of change or creative avoidance, focusing on something less uncomfortable. Figure 3.2 shows how this process can be represented in a causal flow diagram. Exactly how these diagrams work is described in more detail in Chapter 4, but it is worth using one here in order to throw some light on how cultural diversity can contribute to breaking the cycle of deterioration.

As the environment around a team changes, the gap between what the team knows about how to perform and what it needs to know will grow. This creates a need to learn. On a causal flow diagram we show this direct relationship by a '+' sign on the line. The team will respond to this need to learn by increasing their level of understanding, but this may well take some time. However, as the level of understanding increases, the gap between what they know and what needs to be known diminishes (shown by the '–' sign). In systems terms this is a stable feedback loop because it corrects itself: as the need for learning increases, action is taken to remedy this, and the need decreases.

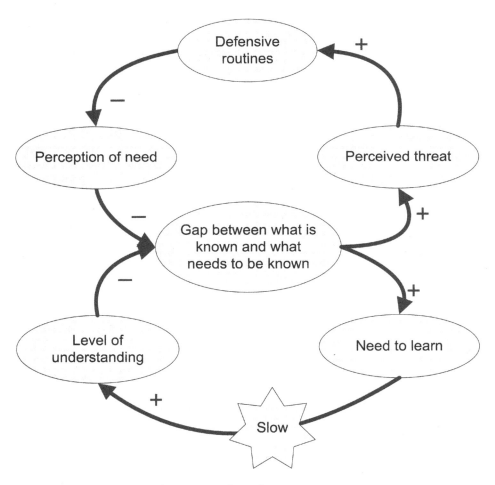

Figure 3.2   How team performance deteriorates

However, the existence of the gap between what is known and what needs to be known also creates anxiety within the team, which they perceive as a threat. After all, something now needs to change. As the levels of anxiety increase, the strength of its defensive routines also increase: team members deny that the environment is changing or they focus on other activities that create the appearance of action but do not actually do anything to close the gap in knowledge. As the defensive routines strengthen, the perception of need decreases. This makes it less likely that the team will learn, and so the gap increases. This second feedback loop is unstable, and, as time goes by, the gap will increase.

This means there is a struggle between the two loops, one closing the gap and the other increasing it, but the problem for the team is that, unless direct action is taken, the loop closing the gap will be working more slowly than the loop increasing it.

There are two things that can be done:

1. The team can be proactive in learning about the changes in its environment so that the stable loop speeds up.
2. The team can examine its defensive routines and suppress them.

Cultural diversity can help with both of these. Different cultural perspectives can help the team to examine the changes in the environment through different cultural lenses by considering such things as:

• relative short- and long-term implications;
• lessons that can be learned from the past;
• what implications there might be for structure or process within the team.

In terms of analysing the defensive routines it is quite possible that the heterogeneity of a diverse team may make the defensive routines that operate more visible. As Senge points out, the strength of defensive routines lies in the fact that they are invisible, that people are not aware they are behaving in that particular way. That is more likely to be true in culturally homogeneous teams in which the shared culture would quite possibly lead to shared defensive routines. However, in a culturally diverse team that has learnt to use its diversity well, the contrast in defensive routines employed should be more visible to all, making it easier to deal with them. When that happens, the unstable feedback loop is extinguished.

CULTURE
AND TEAM
PERFORMANCE

What factors may affect a team's performance? Moxon (1993) suggests four areas: problems with goals, roles, processes and relationships.

Problems with goals

Goal-related problems include:

- how well the team members understand the goals;
- how measurable and specific the goals are;
- whether goals are independent or interdependent and what that may imply;
- ownership of goals;
- potential conflicts or duplications created by goals.

From a cross-cultural perspective a key issue is the attractiveness of the goals. For example:

- Will achieving the goal bring short-term or long-term benefits? People value the relative importance of these according to their cultural background.
- How will the rewards fit into their culture's needs hierarchy? Achieving a goal that brings individualistic rewards may be less appealing to those from a collectivist culture, who may be more motivated by an objective that promotes belonging or security.
- Would the team's goals be seen as promoting career success or enhancing quality-of-life issues? How does this fit in with cultural preferences within the team?
- Where have the goals come from? In a culture with high uncertainty avoidance and power distance it would be important that the goals were seen to be coming from the top down.
- Individualists will compare the team's goals against their own goals and, if they conflict, may well decide to do what is necessary to achieve their own goals, whereas collectivists are much more likely to embrace the team's goals as their own.

How achievable is a goal? It is commonly said that a goal should be just a little bit more than seems achievable, so that its achievement will bring satisfaction and growth, but that it should not seem impossible. But how applicable is this reasoning across different cultures? Consider two of Kluckhohn's dimensions:

1. *Relationship to nature*: do people think they can dominate the outside world, or is it all in the hands of external influences?
2. *Orientation to time*: will what has happened in the past be a problem? If similar attempts have been made in the past to achieve the objective and they have failed, will this discourage people or not affect their confidence?

Also, consider the way of working that may be needed in order to achieve the goals. Will it require close cooperation or significant individual activity? How will this fit in with individualists or collectivists within the team? Remember that collectivists do not always work together harmoniously if they are members of different in-groups.

Problems with roles

Typical problems with roles include:

- how well understood the boundaries between roles are;
- overlaps in roles or responsibilities;
- individual expectations of other people's roles.

Role definition is particularly important in teams where people have different expectations about power distance. In culturally homogeneous teams, expectations about hierarchies and individual roles will be much clearer, but, in teams where values differ, it would be easy for different team members to make quite different assumptions about the extent of their and other people's roles.

Collectivists may be better at adapting to a team's requirements, as they feel a strong need to maintain relationships and work together. On the other hand, individualists may look to find ways to change the team's operation to suit their own needs (Triandis, 1995).

Teams working in low power distance cultures find it easier to cooperate. In high power distance cultures, particularly where there is a hierarchy within the team, subordinates find it much harder to challenge people who are higher in the hierarchy. This can present problems in some situations: Helmreich and Merritt (1998) studied aircraft crew and medical teams operating in stressful situations where, although there was a hierarchy (such as pilot and co-pilot), close cooperation was necessary, with the subordinate providing an indispensable pair of hands or eyes; they discovered that individuals with a high power distance belief found working in this way much more difficult. It is possible that this cultural issue was one reason why the cabin pressurization switch was not operated correctly in the Helios air disaster, discussed in Chapter 2.

Teams operating in low power distance cultures may also be expected to show more innovation, since in high power distance cultures the only people 'allowed' to innovate are the most senior people, who are generally older and therefore probably more attached to traditional ways.

Nevertheless, the strong sense of mutual obligations present in high power distance cultures can strengthen certain aspects of team operations. This also applies to collectivist or quality-of-life cultures, where the personal relationships that develop as part of team-working satisfied desires about connectedness.

What about differences in the team regarding attitudes to achievement and ascription? Team members will have certain expectations about what role they will play in the team and what level of influence they will have. An achievement-oriented person may find it frustrating to have to work with people whom they see as having justified their place in the team not through achievement but through status. For example, an ascription-oriented person of high status would find it difficult to defer to someone with a perceived lower status, whether it is due to factors such as age, gender or religion.

Problems with processes

Process-related problems include those associated with:

- *decision-making* – who makes decisions, what consultation there is and how decisions are communicated.
- *communication processes* – channels for communication, how much information must be communicated, frequency of meetings, attendance policies, and so on.
- *leadership styles* – appropriateness and possibilities for feedback.

How will the team organize its activities? Linear-active members may want to create project plans, identify milestones and allocate precise roles, whereas multi-active members may want to have a general outline plan and let activities evolve.

Team members who have a strong preference for uncertainty avoidance will be keen to have clearly defined, written-down rules and procedures defining how the team operates. Members for whom uncertainty avoidance is not an issue may find rules stifling and frustrating, and may ignore or sabotage rules, seeing them as a restriction on their individual abilities. This can also apply where there is a mix in the team of people with universalist and particularist preferences.

To some extent, processes may define how the team operates on a day-to-day basis. How will these processes seem to people with differing perspectives on specific or diffuse lifestyles? People with a specific approach to work divide their lives up into neat boxes so that when they are working they are just working, whereas those who are diffuse prefer their working and personal lives to overlap. So, for example, if being a team member involves working away from home a lot, that may present problems to people with a diffuse approach to life, as they may not be able to balance the conflicting demands of work and home. Consequently, diffuse members of the team may be talking to friends and family or receiving visitors when specific people feel they should be 'concentrating on their team job'.

What kind of leadership style is most appropriate within the team? If the team is culturally homogeneous, this should be relatively easy to decide, but if, say, people have different attitudes to power distance, some will expect the team leader to encourage participation and to delegate, whereas others will expect the leader to make decisions on their own and the allocation of activities to closely reflect positions within the hierarchy.

How do people communicate? Team members from low-context cultures will communicate using much more direct language, and all aspects of team operations will be more explicit. This could be challenging and potentially offensive to people used to higher-context communication, in which problems are dealt with in a more subtle fashion.

How freely can people communicate and express opinions, especially if they appear to be contrary to those of the majority? The fear of expressing contrary opinions can be sufficiently great that it can lead people into situations where they are prepared to contemplate nuclear obliteration: Janis coined the term 'groupthink' to describe the behavior of the team advising President Kennedy during the planning of the Bay of Pigs invasion of Cuba (Janis, 1972). Apart from the self-censoring that the fear of being different creates, groupthink also causes team members to apply pressure on anyone who seems to be offering a dissenting voice, by doing such things as implicitly or explicitly questioning their loyalty or commitment to the team. Certain members of the team may also see themselves as guards, protecting other members from information that might threaten the team's unity.

Problems with relationships

Relationship problems in teams centre on how team members feel about each other. This includes:

- extent of mutual respect;
- harmony or otherwise of values and beliefs;
- the degree of mutual trust.

Relationship problems can be not only the most intractable within teams, but also have the most powerful effects on performance. Within culturally homogeneous teams relationship difficulties often centre on interpersonal conflicts, but in the culturally diverse team there may be myriad ways in which people can offend or confuse other team members.

For example, what degree of 'closeness' do team members expect? Developing strong interpersonal relationships would be important to people from quality-of-life cultures, but those from work success cultures may find this uncomfortable.

Although collectivists might be expected to find it easier to operate as part of a team, paradoxically they often find it harder than individualists to get to know new people and groups because their social skills are attuned to working with members of a specific in-group (Triandis, 1995). However, collectivists as a whole are more familiar with providing mutual support, and so may be able to help each other adapt to working with other people. On the other hand, individualists can find it difficult to do this as they prefer to work by themselves

Trust is a key factor within a team – without it, team will find it difficult to work together effectively. Attitudes to trust and how to develop it vary from culture to culture. Lewis (2006) distinguishes between high-trust and low-trust societies, and claims that they correspond reasonably closely with his distinction between linear-active and multi-active cultures. People in high-trust societies assume that they can trust people from their own culture until shown otherwise, whereas those from low-trust societies are initially distrustful of people from their own culture. Lewis argues that this is related to how the society is organized: in a country such as China, with a collectivist tradition and strong state control, people spend most of their time interacting with a relatively small number of people, whereas in looser, individualist societies people regularly interact with others from very different backgrounds, which helps them develop a greater understanding of relative strangers and therefore trust them to some degree. It would therefore be expected that team members coming from linear-active cultures would more readily develop a sense of trust than those from multi-active cultures.

How much should team activity extend beyond the working day? In specific cultures people may feel strongly that their involvement with the team should end when they leave work at the end of the day, but people from diffuse cultures may expect the personal relationships developed by working together as a team to extend into their personal lives. Differing expectations in this respect could cause a considerable amount of offence, which could have a serious effect on team performance.

People from collectivist or ascriptive cultures may find it difficult to work with people whom they perceive to have a different status.

Public displays of emotion may cause problems. Neutral people may find constant displays of positive or negative emotion wearing, while affective people may feel that neutral members of the team are rather aloof and not committed to the team's goals. There may be problems with how people perceive acceptable personal space: individualists need a larger personal space around them, whereas collectivists often feel more comfortable closer to others.

When working with culturally diverse teams:

- Be aware of expectations about hierarchies within the team.
- Conflicting expectations between individualist and collectivist cultures can cause tensions in what a team seeks to achieve.

- Look out for conflicts between achievement- and ascription-oriented people.
- Manage different levels of emotional display carefully.

GETTING CULTURALLY DIVERSE TEAMS TO WORK TOGETHER

Given that culturally diverse teams may find it difficult to operate effectively, and perhaps even harmoniously, we need to consider what can be done to harness the definite strengths that they can offer. In the context of improving workplace performance, this may be important in several different ways, perhaps so that the team can work together to solve performance problems or even to overcome performance problems that are caused by the cultural diversity of the group.

There are two levels at which we can consider improving the performance of a team. At the lowest and probably shorter-term level is what we might call conflict resolution, while at a longer-term level we have what is generally called team-building.

RESOLVING CONFLICTS WITHIN A TEAM

As is discussed in more detail in Chapter 5, when people have to make a decision, such as how to resolve a conflict situation, their brains operate both emotionally and rationally. In situations that are perceived to be threatening in some way, as a conflict would be, the emotional response is often stronger, so people tend to instinctively fall back on their normal culturally determined response to that type of situation. This means that individualists will become task-oriented, and will negotiate or bargain. Their low-context culture will lead them to try to make the situation as clear as possible to the other party or parties through extensive and elaborate descriptions. Their analytical–logical predisposition may encourage them to try to explain, perhaps adopting a rational tone of voice, why their position is the correct one and why the other people involved are in error. If emotions start to run higher, they are more likely to use what Jehn calls 'less pleasant behaviour' (Jehn and Weldon, 1996, p. 14) and may resort to expressing anger, being critical or even making threats.

Conflicts between people arising from cultural differences may therefore be extremely frustrating and difficult to resolve, unless the parties can find some common means through which they can communicate. On the other hand, people from a more collectivist culture will feel that the most important thing is not necessarily to win this particular battle, but to resolve it in such a way that the long-term relationship is not threatened or permanently damaged. They may therefore prefer to find an independent third party to mediate – perhaps some authority figure. Their behaviour is more likely to be 'pleasant', and they will rely on the limited direct verbalizations of their high-context, restricted code. They will be more accommodating than an individualist, and, for the sake of 'saving face' – that is, for the sake of maintaining the relationship

– will relinquish their immediate personal goals. Given the choice, they may try to avoid the conflict situation altogether, preferring silence or abstract conversations that allude only obliquely to the conflict.

What about conflicts between people from similar cultures? Some interesting studies by Gabrenya and Barba (1987) showed that conflicts between individualists tended to be resolved quite predictably, because they were used to conflict and negotiation. However, when they engineered situations between people from more collectivist cultures (predominantly Latin American), they found that, contrary to what might be expected, people were less cooperative and harmonious. Decision-making conversations were characterized by more talking and less discussion, clarification and negotiation. Their interpretation of this was that, although the people in the study all came from collectivist cultures, the people with whom they were negotiating were not from their particular in-group. They therefore behaved more like individualists towards these people, but, because of their cultural upbringing, they were less expert in negotiation and conflict resolution as 'pure' individualists.

Conflict resolution is a particular instance where negotiation skills are important: these are discussed earlier in this chapter.

BUILDING A CULTURALLY DIVERSE TEAM

Whether we are talking about conflict resolution or team-building, the general principle to follow when looking to improve how culturally diverse teams work together is broadly the same. It is often referred to as developing a third culture, a culture that 'consists of shared frameworks, value systems and communication systems that evolve when groups of individuals interact to share resources for a common goal' (Casmir, quoted in Adair, Tinsley and Taylor, 2006, p. 6). This contrasts with a multiculturalist approach which encourages different cultures to exist side-by-side, showing acceptance of each other but with little need for exchanges of communication. This would clearly not be acceptable in a workplace team, where communication is essential.

Third-culture-building is also distinct from traditional team-building in that while the latter seeks to make sure that everyone within a team has a shared understanding of task and team issues, the former concentrates on making sure that everyone within a team has a shared set of values, norms and beliefs that they can subscribe to within the team setting. It is not intended to replace team members' individual sets of cultural values (although it is quite possible that a third culture in the workplace may indeed change the way in which a person sees the world in their personal life).

Developing a third culture is an example of what Peter Senge (1990) would see as 'team learning', his fourth discipline in developing a learning organization. He sees team learning as,

'... the process of aligning and developing the capacity of a team to create the results its members truly desire' (Senge, 1990, p. 236). To achieve this, team members need to have acquired the first three disciplines. These are:

- *personal mastery* – not a state of being technically competent, but a process whereby individuals know what they want to achieve, recognize where they currently are and strive to develop themselves to reach their vision.
- *mental models* – the ideas that people within an organization hold about how it works, but which can constrain their thinking unless they are prepared to constantly review and develop the models (described earlier in Chapter 2).
- *shared vision* – a synthesis between what the organization wants to achieve and what its individual employees are looking for, which allows people to provide real support rather than token acknowledgement to a top-down initiative that means nothing to them personally.

Within this construct it is certainly possible to see how the development of an effective third culture within workplace teams would have its place in the drive to achieve a learning organization.

Third culture strength

There are two dimensions to a third culture: its strength and its content. Strength refers to how well established the culture becomes and how clearly defined it is, while content considers what the actual elements of the culture are.

Let us think about the strength of a third culture first. Adair et al. (2006) distinguish between overlapping and identical third cultures (see Figure 3.3).

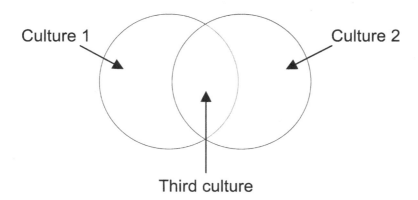

Culture 1   Culture 2

Third culture

Figure 3.3   An overlapping third culture

Source: Adair, Tinsley and Taylor (2006).

When two cultures meet, they will take certain elements from each and put these into the third culture; this therefore represents the overlap between the individual cultures, which still remain as identifiable within the team. Suppose, for example, that a team is composed of a British person, an Italian, a Japanese and a Kenyan. If these people are 'typical' representatives of their culture (which, of course, we must not assume), we might expect to be able to describe them as shown in Table 3.1.

Table 3.1 **Simplified comparison of national characteristics**

	British	Italian	Japanese	Kenyan
Power distance	Low	Moderately low	Moderately low	Moderately high
Uncertainty avoidance	Low	Moderately high	High	Moderately low
Affective– neutral	Fairly neutral	Highly affective	Very neutral	Fairly affective
Individualist– collectivist	Highly individualist	Fairly highly individualist	Moderately collectivist	Moderately collectivist

Note that this table represents a considerable simplification of a real-life situation!

If these four team members developed an overlapping third culture, it might consist of one that was moderately low in power distance and moderately high in terms of uncertainty avoidance. However, the Italian and the Kenyan would continue to express their emotions strongly, while the other two would hide their feelings. The Kenyan might wish that there was a clearer hierarchy within the team. The British and Italian people would continue to operate in their individualist ways, while the Japanese and the Kenyan would yearn for the team to operate more collectively. So there would be a certain amount of compromise going on, but, in other respects, the team members would continue to behave as they always had done.

Now contrast this with an identical third culture (Figure 3.4).

An identical third culture represents a situation where people have come to appreciate the different values and beliefs held by the other team members and have evolved a distinct third culture that represents some sort of consensus. When operating as a team, each of the individual team members will demonstrate the values and beliefs represented by this third culture. So, in our example, the team might:

- operate with a low respect for power distance (so that the team would operate in a fairly consensual and non-hierarchical way),

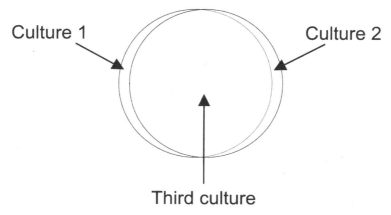

Figure 3.4 An identical third culture

and the Kenyan member would understand why and feel comfortable with it.

- accept some degree of uncertainty avoidance (so that, for example, the team might develop a limited set of rules).
- develop a commonly accepted standard for laughing and crying.
- follow some collectivist principles (team relationships would be considered closely in decision-making, for example).

As might be self-evident, teams with an identical third culture tend to be stronger than those with an overlapping third culture, but although the identical model may be more desirable, it can be much harder to achieve. For example, if the majority of the team are individualists, it will be harder for everyone to give up their individualist ways. Individualists tends to be field-independent and low-context communicators, meaning that they place less importance on context and relationships; as a result, they would find it harder to recognize and appreciate the subtleties of interpersonal cultural issues. It will also be much more difficult to create an identical third culture if the team has a history of high levels of interpersonal conflicts.

Third culture content

The content of a third culture refers to what elements it has. Again, Adair (2006) proposes two types of third culture content: intersection, where it consists purely of elements taken from the individual cultures; and emergent, where it contains elements of its own that are not found in any individual culture. The intersection third culture may be seen as the area of overlap in Figures 3.3 and 3.4, whereas an emergent third culture may be represented by Figure 3.5.

What might this mean in practice? Consider again our four-person team. They have developed an overlapping third culture

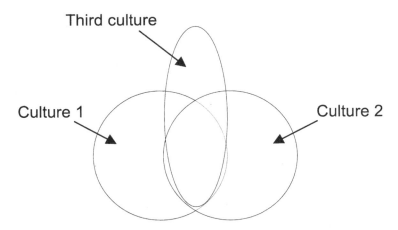

Figure 3.5 An emergent third culture

that is moderately low in power distance and moderately high in terms of uncertainty avoidance, but, as a result of working together, they come to realize that an important aspect of their team-working is focusing on longer-term issues, so this emerges to become a new part of their culture. Of course, this emergent type of third culture can also take place where a team has developed one that is identical, rather than overlapping.

How can a third culture develop?

Whether or not a culturally diverse team can develop an emergent element to its third culture seems to depend to a large extent on the cultural intelligence of its members – in other words, on how good team members are at adapting to different cultural settings. People who are culturally intelligent are those who can travel the world and strike up friendly conversations with anyone they meet. This needs a particular set of qualities: they need to be aware that different cultures do things in different ways; they need to both want to adapt and be able to adapt; and they need to have certain practical skills – for example, being able to speak a foreign language or to at least communicate in some other way.

Interestingly, it also seems to be an advantage for a team to have relatively high levels of task conflict (as opposed to relationship conflict). If task conflict – meaning disagreements about how work needs to be carried out or goals achieved – is managed carefully, it can be innovative and improve efficiencies. So it is quite possible that if team members are constantly disagreeing about processes and procedures, but finding ways to resolve these conflicts, they will develop a distinct subset of cultural values that are unique to that particular team setting.

Emergent third cultures have advantages over those that are merely overlapping. The distinct elements can help create a much stronger sense of unity within the team, and they are likely to lead to more efficient team processes and maximal outcomes.

Building a third culture

So, if it is important for a culturally diverse team to develop a strong and effective third culture, how should it go about doing so? Well, as with meeting and falling in love with a life partner, the principle is simple but the execution is potentially complex. It relies very much on the ability of team members to find out and learn from their associates, which may happen naturally or may need to be facilitated in some way. Each person needs to find out about the beliefs and values of other team members so that a network of knowledge and understanding about how everyone else in the team operates on a cultural level is built.

Each individual then needs to reflect on what these different attitudes and values mean when set against their own, and be prepared to modify or replace some of their own beliefs. These new and modified values then need to be put into practice. This will probably require more than casual conversations between team members: it may need real dialogue in which people question each other's cultural standpoints and assumptions closely in order to develop a better understanding of not only what other people value, but also what they themselves value and why.

This might happen organically, which could take some time, or a manager may, by themselves or with the help of a skilled facilitator, arrange for these conversations to take place. The Johari Window (Luft, 1961) is a tool sometimes used in team-building to help in this disclosure process (Figure 3.6).

	What I know	**What I don't know**
What other people know	The arena	Blindspot
What other people don't know	Hidden	The unknown

Figure 3.6 The Johari Window

Source: Adapted from Luft (1961).

Moxon (1993) refers to topics that both the individual and other team members know about as being 'in the arena', the place where everything is visible and in the open (see Figure 3.6). So if, for example, an affective person knows that someone else in the team feels uncomfortable about public displays of emotion, they can choose to moderate their behaviour whenever that person is around. Correspondingly, if the more neutralist person understands that their colleague is prone to outbursts of emotion, they need not feel that they are overreacting to apparently minor events when they do behave in this way.

On the other hand, if our affective person realizes that her neutralist colleague feels uncomfortable about emotion but has not told them this, they may choose to suppress their natural instincts and not show joy at good news and grief when things go wrong. However, although this may help their colleague to trot along contentedly, it will be at the expense of their own enthusiasm about, and ultimately commitment to, the project.

The third possibility is that the affective person just does not realize that their displays of emotion are viewed as unusual by their colleague. They will therefore persist in behaving in this way, continuing to annoy their colleague.

Finally, the two may be in the unknown zone (see Figure 3.6). The affective person may not realize that their public displays of emotion could be seen by the other person as difficult behaviour, and the neutralist colleague just has a sense that they find this person irritating, but can't quite understand why.

In a team it is therefore important for the arena to be of an appropriate size. Quite what is appropriate will depend on the nature of the team and the relationships with in it: for example, for people who work closely together it would need to be bigger than for those whose working relationship is limited.

How do team members get information into the arena? Adler (2008) suggests a list of questions that team members might like to ask each other in order to develop a clearer understanding of other people's cultural backgrounds and hence expand their mutual arena.

Family background:

- What size family does the colleague come from?
- Do they have brothers or sisters and, if so, how many of each?
- Where are they in the family – oldest, youngest, in the middle?
- What is the socioeconomic status of their family? Are they regarded as being rich or poor?
- What is the history of their family?
- If the family has money, has it been self-made or inherited?
- Is their family respected in their community? If so, why?

Faith:

- Are they religious? If so, what religion do they follow?
- How important is their religion to them?
- How much does their religion influence their personal and professional lives?
- Are they typical of their community?
- How does their religion affect their relationship with you and other people in the team?

Education:

- How were they educated?
- Did they go to a private or a state school?
- To what level were they educated – primary, secondary or higher?
- How does that compare to other people in their country?
- What helps access to education: money, family connections, ability?
- How do they perceive the standard of their education compared to yours?

Family life:

- Are they married?
- If so, who is their partner?
- How did they meet their partner?
- How does their partner affect their working life?
- Do they have children? If so, how many?
- What sort of relationship do they have with their children?
- How much time do they spend with their children?
- Is that typical within their culture?
- Where do they live?
- What kind of house do they live in?
- How would they describe that area?
- What sorts of other people live there?
- Do many other people from an extended family live in the same area?
- What do they think are the most important things in their life?

Career:

- How did they get their present job?
- Was it their own choice, or was it made by someone else?
- How is the job seen by people from their community?
- What is their motivation for working (money, status, responsibility, job satisfaction, for example)?
- What do they want to do in the future?
- How important is their current job to achieving that?
- What do people from their community think about their working with foreigners?
- Do people from their community have foreigners as friends?
- How much do people in their community travel? If so, where do they go?

Culture:

- What do they think are the strengths of their culture?
- What do they see as the differences between their culture and yours?
- What do they see as good and bad points about your culture?
- What would they like to learn about your culture?
- How do your different cultures affect the way in which you work together? (Adapted from Adler, 2008).

Of course, various things may get in the way. Embracing new cultural values can be exciting for some people but threatening to others, which may be connected to a people's attitudes to uncertainty avoidance. Taking on new cultural values takes time, and people must be prepared to invest this time – a long-term orientation to life would help here. It also follows that this process is unlikely to take place within a team that is perceived as being temporary or of a short-term nature. And individuals must have good questioning and listening skills: although facilitated third culture team-building sessions may be of value, real understanding and learning about other people's cultures will take place largely through the hundreds of small, interpersonal exchanges that happen throughout a working day. There are also potential historical or political obstacles. Since many culturally diverse teams come together as a result of overseas investment by American or European transnational companies, there may be a tradition of dominance and submission in the national relationships that must be overcome. Similarly, the power of the parent company may make it politically more difficult for local cultures to fully express themselves and become accepted.

CULTURE AND VIRTUAL TEAMS

Whereas the traditional concept of a team is of a group of individuals working in more or less close physical proximity, new communications technologies make it increasingly likely that teams will be made up of people scattered around the globe, communicating by telephone, e-mail, videoconferencing and collaborative software. What might that mean in terms of culture and team effectiveness?

Jarvenpaa and Leidner (1988) arranged for several different groups of students scattered around the world to collaborate on team projects. Working on the assumption that a team will be unable to work effectively unless its members trust each other, they set out to see if and how trust might develop within a team where the members never actually met each other. A natural assumption might be that these conditions would make it very difficult for trust to develop. For example, trust generally requires people to have some mutually accepted sets of norms, that they interact with each other on a regular basis and that they have some sense that they will continue to work with each other in the future. However, in virtual teams these elements are often not present: people will have no idea about other members' norms, beliefs and values and little idea about their cultural background. Names may provide some clue, but geographical location may be meaningless as they could be collaborating with an expatriate. Interactions may be regular, but they will often be time-delayed; time zones may make telephone conversations difficult so that people rely on e-mail, which breaks the immediacy of the feedback in face-to-face communication. Such teams are often put together to achieve a specific objective and are disbanded immediately afterwards, with little expectation that they will be revived.

However, it seems that, in situations such as this, teams can develop what has been described as 'swift trust'. If roles and responsibilities within the team are clearly identified and communicated, people will make assumptions about each other's capabilities and will feel confidence in the team's abilities at the outset. Indeed, the lack of face-to-face communication may in fact prove to be an advantage, in that each person projects on to other members of the team a similarity to themselves (that may, of course, be completely unwarranted), and in turn quite possibly receives very little information that defines other people as individuals in their own right, with their own set of cultural values. The lack of face-to-face contact with people from different cultural backgrounds may also make it easier for people who are less culturally intelligent to collaborate with others, as they will not have to deal with discomfort related to their expectations about how they 'should' interact.

Of course, culturally distinguishing information can still be sought and provided. Many people, particularly those who are culturally intelligent and curious, will exchange personal information during project communications, but, for those people who do actively seek out information, developing a richer picture of team members is likely to have a positive effect on trust development.

Jarvenpaa and Leidner concluded that cultural differences might therefore have less of an impact on virtual teams than in those that work together face-to-face. The depersonalization of interpersonal contact makes it less likely that cultural differences will get in the way and that individuals might be affected by negative stereotypes that they hold about people from other cultures, arising from miscellaneous factors such as clothing, gesticulation and greetings. In that sense, virtual teams may indeed be representative of the mythical 'global village'.

Culture and Leadership

Western theories about leadership can be a little like fish flapping on the deck of a fishing boat: plenty of action, but without the necessary medium for achieving anything. Leaders can only lead if they have subordinates, and many ideas about leadership often rest on the unstated assumption that the subordinates all have a uniform set of Western values.

For example, for many years people have sought the Holy Grail of a personal qualities checklist for a good leader. Based on the assumption that a good leader can lead anywhere, these 'trait' theories have trawled the dictionaries for positive adjectives. As a result of the failure to find one magical shortlist, these qualities can be qualified as being applicable in this situation or not applicable in that, to the point of rendering the lists useless. Recent interest in charismatic leadership has also struggled to find a consistent definition of what comprises charisma, but there is an admission that a subordinate's perspective is important: what is charismatic in one culture may be unimpressive, or perhaps even offensive, in another.

Reacting against the perceived insensitivities of behaviourism, the human relations school proposed that participation in decision-making, autonomy and responsibility would provide better results. In Western settings this has largely been shown to be true, but this may not be the case in other cultural settings. For example:

- People from high power distance cultures expect leaders to be strong and decisive and do not expect to be consulted themselves. Leaders are leaders because of where they are in the hierarchy, not necessarily because of any particular personal or intellectual qualities.
- For someone from a high uncertainty avoidance culture, being given autonomy or responsibility may be unwelcome and perhaps terrifying.
- Managing someone from a diffuse culture needs to take into account the person's whole life, rather than just their performance in the workplace. This can complicate giving feedback or taking disciplinary action, as consideration must be given to personal factors.

Situational leadership (Hersey and Blanchard, 1977) is a popular model in many organizations, although Guest (1996) suggests that this may be due more to its commercial packaging than to any great effectiveness. The model proposes that the appropriate leadership style in any situation takes into account what the leader needs, the abilities and needs of the subordinates and the requirements of the task. The leader's behaviour has two variables, each of which can be at low or high levels:

- task behaviour – organization and one-way communication about expectations and so on.

- relationship behaviour – two-way communication with the workforce.

As the workforce gains experience, the leader can move through a sequence:

- high task, low relationship for the new workforce (giving orders to get things going);
- high task, high relationship as they get used to the work (establishing a rapport);
- low task, high relationship as they mature (participating with the team);
- low task, low relationship (where the leader can delegate).

Although this concept does take the nature of the subordinates into consideration, it is assumed that there is a process to be followed and that the subordinates all yearn for the day when the work is delegated to them. Well, this may be true in a Western setting, but everywhere?

- In a high power distance setting the subordinates would be most comfortable with a high task way of operating. It may also be preferable to keep to a low relationship way of working as well.
- Where uncertainty avoidance is high, people may prefer to stay with the low task, high relationship, participation stage, as moving on to low leader supervision may prove too stressful. Conversely, in low uncertainty avoidance cultures, people can be quite happy with low task, low relationship (delegation) leadership.

In situational leadership, accounting for subordinates' needs is therefore important, and managers following its principles in a culturally diverse setting must pay careful attention to subordinates' expectations and not necessarily expect to be able to move through the whole four-stage process.

However, more recent work on leadership has brought the importance of subordinates' perceptions into a sharper focus: for example, Lord and Maher suggested that 'the essence of leadership is being seen as a leader by others' (Lord and Maher, 1991, p. 4). As well as stating that leadership is evaluated from its outcomes, they also suggest that perceptions of a leader's effectiveness depend on a fit between what the subordinates think a leader should do and what they do in practice. Therefore, someone who is an effective leader in one culture may be wholly ineffective in another for a wider variety of reasons:

- They may be autocratic in a culture where this is not accepted, or vice versa.

- They may fail to take interpersonal relationships into sufficient consideration when dealing with subordinates.
- In an ascriptive culture they may not have the academic qualifications that are deemed to be necessary or not be old enough, or, conversely, in achievement-oriented societies they may not have a good 'track record'.

Anyone seeking to provide good leadership in a different culture must therefore think carefully about the different values associated with that particular culture and review their own leadership style accordingly. Adler (2008) suggests that a manager faced with leading a culturally diverse team has a choice of three strategies: parochial, ethnocentric or synergistic.

She suggests that the most common reaction is to adopt a *parochial* approach: the leader sees the diversity and shuts their eyes, pretending that it does not exist or that it will have no effect on how the organization or their team will operate. A parochial leader may well project their own culture on to anyone who seems different. Adopting this approach means that not only will they fail to deal with any of the problems that the diversity might bring (if diversity is not acknowledged, it cannot be seen as a potential source of problems), but, perhaps more importantly, will also be unable to harness the creative potential offered by the multiple perspectives.

Another approach is to see the diversity as a source of difficulty and as a problem that can be overcome by 'doing it my way'. This *ethnocentric* approach to leadership assumes that the leader's culture is good and that all others are, by definition, bad. A manager following this approach will try very hard to ensure that their team does not contain anyone from a different culture and, if it does, will try to force these 'deviants' to accept their own way of working. As with the parochial style of management, this approach will make it impossible to solve any diversity-related problems or utilize the positive potential, but, in addition, it is ethically unacceptable and, depending on the jurisdiction where it is happening, potentially illegal.

The third possibility is *synergistic*: the manager sees the cultural diversity and recognizes that it is potentially a source of both strengths and weaknesses. Synergistic managers will attempt to, '... manage the impact of cultural diversity rather than manage the diversity itself' (Adler, 2008, p. 107), Managers and, indeed, organizations that look for cultural synergy will actively seek out diversity within the team or organization and build processes around it to make sure that the problems it might cause are resolved quickly and easily and that its benefits are exploited to the full. Such managers look for ways to help a third culture to develop. They will encourage team members to expand their Johari Window arena by getting to know other members of the team.

A PERFORMANCE
AID TO HELP
TEAM LEADERS

If you are managing a culturally diverse team you may find Table 3.2 useful. You might want to make copies and complete them by reflecting on what cultural glasses different members of your team might be wearing. But remember that this should not be an exercise in writing down stereotypes: the idea is to encourage you to reflect on how other members of your team might view what is happening around them. You could then use this to frame a conversation in which you can explore your initial assumptions and hence expand your own Johari Window arena.

Table 3.2   Initial ideas about team members' perspectives

Team member		
Team issue (optional)		
Indicator	**Possible orientation**	**Possible implications for their view of the issue**
Individualism–collectivism		
Power distance		
Uncertainty avoidance		
Work–life balance		
Long-term orientation		
Universalism–particularism		
Affective–neutral		
Specific–diffuse		
Achievement–ascription		
Linear- or multi-active		

Culture and the New Arrival

A special, and usually temporary, instance where culture has a profound effect on performance is for the new arrival in a culturally diverse organization, the most striking example being for the expatriate arriving to start work in a foreign country.

Expatriates are an important and growing part of the international workforce. Many organizations see offering the opportunity of global travel and of working in exotic locations as being an important way of attracting and retaining quality employees. Similarly, many people are attracted to the idea of working in another country for any number of reasons – for example, the perceived glamour, wider work experiences, a chance for promotion and so on – and will look for employers who can offer this. But, for many, the experience can be disappointing when the location turns out to be less glamorous and exciting than anticipated, when the climate proves difficult or (what we are interested in here) when it proves difficult to perform effectively in the workplace.

THE PROBLEMS OF ADAPTING TO EXPATRIATE LIFE

A major reason why many expatriates struggle when arriving in an alien culture is inadequate preparation, as many companies offer only token training to help an employee prepare for, and adjust to, living and working in a foreign culture. Training often focuses on surface behaviour issues, such as when and where to use your left hand or how to say 'no'.

Less well covered are those deeper cultural values which are the focus of this book. The net result is what someone preparing me for my first overseas experience working as a volunteer in the Sudan described as the 'bathtub effect'. You climb over the plughole end of the bath, dive into the water and everything is exciting, the noises, the colours, the sunlight, the different foods and so on. That feeling of euphoria may last a few weeks after which the routine of working life becomes more apparent and you start to experience some of the frustrations of working in a foreign culture – the heat, the cold, the strange manners that people have, the lack of familiar comfort foods, the inability to understand a local language, for example. And morale plummets as you slide down towards the plughole. There then follows a slow and extended period of adjusting, or not. As time progresses, you either come to appreciate and enjoy the difference of life around you as you float and eventually climb out at the end of the bath, or you find it increasingly frustrating and sink. If the latter happens, you may retreat within yourself, seeing everything in the host country as being 'bad' or threatening.

THE SCALE OF EXPATRIATE UNHAPPINESS

If that is the expatriate's experience, before long they will want to return home, bringing to a conclusion what will have been an expensive experience for their employer and a possibly psychologically damaging experience for the expatriate. This is not something that happens just occasionally:

- The turnover of staff on expatriate assignment is 25 per cent compared to 13 per cent for people working in their home countries (Brookfield Global Relocation Services, 2008).
- At the end of their assignment 20 per cent of returning expatriates want to leave their company (Adler, 2008).

Supporting expatriate workers is also extremely expensive: Birdseye and Hill (1995) reported that in the mid-1990s the cost of maintaining an American employee with a basic salary of $100,000 and a family of two was over $138,000 if the assignment was in Paris and $220,000 if it was in Tokyo. And these figures do not include the cost of the below-expected performance while the employee was at the plughole end of the bath. Given these figures, it is very surprising that 65 per cent of American firms send their employees off on expatriate assignments without providing them with any orientation (Wilson and Dalton, 1999).

Whatever an individual's reaction in the longer term there will undoubtedly be a period when they will feel unhappy and therefore be unable to contribute effectively in the workplace. An expatriate's manager will therefore have an important role to play in supporting the new arrival to try to minimize the feelings of dislocation and unhappiness. Much of this role will focus on helping the new arrival to come to terms with the physical aspects of the new environment, but managers should realize that these problems may be just surface issues and that longer-term happiness will only be achieved if the expatriate can learn to understand, and perhaps embrace in some ways, local beliefs, values and norms. Here, we return to the importance of the third culture.

SELECTING THE RIGHT PERSON FOR EXPATRIATE LIFE

Even more important is the role played by managers responsible for selecting employees for expatriate assignment. Wilson and Dalton (1999) suggest that there are three main factors that influence a person's suitability for an expatriate assignment: personality, early-life experiences and family readiness.

Personality

In Chapter 1 we saw how an individual's personality can be classified according to their rating in the 'Big Five' different categories (as summarized by the mnemonics CANOE or OCEAN), although it is important to remember that some studies have shown that this categorization does not necessarily apply in Eastern cultures. As applied to expatriates, these are:

- **O**penness – the expatriate needs to be curious about their new life and what goes on around them, to be prepared for differences and to be ready to make changes.
- **C**onscientiousness – the expatriate needs to be committed to achieving workplace objectives. If they are, they are more likely to be able to overcome culture shock[1] issues.
- **E**xtraversion – if the expatriate is energetic and keen on finding company they are more likely to adjust quickly to their new

---

1   The coining of the term 'culture shock' is generally attributed to the Finnish-Canadian anthropologist Kalervo Oberg, who used it in a 1954 lecture when describing the four stages of adaptation to a new culture (the honeymoon phase, culture shock, recovery and adjustment). See Oberg, 1954.

lifestyle. Someone who is introverted may become even isolated because they do not seek out other people's company.

- **A**greeableness – being cooperative and compassionate makes the expatriate more likely to get on with people, even if they have different cultural values.
- **N**euroticism – culture shock may make someone who is prone to emotional instability veer off in a direction that makes good workplace performance difficult. Emotionally stable people may be more likely to adapt quickly to living in a different culture.

According to Wilson and Dalton the most important of the Big Five characteristics are conscientiousness (as rated by their home-country boss) and agreeableness (as rated by their host-country boss).

Employers considering sending someone on an expatriate assignment should therefore think about the individual's possible personality profile, and they may even want to consider asking them to complete some form of personality assessment. If someone does seem to have a personality type that would make adapting to life in a different culture more difficult, it would be a good idea to consider whether or not they would benefit from some pre-departure training or, in more extreme cases, whether or not that person should go on the assignment at all.

Early-life experiences

In looking at the likelihood of members of a team developing an effective third culture we discussed the idea of cultural intelligence – that some people are more sensitive to others' cultural differences and better able to get on with them. Wilson and Dalton suggest that this is strongly affected by experiences in a person's early life. So, for example, people who have lived in foreign countries as children, who have families containing different cultures, who live in cosmopolitan settings or border towns may be more familiar with cultural differences than people who have led a more sheltered life.

Family readiness

For expatriates with dependants – a partner, possibly children and members of an extended family – it is crucial to consider the family's ability is to provide the expatriate with the level of support they will need. There are a number of different facets to this.

What stage is the family in? In any family there is a window of opportunity when expatriate life is more feasible. No children or very small children may present fewer difficulties than children who are of school age. People who have aged or infirm parents or other dependants could find themselves constantly having to worry about someone back home or having to make sudden, and possibly extended, return journeys.

How big is the family? In individualist societies the family that an expatriate tends to consider when deciding whether to relocate is generally nuclear – a partner and children. However, in collectivist societies extended families will include brothers, sisters, parents, grandparents, nephews and nieces. Someone with responsibility for members of an extended family may find it very difficult to be geographically distant, even if they receive handsome financial recompense.

What about the partner's own life experiences and personality? A partner's preparedness for life in a foreign country will have an indirect bearing on the expatriate's performance at work, since, if the partner cannot settle, the expatriate will not be able to concentrate fully on their work. This can be particularly significant for a female partner, who may find the expectations about women's behaviour in society is quite different to anything they have experienced before.

What will the partner's role be in the host country? Very few expatriate assignments can find suitable working opportunities for a partner as well. So, if both members of a couple are working in the home country, the partner may find themselves having to temporarily abandon their career in order to support the expatriate. If this happens, it could become a source of considerable tension within the relationship, again with negative effects on performance.

What schooling and childcare arrangements are available in the host country? If the expatriate has children of school age or their partner is also going to be working in some way, they will need to feel assured that there are adequate schooling or childcare arrangements available. Spending some time in a foreign country can be hugely beneficial to a child in terms of finding out about different cultures or learning a language, but it may present problems in terms of examinations and keeping up with studies so that they can return to the home country's educational system without too many difficulties.

Culture and Performance Management

Performance management is a process that many organizations adopt with the aim of encouraging and supporting employees' good performance. It generally works through each member of staff working with their line manager to develop an individual performance agreement, based on objectives that are often directly linked to corporate and departmental objectives. The performance agreement leads to some form of development plan, which identifies the responsibilities that the individual will take on over the coming year that will help them achieve their objectives. Throughout the year there will be performance reviews to assess their progress in achieving their objectives.

As with management practices, performance management has grown out of Western business thinking (in particular, management by objectives) and so embodies Western cultural values. In the context of performance management the key cultural indicators here are North American individualism, a low power distance regulating the relationship between managers and their subordinates, a preference for success in the workplace as opposed to high quality of life, a focus on short-term goals and advancement through achievement rather than through ascription.

When operating a performance management system with a culturally diverse workforce it is therefore important to think about how different cultural perspectives may affect how well the system will work.

For example, a key element within the performance agreement is often some assessment of the individual's competency. Many organizations have a competency framework which lists a number of competencies that have been deemed to be important to the organization's work. These often include factors such as communication, achievement and results orientation, and leadership. The challenge in a culturally diverse setting is in judging how strong an individual is within each of these competencies.

Consider communication. A framework may say that an employee should be able to 'clearly convey information and ideas'. Who judges what constitutes being clear? Someone from a low-context culture might expect the individual to have a history of always providing comprehensive information and guidance to other team members when trying to 'convey information and ideas'. However, if that person were from a high-context culture, their preferred pattern might be to provide a minimal amount of information verbally, knowing that the operational context would provide the other information necessary. Now, behaving in that way might be effective, but equally it might not be. The important thing is that the person making the evaluation must not assume that clearly conveying information and ideas always requires a specific pattern of communication.

As a second example consider the competency of achievement and results orientation. People in many cultures are not driven by the need to achieve the types of result that an organization may want, preferring a working pattern that gives them what they feel to be a high quality of life. However, that does not necessarily mean that they are 'slackers' and that they do not contribute to the organization's success. It could be that they recognize the value that the organization brings to their life and work just as much as other people who have an achievement and results orientation, but that they are just careful to balance their work and life commitments. The danger is that this would not be recognized by a more results-oriented manager making an assessment about this particular competency.

The performance review is aimed at another key element in the performance management process. The traditional, Western view of the manager–subordinate review process is that the manager provides constructive feedback and that there is an open and honest exchange of views. This is, of course, sometimes challenging within cultures that are homogeneously Western, but it can be particularly fraught where there are cultural differences. For example, criticizing someone with a collectivist perspective about some aspect of their performance can be very damaging if not done appropriately, as it could be interpreted as saying that this person is letting the team down, which would be a serious loss of face issue. The commonly accepted way of motivating someone from a Western culture to higher levels of performance is to offer praise and encouragement, whereas it is suggested that Japanese people, for example, are encouraged to perform better after receiving negative feedback (Ide, 1999).

In addition, the 'open and honest exchange of views' may be completely impossible with a subordinate who has a strong sense of power distance and for whom the idea of saying anything that would challenge the authority of their line manager is unacceptable. A Western manager faced with a member of staff behaving in this way might, if they were not culturally aware, interpret this as a sign of having something to hide, or worse.

There is clearly much more that could be said about the difficulties of operating performance management systems in culturally diverse settings. Some parts of the process may work if people involved are sensitive to the cultural complexities at play, while other parts may not be able to function at all without extensive cultural adaptation.

Summary

This chapter has looked at how different cultural perspectives have an effect on a number of different general management areas, including negotiation, decision-making, team-working, leadership and performance management, as well as on the specific challenges of arrival in a new culture.

Figure 3.7 summarizes what we have covered in this chapter.

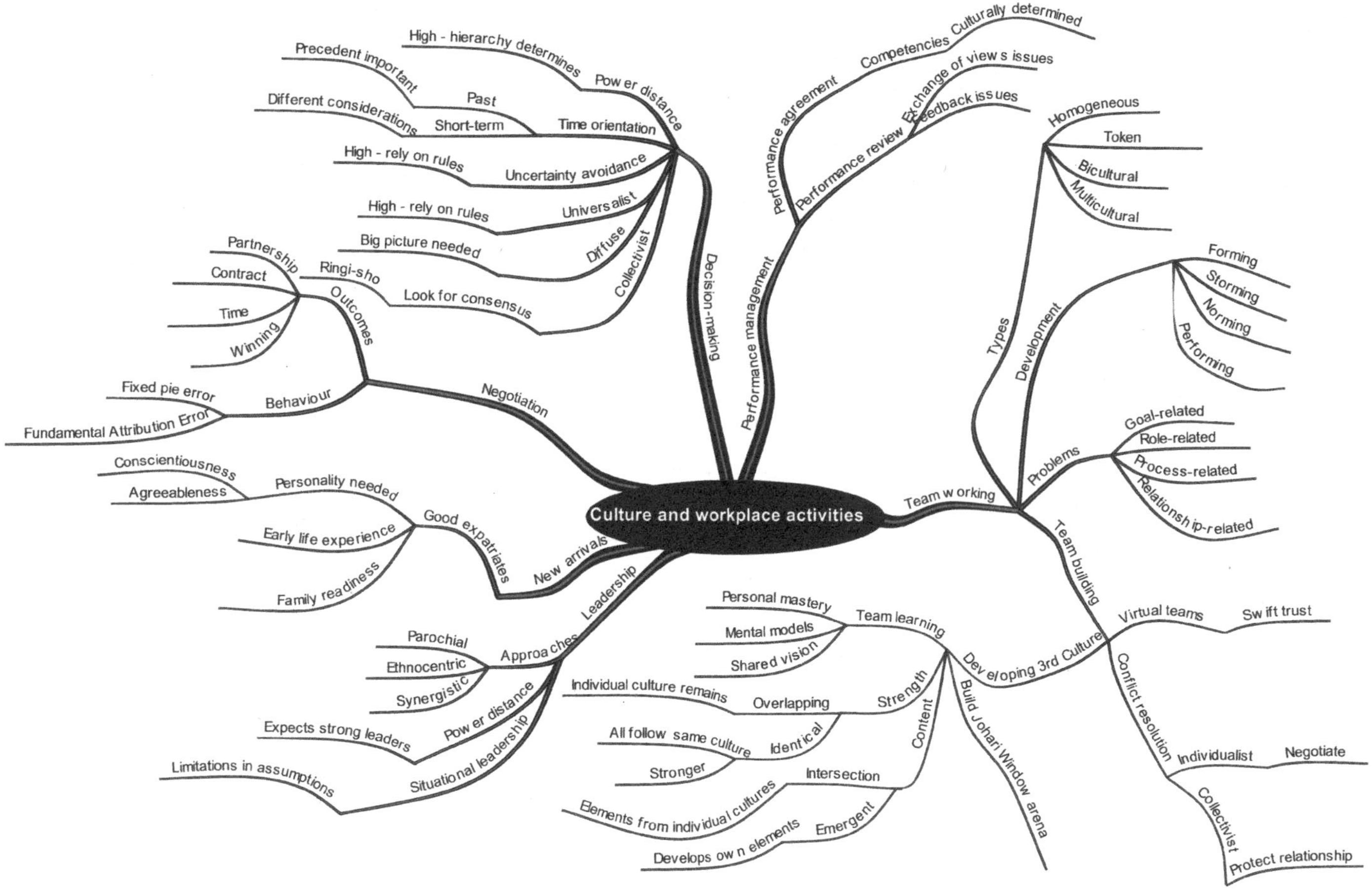

Figure 3.7 Mindmap summary of Chapter 3

4 The Systems Approach

KEY POINTS

- Considering organizations as systems gives us a useful tool to help analyse workplace performance.

- Causal flow diagrams provide a useful way of graphically representing an organizational system.

- Soft Systems Methodology is a useful process to follow when exploring organizational problems.

The Importance of the Big Picture

First, a poem – 'The Blind Men and the Elephant':

It was six men of Indostan
To learning much inclined,
Who went to see the Elephant
(Though all of them were blind)
That each by observation
Might satisfy his mind.

The First approach'd the Elephant
And happening to fall
Against his broad and sturdy side,
At once began to bawl:
'God bless me! but the Elephant
Is very like a wall!'

The Second, feeling of the tusk,
Cried, 'Ho! what have we here
So very round and smooth and sharp?

To me 'tis mighty clear
This wonder of an Elephant
Is very like a spear!'

The Third approached the animal,
And happening to take
The squirming trunk within his hands,
Thus boldly up and spake:
'I see,' quoth he, 'the Elephant
Is very like a snake!'

The Fourth reached out his eager hand,
And felt about the knee.
'What most this wondrous beast is like
Is mighty plain,' quoth he,
''Tis clear enough the Elephant
Is very like a tree!'

The Fifth, who chanced to touch the ear,
Said: 'E'en the blindest man
Can tell what this resembles most;
Deny the fact who can,
This marvel of an Elephant
Is very like a fan!'

The Sixth no sooner had begun
About the beast to grope,
Then, seizing on the swinging tail
That fell within his scope,
'I see,' quoth he, 'the Elephant
Is very like a rope!'

And so these men of Indostan
Disputed loud and long,
Each in his own opinion
Exceeding stiff and strong,
Though each was partly in the right
And all were in the wrong.

So oft in theologic wars,
The disputants, I ween,
Rail on in utter ignorance
Of what each other mean,
And prate about an Elephant
Not one of them has seen!

by John Godfrey Saxe (1816–1887).

You may be familiar with this story: it is one that appears in a number of Eastern traditions, including Sufism, Jainism, Buddhism and Hinduism. Saxe's summing up refers to 'theological disputants', but the gist of his story could apply to many people grappling with a workplace performance problem: they see what they think is the problem and, from that, decide what a solution should be. For example:

- Sales are down; we need more advertising.
- Too many mistakes are being made; people need training.

So advertising is commissioned, training is delivered and what happens? The manager is left with a wall, a spear, a snake, a tree, a fan or a rope, but not a better elephant. Like each of the blind men, the manager has looked only at one part of the problem and has failed to look at the other connected parts and, most importantly, to consider how they are connected. This is an example of reductionism, the principle whereby, in order to understand the functioning of something complex, we break it down into its constituent parts. Some people blame Descartes and his principle of rational analysis for this, but in truth the whole of Western civilization is based on the study of individual objects and their properties rather than of relationships, which has been a feature of Eastern civilization. As discussed in Chapter 1, one way of characterizing many Eastern cultures is as collectivist, where great importance is placed on relationships and harmony. It is therefore not surprising that the blind men and the elephant story appears in many different Eastern belief systems as a way of illustrating foolishness.

So while the East has made slow but steady progress, concentrating on maintaining harmony, the West has pushed ahead with making ever more disconnected changes aimed at making short-term changes to carefully defined aspects of life or business, and failing to appreciate the wider or longer-term implications of these changes.

So, for example, in the 1990s the Western business world embraced business process re-engineering (BPR), wherein organizations pulled apart their individual activities, decided which ones were fundamentally important and discarded the rest. The aim of BPR was to make radical changes that would generate quick improvements to an organization's performance. However, after a few years of happiness it was realized that the short-termist and technology-driven nature of BPR interventions failed to consider human aspects of organizational life, and the original radical approach fell out of favour.

On a more global scale, Western technology has focused on developing more and more ways of consuming energy with relatively little attention paid to finding methods of energy generation that did not rely on burning what remains of a finite supply of fossil-fuel energy. The consequence of this has been the release of millennia's worth of carbon into the atmosphere, which could spell catastrophic consequences for everyone in the world.

Similarly, many countries are exploited for their raw materials in order to provide short-term gains for Western corporations at the expense of long-term global peace and security.

On the other hand, collectivist Japan developed the principle of *kaizen* or 'good change'. When following a *kaizen* principle, an organization constantly makes small changes to improve performance, rather than making one-off large changes. There is an emphasis on long-term success, reflecting the culture's long-term orientation. Similarly, the Japanese motor industry developed *kanban*, or just-in-time stock control. By keeping a close watch on stock levels and making sure that this information was made available appropriately, suppliers could adjust their production and delivery to keep the stock held in the car assembly plant to a minimum. The system works as long as relationships (personal and technical) work well. And, of course, they generally do in the relationship-oriented Japanese society.

Western management principles in general tend to be reductionist in nature, looking at individual elements rather than the combination of elements and their interconnectedness – a reflection of an individualist culture. It would therefore be useful to consider how we can take a more holistic look at performance issues through the use of a systems approach.

The Development of Systems Thinking

In the West, systems thinking made something of an appearance in 1917, when the Russian Alexander Bogdanov published his ideas about 'tectology', saying that complex objects could only be understood by looking at the way in which they organized themselves. However, his ideas fell foul of Lenin and Stalin, and systems thinking lay dormant until the 1950s when the Austrian biologist Karl Ludwig von Bertalanffy presented his General Systems Theory. This picked up on the idea that there could be a generic methodology for looking at how scientific systems might be analysed, and these ideas were then taken forward and applied to the way in which organizations work by a number of people – in particular, Kurt Lewin, Peter Checkland and Peter Senge.

Systems thinking has evolved in various ways to help explain different types of systems. For example:

- *hard systems*, in which inputs and outputs are clearly defined (for example, IT systems) and approaches such as the Structured Systems Analysis and Design Method (SSADM) are used.
- *soft systems*, in which inputs and outputs are not clear (as in most organizational situations), with Peter Checkland's Soft Systems Methodology (SSM).

Issues within organizations are usually fuzzy and complex, so in this book we lean much more towards the soft side of systems. Adopting a systems approach to analysing performance problems can be a very powerful tool, as it encourages a more holistic look at what is happening. Through this you can feel more confident about finding solutions that deal with root causes of the problem rather than identifying sticking-plaster solutions that, while they may work to some extent in the short term, fail to deliver any long-term benefit and may actually have side-effects that can make things worse.

What is a System?

The *Oxford English Dictionary* defines a system as '... a set of objects or appliances arranged or organised for some special purpose'. From this we can deduce that a system needs to have certain elements:

- an input – something entering the system that will contribute to the purpose;
- an output – the purpose of the system;
- a transformation – something that happens to the input to convert it into the output;
- feedback – information circulating within the system that ensures that the transformation produces the output that is required.

Implicit within this definition is the core feature of a system – that by putting together individual items in a particular way they will do something in combination that not one of the items on their own can do. This is called an *emergent* property. So, for example, a wheel on its own can turn and sprockets can engage with a roller chain and not do much else, but when we combine these with some other handy items, such as a crossbar and a saddle, we have an emergent property that makes a form of transport possible: the bicycle.

Let us now think about a water heater, a simple physical example of a system. We shall define it as a system to convert cold water into hot water. The input is cold water; the boiler transforms the cold water to hot water which is then delivered as the output. A thermometer measures the temperature of the water as it leaves and provides feedback that regulates the level of heating so that the water is not too hot or too cold.

We can represent this in a simple diagram as shown in Figure 4.1.

It is easy to say that a thermostatic water heater is a system, but it is harder to say that an organization is a system with clearly defined inputs, outputs and transformations. However, we can look

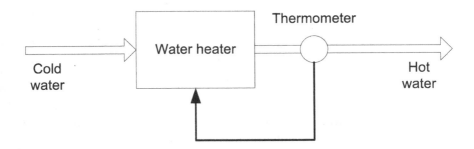

Figure 4.1   Water heating principle

at an organization as if it were operating *as a system*. This is very different and gives us a useful analytical tool, as we can look at what is happening within the organization, reduce this to some form of input–output–transformation system and see what we can learn, both from the process of imagining it to be a system and by looking at the differences between the 'theoretical' systemic behaviour and what happens in practice.

Organizations can be regarded as operating as systems at many different levels. For example, a car factory could be a system that takes in metal, electrical components, human endeavour and intelligence and combines these to produce motor cars. Feedback in the form of the level of sales or customer complaints affects the transformation process so that more or fewer cars are made, inherently faulty components are improved, and so on.

At a micro-level each individual function within the car factory is another system. Consider the area holding stocks: individual components are the input, components delivered to the production area are the output, and the transformation is the storage area. The numbers of components delivered for production feeds back into stock control management processes to make sure that an appropriate number are ordered as replacements.

We now need to be able to examine the system's behaviour, and we can do this diagrammatically using something like Figure 4.2. Diagrams like this can be presented in different ways and have various names, including causal flow diagrams (Jones, 1995), sign graphs (Open University) or just plain system diagrams (Senge, 1993).

Figure 4.2 shows how the level of heating is related to the water temperature. We draw boxes labelled with the key *levels* in the system (notice not 'states', such as 'hot water'). There is a direct relationship between the level of heating and the temperature, so, as the level of heating applied increases, the water temperature rises, and we show this by a '+' on the arrowed line. In the physical water heater system, a thermometer measures the temperature of the water being provided and regulates the level of heating, so that, as

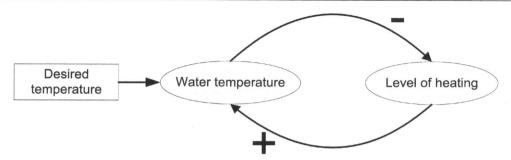

Figure 4.2   Water heating system

the water becomes hotter, the heater turns itself down so that the water slowly approaches the desired temperature. In the sign graph we show this by a '–' on the line. It is important to realize here that the + and – used on these lines actually correspond to direct and inverse relationships and not increases and decreases. So the + means that as one quantity increases the other increases, or that as one decreases the other also decreases. Conversely, the – means that as one quantity increases the other decreases.

We have also indicated that there is some input to the system in the form of the desired temperature setting. You can see that this is a stable (or balancing) feedback loop: as the water gets hotter the heating goes down, and then if the water cools down the heating will increase. The equilibrium within the system is determined by the temperature setting.

Now let us think about the car factory system, which we define as a system to convert parts into motor cars that can be sold. This could be represented by Figure 4.3

Here, as more and more cars are sold, the demand for parts will increase. Then, as more parts are supplied there are more cars available for sale, so sales can increase. Both lines have a + to show that an increase in one causes an increase in the other. Now this is a very different situation, as there is nothing to stop the level of sales increasing as long as the supply of parts can keep pace. (Oh, how motor manufacturers wish it were that simple!) This is an

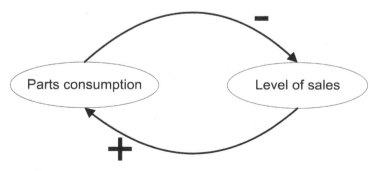

Figure 4.3   Car factory system

example of an unstable feedback loop, as it shows that things will keep increasing rather than settling on a particular level determined by an external input.

THE IMPORTANCE OF DELAYS

Let's now return to our water heater system. As we saw, this is a stable system where the water temperature will rise slowly to an externally determined level as the level of heating supplied is reduced. We can show this on a temperature–time graph, as in Figure 4.4.

In this graph our water heating system is shown by the line labelled 'Perfect system', and you see that the temperature slowly approaches the desired level. However, in a real-world system this would not be possible. For example, the heating element will always have some residual heat even after the energy supplied to it is cut off, so it will continue to heat the water. Careful design could minimize this, but then we need to consider what we exactly mean by the 'desired temperature'. If we want the water to be at 60°C, do we mean that 60.1°C is too hot and 59.9°C is too cold? If that is the case, then we must design a system that will switch off at 60.1°C and switch on again at 59.9°C. In practice this would mean that the heating system would be constantly switching on and off, and it would fail quickly. So we must accept some tolerance, perhaps designing the thermostat so that 60°C means anything between 57°C and 63°C. Our real system, therefore, would display a temperature–time graph more like that shown in the 'Real system' line, where the temperature overshoots, the heating switches off, the temperature falls off, the heating switches on, and so on.

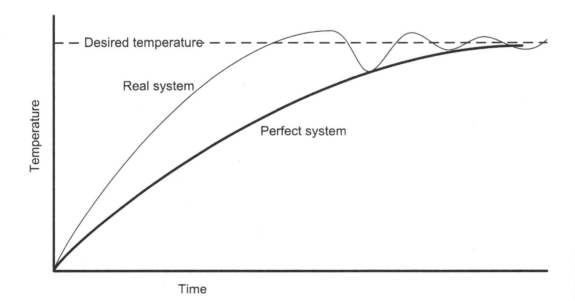

Figure 4.4 Temperature against time

This over- and undershooting is called *hysteresis* and is found in all dynamic systems. We experience it every time we sit in a car. Car suspension systems rely on two components: a spring and a shock absorber. If a car did not have a spring, the ride would be very hard, so the spring system allows the body of the car to move up and down gently as the wheels pass over holes and bumps in the road. However, the weight of the car body would cause the car body to quickly settle into a regular up-and-down motion, which would become very uncomfortable and prompt car sickness all round. So, along with the springs we have a shock absorber system, which slows the up-and-down movement. Now, the art of the car designer is in balancing the effects of the springs and shock absorbers. Cars with a 'soft ride', such as old American cars, are good for travelling in straight lines on good roads as the springs smooth out any slight imperfections in the road. However, when the car hits a bump it moves up and down dramatically. Conversely, a vehicle designed to go over uneven surfaces, such as an off-road four-wheel drive, has much stronger shock absorbers, but these can make travelling on smooth surfaces rather hard.

Hysteresis can cause health problems in our water heating system, as another of its effects is to create time delays between the input and the output, which can have a dramatic effect on how the system operates. We have probably all stayed in hotels in which the shower system is difficult to operate because there is a long time delay between turning the temperature control and the change in temperature of the water. Shivering under the cold water, we then turn the temperature control up slightly to no immediate effect, so we turn it up more, and suddenly extremely hot water jets out of the shower head, making us leap out of the shower, potentially injuring ourselves.

Now, what is the significance of all this in organizational systems? Let's go back to the car factory. As sales increase the demand for components will increase, but, for many different reasons, the suppliers may not be able to respond immediately: there are not enough suppliers, they need to invest in new equipment to produce more components, and so on. So instead of more components allowing higher sales, sales may stagnate as there are not enough vehicles available to meet the demand.

When this happens the sales department may see the reason for the sales problem as a shortage of components, so they react by ordering more. But this does not solve the problem, as these extra components will still not arrive in time, and, when they do, the company will find itself with higher stock levels than it needs and a cash-flow problem caused by the purchase. Panicking, the company slashes its orders for components, but then finds that, as sales pick up again, they have a shortage. The delays in the system are causing a constant crisis in over- and undersupply of components.

These problems could be avoided by recognizing the inevitable delays in the system and planning stock purchases to take these delays into consideration. This is what the Japanese *kanban* system does. Manufacturers using such just-in-time methods have a clear understanding about how each part of the system works and how quickly it can react to 'bumps in the road'. The collectivist nature of the society means that relationships between people and organizations are strong, and so the communication necessary for the system to work smoothly without unexpected delays is much easier.

Causal Flow Diagrams and a Performance Problem

Let's think next about how we might use a causal flow diagram in looking at a performance problem. I worked once with some civil engineers who were responsible for road-building in a West African country. The country had been through a civil war, and its roads were in a terrible state, so it was extremely important to get roads rebuilt so that the country's economic development could be speeded up. We might represent this system to build roads in a causal flow diagram (Figure 4.5).

On its own, this feedback loop would lead to steady growth of both factors: road-building would improve communications so that businesses could prosper, increasing the national GNP, which would make it possible to invest in more roads – a virtuous circle. However, this is a very slow process, and it would take several years before this cycle could be seen to be working. These civil engineers were, however, more concerned with getting construction materials from the docks. The war had destroyed much of the harbour infrastructure, and unloading construction materials and transporting them to the various depots around the country was proving very difficult. So

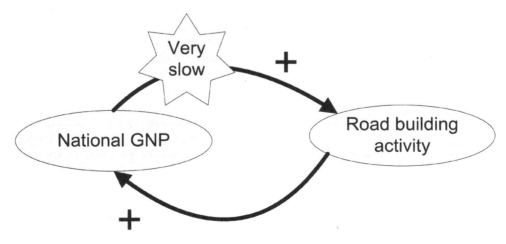

Figure 4.5   Road-building and national prosperity

the difficulties in supply of construction materials were slowing the road-building activity, which meant that the demand for construction materials was suppressed – a loop that was making progress increasingly difficult as time went by.

As a consequence there was a major project underway to rebuild the port area, so that, when this was completed and the port was working efficiently, the current vicious circle would be replaced by a virtuous circle (Figure 4.6). Construction supplies would flow from the docks, road-building would proceed apace, the country's economy would boom, more materials would come from the docks and everyone would live happily ever after. However, a few things were being overlooked here.

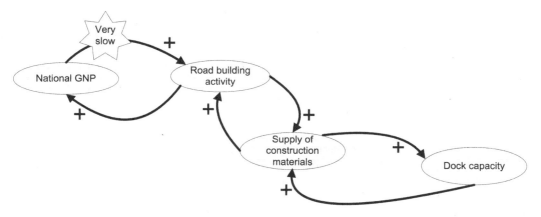

Figure 4.6   The impact of port reconstruction

The civil engineers pointed out that there were a few other problems affecting road-building in the country. There were not enough local companies able to take on the construction work available for various reasons, such as the effects of the civil war and government requirements for a minimum of three companies to tender for all contracts offered.

Also, it was impossible to find enough construction vehicles, especially lorries able to transport large quantities of gravel, hard-core and so on. The main reason for this was that the existing roads were in such poor condition that lorries were constantly breaking down, and keeping them roadworthy was difficult because of a shortage of spare parts. And one of the reasons for that was – yes – the problems in the docks.

Figure 4.7 overleaf shows the effect of these other factors.

Increasing dock capacity would make more spare parts available, which would then increase vehicle reliability. Increased reliability would lead to less demand for spare parts and would also improve availability. And, of course, increased vehicle reliability would

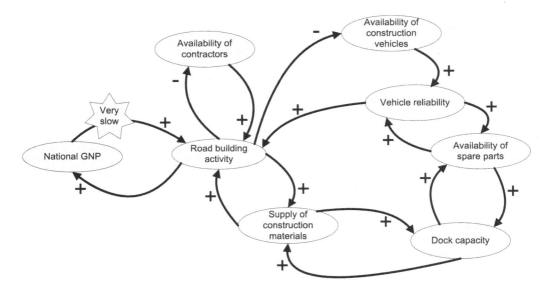

Figure 4.7   Other factors affecting road-building

increase road-building activity. This all looks wonderful, but we have a problem.

Consider the loop involving the availability of construction vehicles. As road-building activity increases, the number of vehicles available decreases. As the vehicles that are available are used more and more, they break down more frequently, so decreasing availability means decreasing vehicle reliability, which feeds back into the road-building activity, creating a stable loop. This is an example of what Peter Senge (1993) calls a 'limits to growth' archetype, because, regardless of anything happening in the rest of the system, this loop acts as a brake on the central activity of road-building. Combining this stable loop with the other systems means that the overall road-building system will reach equilibrium where the effects are in balance. Whatever we do to improve the efficiency of port operations, road-building will always be limited by the lack of heavy vehicles. As Senge says, '... the system has its own agenda' (1993, p. 84), which, in systems terminology, is an emergent property. This means that the number of construction vehicles act in the same way as the thermostat setting in the water heating system in Figure 4.2: the only way in which we can increase road-building activity above the equilibrium level is to provide more construction vehicles.

In a system with a stabilizing feedback loop the overall system equilibrium is always determined by the parameters within the *stable* loop.

The above example shows how useful it can be to represent an organization's dynamics in systems terms, and how limiting it can be to try to improve its overall performance by tinkering with just one part of the system. It is extremely enlightening to reflect on a workplace situation and to try to work out the causal relationships. Drawing system diagrams is a very powerful way of increasing your understanding of the situation because you are creating a visual network which parallels the way in which your brain works. Intelligence comes from the interconnectedness of individual neurons in the brain, and presenting it with information in this visual format makes it much easier for us to understand what is happening and to learn. And, although it is preferable to develop an accurate representation of what is happening, do not worry if things are not 100 per cent correct: just the process of drawing the diagram will have moved your understanding on considerably.

PRINCIPLES FOR DRAWING CAUSAL FLOW DIAGRAMS

Causal flow diagrams are a very useful tool for trying to develop a deeper understanding about what is happening. Here are some principles to follow when drawing diagrams.

Don't be afraid of making a mistake

The purpose of causal flow diagrams is to improve your understanding about what is happening, so don't worry about making a mistake about the direction of a relationship. Errors will quickly become apparent as you draw the diagram, discuss it with other people and see how it maps against reality, and you can use these errors to reflect on why you made your initial decision.

Define your issue carefully

Make sure that your starting-point is sufficiently well defined and that it is expressed as a variable quantity, so that it can go up or down. Avoid adding a direction to the quantity, as increases or decreases are conveyed through the connecting lines: 'road-building activity' is better than 'increased road building activity'. Similarly, express positive themes: 'activity' and not 'inactivity' as negative themes increase the degree of mental gymnastics you need to perform to understand the diagram.

Make drivers explicit

When thinking about how something changes over time, make sure that your diagram includes the factors that cause that change. In our example above, increasing dock capacity will increase vehicle reliability in the country, but the reason for this needs to be expressed. This is because each individual driver can have more than one effect on the system, and missing anything out could have a big effect on the operation of your system.

Define your boundaries

The process of drawing causal flow diagrams can become very absorbing and stimulating, and it is all too easy to find yourself wandering off in unintended directions. If you find yourself doing this, think about whether the issues you are exploring are relevant to the central issue and whether they will have a significant effect.

Acknowledge delays and time factors

Delays and time factors are crucially important in system diagrams, so label them. If road-building increased the gross national product quickly, the importance of the other factors in Figure 4.7 would become much less significant.

Cultures and Causal Flow Diagrams

So far, we have seen how we can use causal flow diagrams to increase our understanding of what is happening in an organization. However, it is also instructive to look at what they can tell us about cultures.

Let us consider collectivism. In Chapter 1 we saw how collectivism seems to inevitably be replaced by a more individualist culture as societies become wealthier. Many different reasons have been proposed for this, but a systems analysis allows us to consider the mechanisms by which this might happen.

First, we define the collectivist system as one in which individuals are encouraged to think about the needs of the group in preference to their own. This has many different implications, but one is that status is more important than achievement, as status reflects a degree of connectivity within the in-group. We can therefore draw a causal flow diagram like Figure 4.8.

The collectivist society encourages a respect for status, so ascription is encouraged, and this reinforces the attitudes towards collectivism.

Now, looking at Figure 4.9, consider one of the side-effects of ascription. It encourages trust within businesses, as the people appointed to key positions are accepted members of the in-group. Trust means that the company operates effectively and the business succeeds. As the business prospers, the need for people increases. However, this is where a problem can develop. The in-group can only be so big, and sooner or later there will not be enough suitable members to take up positions within the business, so the availability

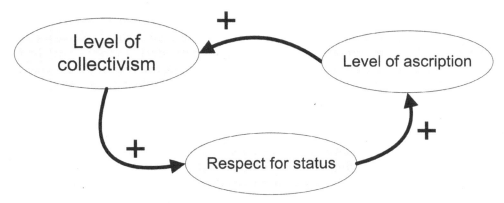

Figure 4.8   Collectivism and ascription

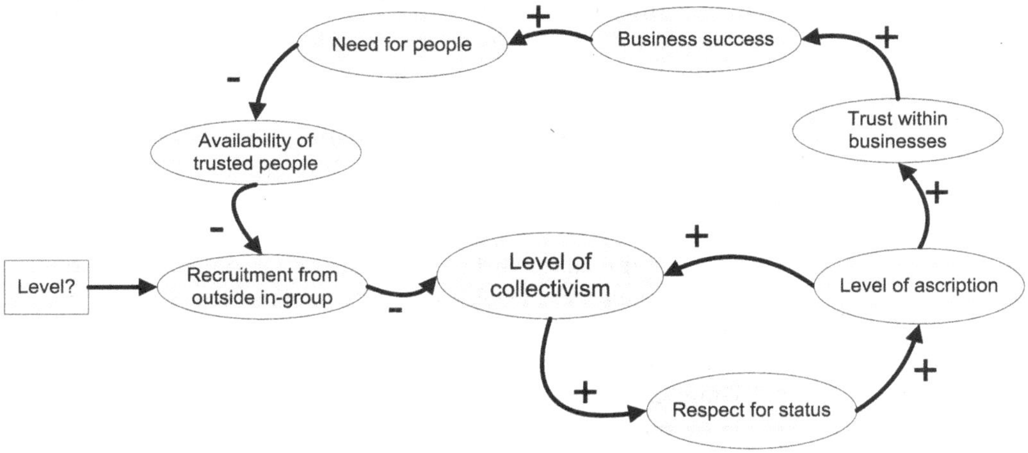

Figure 4.9   Collectivism and economic success

of trusted people will go down. As the availability goes down, the number of people having to be recruited from outside the in-group will increase. Now, these people will not necessarily see the rewards of mutual loyalty and obligations as adequate compensation, so they may need to be rewarded by salary systems and bonuses that are more appropriate to an individualist outlook. So, as recruitment from outside the in-group increases, the commitment to the level of collectivism within the business will decrease. As with the availability of construction vehicles in Figure 4.7, we have a stabilizing feedback loop, where its significance depends on the level of recruitment from outside that is tolerated. The higher this level, the greater the negative impact on the level of collectivism, and, with increasing economic success, one might reasonably expect this level to constantly increase. This seems to be the current experience in China, where young people entering the booming economic system have different expectations and values to the older generations.

Now, in many respects, this is a simplistic analysis of the situation. There are many other perspectives to economic growth that you could examine, but it is likely that most of them will also create a stabilizing feedback loop. Interestingly, some time in early 2009, during the depths of the global economic crisis, I listened to a radio discussion about whether a side-effect of the crisis might be a return to 'family-operated businesses', because one effect of the crisis (and perhaps also a cause) had been a collapse in business trust. I leave it to interested readers to explore causal flow diagrams that might help to shed some light on this possible outcome!

The limits-to-growth loop introduces an important feature of the logic of causal flow diagrams. Note that in the limits-to-growth loop in Figure 4.7 there were two '+' and one '–' relationships. In

Figure 4.9 the loop contains five '+' and three '–' relationships. There is a rule that if a loop has an *even number* of indirect relationships, the loop is *reinforcing*, but if it has an *odd number* of indirect relationships, the loop is *stabilizing*. This provides a handy way of looking at a loop and predicting its behaviour.

The following steps show you how to draw a causal flow diagram:

- Identify the factors influencing the behaviour in the system.
- Express factors as levels of activity (not as states).
- Decide how factors influence each other.
- Draw lines with a '+' to show direct relationships.
- Draw lines with a '–' to show inverse relationships.
- Look out for reinforcing loops (all direct relationships or even number of inverse relationships).
- Look out for stabilizing loops (odd number of inverse relationships).
- Play around with different factors to increase your understanding of relationships.

Soft Systems Methodology (SSM)

Earlier in this chapter we referred to Structured Systems Analysis and Design Methodology (SSADM) and contrasted it with Soft Systems Methodology (SSM). SSADM is a process for analysing such things as manufacturing processes and software designs and, although effective in those areas, cannot be applied very easily in the much less well-defined areas of organizational problems. In contrast, SSM has been developed specifically to look at these types of problem, but could also be regarded as the general case methodology with the ability to examine all types of system. If inputs, outputs, transformations and objectives are rigidly and clearly defined, SSM can be seen to reduce to SSADM (Checkland and Scholes, 1990).

Originally developed by Peter Checkland at Lancaster University in the 1970s, one of SSM's most satisfying tenets is that its real value is in encouraging the analyst to constantly reflect on how their analysis relates to real life, and to move backwards and forwards in the analysis process to continually deepen their understanding. This is very much the philosophy in the later problem-solving chapters of this book where constant reflection and refinement is encouraged, and where the choice of problem-solving tools is intended to encourage this behaviour.

Although I do not follow the Soft Systems Methodology rigorously in this book, I do make use of many of its concepts where helpful. Noting that, let us look at the key elements of the SSM process.

IDENTIFYING THE
PROBLEM

The process starts by someone recognizing that there is a problem and that it is sufficiently serious to warrant some attention. As Checkland says, 'the situation itself, being part of human affairs, will be a product of a particular history, a history of which there will always be more than one account' (Checkland and Scholes, 1990, p, 28). This is extremely important, because it introduces the notion of system perspectives – that what is a problem to one person may be a different issue to another and, by implication, what one considers to be a good solution may be inappropriate to someone else. This has particular significance in cross-cultural workplace settings: for example, where there are concerns about the performance of a particular work team, the definitions of the problem could be that:

- internal relationships within the team are not harmonious (from the perspective of someone with a collectivist, Confucian cultural background).
- sales targets are not being met (from the perspective of someone with a short-term orientation).
- decision-making within the team is too autocratic (from the perspective of someone from a low power distance culture).

And so on.

CONCEPTUALIZING
THE PROBLEM

Once the problem has been identified, it needs to be described in some way, and in SSM this is done by drawing a 'rich picture'. Its purpose is to capture and express salient features of the current situation, including elements, processes and associated emotions, and it is often created collaboratively and drawn by hand on a large sheet of paper so that different people can add their thoughts to it.

Rich pictures need not be works of art. Their purpose is to summarize what is happening and to illustrate relationships. The act of drawing the rich picture usually acts as a powerful stimulus to thinking about underlying issues.

Using rich pictures to develop an understanding of a workplace problem is covered in more detail in Chapter 6.

IDENTIFYING
SYSTEMS

With some understanding of what is going on, the analysts can next identify some ways in which this can be described as a system. Checkland and Scholes (1990) stress the importance of identifying both 'primary task' and 'issue-based' systems in order to make sure that thinking is kept clear and open. Primary task systems relate closely to the visible activities of an organization. For example, a bookshop could be:

- a system to convert unsold books into sold books.

On the other hand, an issue-based system might be:

- a system to encourage more coffee consumption;
- a system to help like-minded people meet each other.

Once upon a time bookshops just sold books, but then they realized that a bookshop potentially provided an ideal setting for a coffee shop as well. Then some bookshops noticed that people's eyes sometimes met in the classic fiction section, so the idea of singles' evenings was born.

Drawing up a list of ways in which an activity may be described stimulates thinking about what is going on and what needs to be considered. So, if you were considering how to improve the performance of a bookshop, you should think carefully about both primary task and issue-based systems.

Identifying different systems is similar to the process of defining and redefining a problem statement, as discussed in Chapter 4.

DEVELOPING
A ROOT
DEFINITION

A root definition defines the core purpose of the activity and is derived by reflecting on the different systems suggested. When following SSM strictly, the root definition needs to be expressed fairly precisely and to contain specific elements. Checkland and Scholes use the mnemonic CATWOE to summarize:

- **C**ustomers – who are affected by whatever the system transforms,
- **A**ctors – the people who implement the transformation,
- **T**ransformation – what actually changes,
- **W**eltanschauung – the world-view which underpins this particular root definition,
- **O**wner – people who could stop the transformation,
- **E**nvironment – given elements outside the system.

What is particularly interesting here is the concept of *Weltanschauung*. Because so many system definitions are possible in any particular case, any final choice for a root definition will depend on the interests of the analysts, and so will reflect their interests, cultural perspectives or priorities. For example, the *Weltanschauung* in the case of the bookshop system could be:

- Selling books is important to ensure the financial security of the bookshop.
- Bookshops provide an important and useful place where people can meet, so helping social harmony.
- Selling books provides a way of attracting people who may be interested in other purchases.

The choice of *Weltanschauung* is therefore extremely important when following SSM, because it has a profound effect on what insights the process gives. This is the reason for some criticisms of the method. Flood and Jackson (1991), for example, point out that since its choice is often influenced by dominant cultural assumptions, the whole process may fail to challenge existing power structures because it supports existing decision-makers.

Since SSM stresses the importance of analysts, customers, actors and owners working together to explore what is happening, in a multicultural setting the opportunity to discuss a relevant *Weltanschauung* would stimulate a very useful discussion.

BUILDING A CONCEPTUAL MODEL

The next stage is to use the root definition to build a *conceptual model* of the system – that is, a model of what the real-life system might look like. A first draft of the model would use all the transitive verbs in the root definition, and would show which activities are dependent on others – that is, which activities require significant amounts of information, materials or energy from another activity.

The conceptual model is then compared with reality in order to open a discussion about what is happening, considering questions such as:

- Does this activity in the model happen in real life?
- Are the dependencies represented correctly?
- Are there any real-life activities that are not represented in the model?

Again, the purpose of this discussion is not to develop an accurate model, but to serve as a prompt to a discussion that will assist in identifying changes that will help real-life processes work more effectively.

Summary

Systems thinking encourages us to take a wider look at what is happening in a given situation, so that we take into consideration the complete network of influences and relationships at play. This makes it easier for us to identify root causes of problems, elimination of which will lead to identifying solutions that are more effective than those we would employ if merely tackling the symptoms displayed.

In particular, Soft Systems Methodology can provide a very useful process to follow when looking at a workplace performance problem. In Chapter 5, 'Solving Workplace Problems', we will use a number of its ideas in a systematic approach to analysing performance problems and finding solutions.

Figure 4.10 summarizes what we have covered in this chapter.

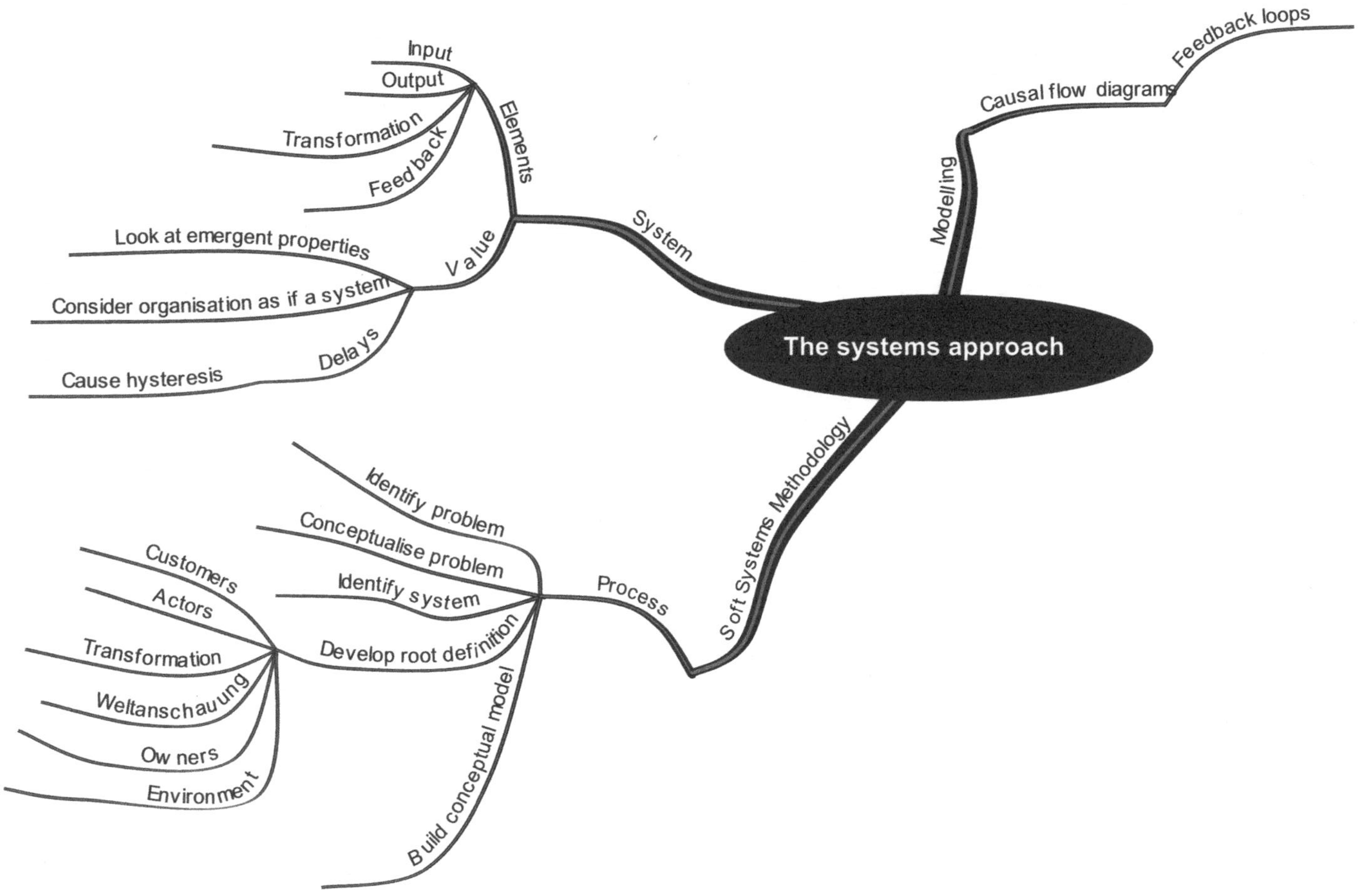

Figure 4.10 Mindmap summary of Chapter 4

5 *Solving Workplace Problems*

KEY POINTS

Our ability to solve problems is affected by a number of factors, including:

- environmental obstacles (a lack of time or other resources);
- intellectual obstacles (not knowing a suitable process to follow);
- physiological obstacles (how our brains deal with problem-solving);
- cultural obstacles (related to how we view the world around us).

> *Reason guides but a small part of man, and the rest obeys feeling, true or false, and passion, good or bad.*
>
> Joseph Roux (1725–1793).

Describing Problems

Earlier chapters looked at the differences in how people from around the world approach the workplace, and then at ways of analysing performance problems. In this chapter we move on to see how we can pull these two strands together into a coherent process for problem-solving. What we will look at here are some background ideas about problem-solving and a seven-step process for problem-solving that will enable us to develop holistic solutions. At each stage we can consider how cultural issues can impact on the process. In Part 2 of the book, Chapters 6 to 12 look at practical ways in which you can carry out each of these steps, focusing on techniques that can take cultural aspects of performance into consideration.

Describing Problems

Problems can come in many different shapes and sizes, and they have attracted a great number of adjectives:

- *Simple* problems have clear structures and requirements for solutions (but may not be simple to solve).
- *Complex* problems include many different factors, but may have limited requirements for solutions.
- *Well-defined* problems are those where the various issues involved can be expressed easily.
- *Ill-defined* problems are those where the various issues involved cannot be expressed easily.

Organizational problems are usually complex and ill-defined. It may be difficult to define what the actual problem is, the contributory factors may be obscure and there is probably no clear right or wrong answer. It is also quite likely that the problem you are investigating will be, in some way, connected with other problems that other people are struggling with.

What Can Make Problem-solving Difficult?

When we are faced with a problem there are many different things that can prevent us finding an effective solution. We can put these obstacles under four headings: environmental, intellectual, physiological and cultural.

We shall first briefly consider environmental and intellectual obstacles and then move on to look at physiological and cultural ones, which are interconnected.

ENVIRONMENTAL OBSTACLES

Finding solutions to problems can be very difficult and requires a considerable investment of such precious commodities as thought, concentration and time. These are often in short supply in a modern workplace, where open-plan offices expose us to a constant bustle of people talking and ringing telephones, and lean staffing levels mean that everyone is pressed for time.

None of this helps with problem-solving, which is, more often than not, a task that requires patient mental effort. It is a creative activity, and creativity is not something that can be simply turned on and off as necessary. I am sure that many of you reading this will recall incidents where you have thought of the answer to a problem in an unlikely setting – maybe while practising yoga or riding a bicycle through the countryside. This phenomenon is sometimes called *incubating* and is thought to be a consequence of subconscious problem analysis going on within our brains. Sadly, unless you are self-employed or work for an unusually enlightened employer, these are not normally acceptable problem-solving strategies, even if you are grappling with the most intractable of issues.

INTELLECTUAL OBSTACLES

As both intellect and culture are connected with processing within the brain, it is useful to distinguish here that intellectual obstacles refer to those related to reason and knowledge, rather than the emotional activity associated with culture. This is, admittedly, a somewhat rough and ready distinction, but it helps in this case.

We can identify perhaps three ways in which our intellect can let us down when trying to solve problems:

1. We lack knowledge of problem-solving techniques.
2. We over-rely on previous experience.
3. We stereotype the problem.

Problem-solving is not generally taught in schools or universities, or in the workplace for that matter, although it is in fact a discipline in its own right, with a significant body of literature and a wealth of different approaches that are applicable in different areas. While it is probably true that some people are naturally better than others at solving problems, it is generally true that studying and learning specific techniques can improve performance significantly. It is hoped that, by the time you have studied the relevant chapters in this book that this will no longer exist as an obstacle.

As we grow older we acquire a vast amount of experience and information. Much of this is of little use, but that which is useful is stored away so that we can recall and use it when necessary: this is a very efficient arrangement and saves us a lot of wasted time. Unfortunately, we can sometimes look at a problem and think that it is very similar to a problem we had just a while ago; we recall that when that happened we did such and such, and decide that we should probably do the same thing again. As Monsieur Roux observes in the quotation that opens this chapter, feeling and passion are getting the better of reason, with a feeling about a solution that we liked before stopping us from analysing things in a more reasoned way.

This is a manifestation of a pattern known as *confirmation bias*, which is where we make assumptions about how something is and then interpret evidence connected to the situation in a way that supports our assumptions. In the context of problem-solving we often have a preconception as to what the solution should be and then interpret the available information in such a way that our preference is justified. There is even a word for the process: the *Oxford English Dictionary* defines 'satisficing' (a combination of 'satisfy' and 'suffice') as to 'decide on and pursue a course of action that will satisfy the minimum requirements necessary to achieve a particular goal'. What we do is look at the problem, decide what the solution is and then look for justifications for this particular solution (and, of course, ignore anything that says that this might just not be the best thing to do).

Satisficing is, of course, helped by stereotyping. As with making assumptions about how people of a different age, race or religion, for example, will behave, we assume that problems that look somewhat alike are all caused by the same root cause and will respond to the same solution. As soon as we do this we define all sorts of inappropriate limits to the problem, setting boundaries that do not exist and imagining constraints that are not there. Shutting down the real range of options is, of course, what 'lateral thinking' problems exploit: given simple descriptions of a scene, we create our own mental definition of the problem which often excludes the possibility of the real interpretation. This is because human brains like to look for patterns. Wertheimer's Laws of Gestalt include 'the law of continuity' – that our brains try to reorganize possibly random shapes, lines or dots into a meaningful image. Similarly, many people take great comfort in interpreting random, one-off events as the results of conspiracies, whether they be presidents being shot or princesses killed in car crashes. For example, a lone gunman killing President Kennedy is unsettling because there could be any number of deranged people out there with a gun, and we could be a victim. However, imagining that the assassination was a CIA plot reassures us, as very few of us could imagine that we would be a specific target for a government-appointed hitman.

As well as potentially being explained by our need to see patterns where there is only randomness, conspiracy theories can also be interpreted as another example of confirmation bias. For example, if we had childhood experiences of being bullied by groups of other children, we might be more disposed to see violent acts as being premeditated and directed rather than as random.

Finally, as Morgan Jones (1995) points out, we tend to hang on tenaciously to things we believe in, even when they are patently not true: for example, women thinking they are fat when they are not and men believing they have hair when it has long gone. In reality, we look at our beliefs as if they are possessions and are reluctant to give them away.

PHYSIOLOGICAL OBSTACLES

Your reason and your passion are the rudder and the sales of your seafaring soul.

If either your sales or your rudder be broken, you can but toss and drift, or else be held at a standstill in mid-seas.

For reason, ruling alone, is a force confining; and passion, unattended, is a flame that burns to its own destruction.

Therefore let your soul exalt your reason to the height of passion that it may sing:

And let it direct to your passion with reason, that your passion may live through its own daily resurrection, and like the Phoenix rise above its own ashes.

From *The Prophet*, Kahlil Gibran (1883–1931).

There are two types of physiological obstacle that can jump up in front of us when we try to make a decision. The first is an innate feature of our human physiology, while the second, although physiological, is locked in a reinforcing feedback loop with our cultural values system.

This innate feature derives from the way in which our brains work in response to a problem. It has been suggested that two different parts of the brain are involved in decision-making: the amygdala and the neocortex. The amygdala is a small processing unit located on the underside of the brain, just at the top of the brainstem, and it is responsible for emotional reactions to the world around us. The neocortex, on the other hand, handles rational decision-making processes. They are both able to control how our body reacts to the world around us.

When we are presented with a problem both the amygdala and the neocortex play a part in helping us identify solutions. The problem might evoke a strong emotional response, in which case we may pay less attention to the rational analysis provided by the neocortex. This clearly has potential benefits if the problem presents a physical danger, and has parallels with blindsight. This is the observed phenomenon where people who have suffered damage to the visual cortex area of their brain, meaning that they cannot consciously see, can still sense movement in front of them, allowing them to make certain decisions about what to do in response.

However, while the alternative responses of the amygdala and neocortex are sometimes presented as in conflict, it is probably essential that they both do function. Daniel Goleman (1995) discusses a number of medical cases in which people have suffered brain injuries or undergone operations that have resulted in their amygdala no longer being functional in the decision-making process. When this has happened, people can fully understand and articulate the rational arguments involved in a particular decision, but may be incapable of making a final decision. After all, in most cases we make decisions by to a greater or lesser extent considering the pros and cons of the situation rationally and then finally making an emotional decision about which solution we prefer. The trick, of course, is in getting the balance right.

Being aware of these two separate processes going on and managing them is what Daniel Goleman discusses in his popular book *Emotional Intelligence*. He suggests that emotional intelligence requires that we:

- can recognize our own emotions;
- can manage these emotions when they rise up inside us;
- are able to use emotions to motivate us to achieve things we need to do;
- can recognize emotional reactions in other people;
- can manage the interplay of emotions in relationships so that they can prosper.

In terms of the decision-making process, the first three are of particular interest to us. We need to be able to recognize when our response to a workplace problem is an emotional one and to manage that appropriately. Being able to use emotions allows us to work creatively, which is of great importance when analysing and trying to find solutions to problems.

Also happening inside our heads, when we are faced with a problem, is a process of problem classification and solution selection. As we grow older and gain more experience of the world around us, we classify things that happen around us into different categories of incident and develop strategies for responding to each particular category. This makes it quite likely that we will react rather predictably and find ourselves selecting solutions from a relatively small bank of possibilities, rather than living dangerously and trying something completely different.

Further complicating our emotional response is the mood that we are in when the problem occurs, so that how we react can be very different if the sun is shining, we are thinking fondly about our partner or if our football team has just won an important game. Or, for that matter, as scientists have shown, whether or not we are holding a warm drink, as it seems that having a cup of tea or coffee in one's hands disposes us to think favourably about the world around us (Williams and Bargh, 2008). So, clearly, when considering our response to a non-dangerous problem we need to slow down, let our immediate emotional response pass, and move on to a more rational approach.

The other physiological response is connected to our values system, and concerns whether or not we are field-dependent or field-independent perceivers. Witkin's and Goodenough's (1977) distinction was described in Chapter 2, but to reiterate:

- Field-dependent observers take into account the background or environment of an object.

- Field-independent observers focus on the object and take less account of its environment.

Field dependence is generally associated with people from collectivist cultures whereas field independency is associated with individualists. It seems as if the way in which adults interact with babies and small children encourages them to focus on the world around them in a particular way, and 'trains' brains and eyes to work together in such a way as to emphasize some aspects of the surrounding world and to de-emphasize others. For example, Nisbett (2003) discusses how East Asian children learn verbs at a much faster rate than do Western children. He advances two ideas to explain this. First there is a tendency for most Western languages to position verbs in the middle of sentences, surrounded by nouns, while in Eastern languages they are placed at the more visible beginning or end of sentences. Second, Western and Eastern parents talk to babies and small children differently: Western parents label objects when teaching their children to speak (emphasizing nouns) whereas Eastern parents describe activities and transactions (emphasizing verbs).

It is perhaps therefore not surprising that, when presented with a problem, field-independent people are more likely to focus on the specific manifestation of the problem whereas field-dependent people will reflect more on the connections between this manifestation and the setting in which it occurs.

CULTURAL OBSTACLES

We can see differences in cultural approaches to problem-solving right from the very first stage of identifying a problem. People from Western, individualist cultures seem to be better at seeing problems, for example, than those from Eastern cultures. Indeed, where the relationship of a culture to nature is dominant, the whole of existence might be seen as a problem that needs to be overcome, whereas to people whose relationship to nature is subordinate, the feeling that life's vicissitudes are due to external factors over which you have no control can remove the notion that anything is a problem at all.

Western thinking is largely derived from ideas that were formulated during the classical Greek period. A key concept that the Greeks introduced was that of *personal agency*, the idea that people are in charge of their own lives and can influence the environment around them. Nisbett (2003) points out that a definition of happiness for an ancient Greek was to be able to pursue excellence, freed from any constraints. Control over our environment introduces the idea of a goal or objective – a state of being that we want our environment to be in – and from this developed the Western tradition of logical analysis and causal attribution: by deciding on an appropriate series of actions, we can achieve any objective. Conversely, if we have an undesirable situation, we can work backwards to figure out what needs to be changed. Anyone who has been brought up in a Western setting such as this is totally immersed in the logic of cause and effect, and hence problem-solving.

So while Westerners are good at thinking backwards, people from Eastern cultures are more confident about thinking forwards. Nisbett discusses how this manifests itself in the different ways in which history is taught in American and Japanese schools. In an American classroom a teacher typically starts by explaining what happened, and then, through asking lots of 'Why?' questions, encourages students to detect the causal relationships. In contrast, Japanese teachers explain in detail the context of a given situation and then encourage students to consider subsequent events: thinking forwards and not backwards. Being educated in this way makes people much better at thinking through consequences and anticipating change.

The Western tradition of logical analysis and causal attribution is undoubtedly powerful and has been a major reason why the West has been responsible for scientific and technical advances during the last 500 years. However, its reductionist tendencies can often simplify matters to the point where essential contextual factors are ignored or overlooked.

The perceived ability to discuss a problem can be different in achievement-oriented and ascriptive societies. The emphasis in achievement-oriented culture on individual activity encourages people to draw attention to something that might need rectifying: if it is indeed a problem and is rectified, that person's personal kudos will be enhanced. By contrast, in ascription-oriented cultures individuals must take careful account of their status within a group before mentioning anything that could reflect badly on, or have negative implications for, more senior members of the organization.

A Process for Solving Problems

There is a large body of literature dedicated to problem-solving methods, which together present a huge number of possibilities for the would-be problem-solver. Most methodologies are designed for specific types of problem – for example, to promote innovation or to troubleshoot problems in more or less mechanical systems. We looked at one such problem-solving system, Soft Systems Methodology (SSM), in Chapter 4 and saw how this used a somewhat iterative approach to help the problem-solver develop a deeper understanding of a problem in order to identify potential solutions. A variation on this method will be used in this book.

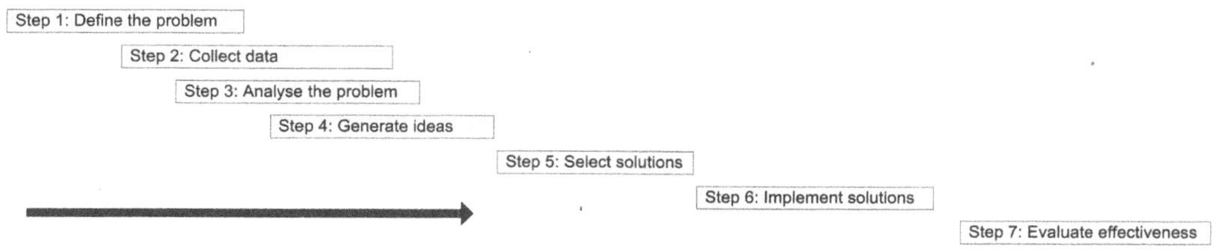

Step 1: Define the problem
Step 2: Collect data
Step 3: Analyse the problem
Step 4: Generate ideas
Step 5: Select solutions
Step 6: Implement solutions
Step 7: Evaluate effectiveness

Figure 5.1   The problem-solving process

Of course, in a book of this nature it is pertinent to reflect on the cultural values that this methodology represents. Were I not British of Anglo-Saxon stock, then my suggested approach might dwell more, for example, on the lessons that we should take from historical precedent or I might rely less on logical dissection and more on intuition. However, pragmatism means that we must start from somewhere, and, while I acknowledge the cultural bias implicit in this methodology, throughout this book we will seek to draw on cultural differences that are of significance at each stage, and in this way develop a methodology that takes these into due consideration.

There are essentially seven steps to follow, as shown in Figure 5.1 above.

Although in essence this is a linear process it is important to realize that one step does not rigorously follow another. Instead, it is perhaps more like waves lapping on a beach as the tide rises: you progress through one stage and realize that you need to return to the previous stage for more information or more analysis, and so you slide backwards only to move forwards again with a little more impetus.

Let us look at each of these steps.

Step 1: Define the problem (Chapter 6)

A problem exists when someone feels that something around them is not quite right and it is making them feel uncomfortable. If you or someone else finds themselves in this position in the workplace, you have to decide whether or not to invest any time in putting things right, and a decision on this is going to depend on just how big the problem is.

You may recall that we discussed this subject in Chapter 2, where we looked at the Mager and Pipe performance flowchart. Before spending any time investigating a performance problem you need to ask, 'Is the problem serious?' If you think that it is not, you do not need to do any further analysis but should monitor the situation, because, if something is starting to go wrong, the chances are that it will get worse rather than better. The seriousness of the problem depends on its costs, which can be financial, regulatory or ethical. To a certain extent, regulatory and ethical issues can be given some financial value. What you define at this stage is the cost of doing nothing.

If this cost does look as if it is more than you want to bear, you need to start on the problem-solving process, and the first step is to define the problem. To do this, it is useful to consider the answers to five questions: who, what, where, when and how big:

- *Who* is the person or group that we are concerned about?
- *What* is it they are doing (or not doing) that concerns us?
- *Where* do we see this happening (which office, department or geographical location, for example)?
- *When* did we start to see this happening and how often does it occur?
- *How big* is the effect of what is happening?

Answers to these questions will help you to write a *problem statement*, which will be the starting-point for the problem-solving process. In fact, the answers will help you write a number of problem statements, because, as we have discussed in the earlier chapters in this book, perceptions of problems are culturally defined so that the same situation can look quite different to people from different cultures. We will see how developing several different problems statements for a single problem can help us identify different root causes and hence different solutions.

You can find out more about this stage of the problem-solving process in Chapter 6.

Step 2: Collect data (Chapter 7)

In Step 2 you collect information about the problem. You need to identify who is involved and what is happening at the moment, and define what should be happening.

There are a number of different ways in which you can collect data. You can:

- look for information about previous investigations into the problem – other people may have gone this way before and left their analysis on a dusty shelf.
- examine quantitative information, perhaps stored in records or computer systems.
- carry out interviews with a range of people involved in the problem.
- send out questionnaires.
- have a go at the jobs involved in the performance yourself and see what challenges you can find.
- observe people carrying out the performance.

Step 3: Analyse the problem (Chapter 8)

In many ways, the analysis stage is the crucial part of the problem-solving process. This is where you need to pick the problem apart and identify what the root causes are. In Chapter 8 you will look at some powerful techniques that you can use to help you get inside the problem and analyse it more effectively.

These techniques draw heavily on systems thinking and on the use of visual representations of a problem to make it easier to see the interconnection of causal factors.

Step 4: Generate ideas (Chapter 9)

In the generating ideas step described in Chapter 9 we look at some ways of identifying potential solutions. The important thing at this stage is to come up with as many potential solutions as possible, and this will therefore entail drawing upon different ways of working with a small team of people committed to helping you with your problem-solving with the aim of generating an initial long list of ideas.

The chapter also looks at how to use the Mager and Pipe performance flowchart, first described in Chapter 2. Unlike brainstorming, this is a systematic way of approaching problem analysis, but this does not necessarily mean that it is better or worse. In fact, as with many parts of the problem-solving process, you can achieve better results by adopting both creative and systematic approaches.

Step 5: Select solutions (Chapter 10)

Step 4 generated a long list of potential solutions, and in Step 5 you need to evaluate these ideas and select a number that, when implemented together, will eliminate your problem.

In Chapter 10 we look at some techniques you can use to help you make some rational comparisons between what might be quite different types of solution.

Step 6: Implement solutions (Chapter 11)

Having identified your potential solutions, you now need to put them into practice. Chapter 11 looks at some of the issues you need to take into consideration when seeking to implement both organizational changes and those involving the delivery of training solutions.

Step 7: Evaluate effectiveness (Chapter 12)

The final step in the problem-solving process is to see how successful your solutions have been, once they have had time to take effect. At this stage you need to go back to your initial data and see just how serious the problem originally was. Quantifying the size of the problem at the beginning of the process is essential if you are to be able to prove to problem owners just how effective your process has been.

THE RELIABLE CONSTRUCTIONS CASE STUDY

Chapters 6 to 12 look in detail at each step of the problem-solving process. Each chapter explains the principles involved in carrying out that particular stage and then uses a case study to show how these principles might be applied in a typical problem.

The case study looks at a problem afflicting Reliable Constructions Ltd, a British company working on a construction project in a newly industrializing Eastern European country. It should be noted that

Reliable Constructions Ltd is a completely fictitious company, but that the problem described is based on a real-life example. In each chapter we use the various ideas and techniques discussed for each step to show how they help the company's problem-solving sleuth.

The aim of this case study is to show you how to follow the problem-solving approach to pull apart a workplace performance problem, considering cross-cultural issues along the way. For this reason it has been simplified, and the careful reader will probably question why certain aspects of the problem have not been covered or discussed in more detail. Certainly, if you were the real troubleshooter you would be doing this, but here this runs the risk of obscuring basic principles, and might also make the process seem rather intimidating and perhaps excessively time-consuming.

If time and other resources are limited, problem analysis can be done quickly. The important thing is to do it.

Summary

This chapter has summarized the environmental, intellectual, physiological and cultural issues that can hinder finding solutions to problems. It has also introduced us to a seven-step process for problem-solving, and the following chapters explore each of these steps in more detail.

The Practice

CHAPTER 6

Step 1: Define the Problem

KEY POINTS

Put together a team of people who can work together to help solve the problem.

Define your problem by establishing:

- what the problem is;
- how serious the problem is;
- whose problem it is;
- when the problem occurs.

Develop a number of different problem statements, each defining the problem in a different way.

Figure 6.1   Step 1 in problem-solving

Getting Off to a Good Start

The first stage in problem-solving is to recognize that there is in fact a problem. But, what is a problem? One definition is that a problem exists when someone feels that something around them is unsatisfactory. This, of course, implies that the existence of a problem depends on each individual viewer's perspective, which will be shaped very much by their culture. So problems are relative, and there cannot be a single absolute definition of any particular unsatisfactory situation.

This is very important, because if you do make the assumption that a problem can be defined in only one way, you may immediately close down any number of possible solutions.

In this chapter we will look at how you can make sure that you keep your options for problem-solving as open as possible. Even before we consider cultural diversity there are a number of techniques we can use to ensure that we try to describe a problem in different ways: multiple cultural perspectives just add to the richness of our initial picture.

There are some key questions to ask about any problem:

- What is the problem?
- How serious is it?
- Whose problem is it?
- When does the problem occur?

Let's take a look at each of these in turn.

What is the Problem?

This is perhaps the most fundamental question, and is also the one that may be hardest to define in a culturally diverse setting. Thinking back to Soft Systems Methodology (SSM), a description of what the problem is depends on each observer's *Weltanschauung*, their world-view.

Say, for example, there is a problem with a team which is not achieving the level of sales required. This problem can be perceived in different ways:

- 'We are not hitting our sales targets,' says the individualist with a short-term orientation and a masculine outlook.
- 'The marketplace is changing. Our competitors are suffering as well,' says the person who feels that they are subjugated by nature.
- 'Our relationships with our customers are difficult,' says the collectivist with a long-term orientation and a belief in harmony.
- 'The management structure in this team is stifling,' says anyone who thinks that the management structure is too strongly based on achievement (or perceived status) or that decision-making is too hierarchical (or not hierarchical enough).

Of course, looking at this list of problem descriptions leads you to think that perhaps they are all true, at least to some degree. And, if someone thinks something is a problem, then that observation needs to be addressed in some way, even if its significance is not great.

Herein lies one of the advantages of looking at a problem through cultural glasses: it immediately prompts you to think about what is really going on, rather than jumping straight to conclusions.

Starting with a single problem statement makes a problem seem simpler, and we refer back to previous experience to see how we have solved this type of problem in the past. This reductionism encourages managers to look for a specific solution to a specific problem, so that an instinctive response to the problem, as first described above, would be: 'The team needs sales skills training.' Training may be a possible solution, but the different perspectives on the problem could lead a manager to consider other areas that need to be addressed as well.

So, what should you do, as a manager, to find an answer to the question 'What is the problem?' You should:

- seek the opinions of people within the group involved with what is happening, making sure that you talk to a representative number of people with different organizational and cultural outlooks.
- formulate and reformulate problem statements, as described below.

Implicit within the idea of asking what the problem is, is to establish what people would regard as not having a problem. What would be going on if people felt completely comfortable about the situation? Sometimes this can be easy to define: for example, sales targets are being exceeded, project deadlines are being met or teams are keeping within budgets. However, it can often be difficult in the case of softer organizational problems to come up with satisfactory or measurable criteria for acceptable performance. If at all possible you should try to do this, as, in the final stage of the process, you will want to evaluate the success of the solutions you have introduced and, if you have no criteria of success defined from the outset, it will be, by definition, impossible to prove that you have achieved what you set out to do.

How Serious is the Problem?

We first encountered this question when looking at the Mager and Pipe performance flowchart in Chapter 2 (see Figure 2.7). You might recall that this provides a structured way of picking apart a performance problem using a sequence of yes or no questions, and that the very first question to ask is, 'Is the problem serious?'. If the answer to this is 'no', then you are advised to do nothing for the time being, but to keep an eye on the situation in case things get worse.

Of course, 'seriousness' is rather subjective, and we looked at some ways in which it can be quantified, in that it can cause financial, regulatory or ethical difficulties.

FINANCIAL EFFECTS

Financial difficulties are the most quantifiable of these three and, as such, are perhaps those with the least culturally determined angles. Are sales too low? Is the level of rejected parts too high? Is the market share too low? Culture, however, may have its part to play in deciding on the measure of financial seriousness. For example, Western businesses tend to measure success by reference to short time horizons: 'Are we meeting sales targets?' or 'What is the share value today?' On the other hand, Japanese businesses have tended to adopt a more strategic view of success, with long-term development of market share being a more important criterion. What is therefore serious to a Western organization might be a matter of little consequence to one whose culture is more long-term-oriented.

The 2008 'crisis of capitalism' has led many observers to comment on the apparent failings in the short-term, profit-driven motivation behind classical capitalism in its Western form, and it is possible that all businesses will, as a consequence, start to measure the seriousness of a problem using longer-term timeframes.

REGULATORY EFFECTS

Regulatory problems occur when what is happening in the workplace puts the organization into contravention of either local legislation (for example, in terms of workplace health and safety, terms and conditions of employment or even financial management) or foreign legislation that applies to the business's products (for example, through using chemicals in the manufacturing process that are banned in other countries). Any country's legislation, of course, has its roots in that society's culture and is arguably the most explicit and clearly defined manifestation of a society's values. It might be relatively easy to quantify the seriousness of a regulatory problem by asking the following questions:

- If this malfeasance came to light, what sanctions might be brought against the business?
- What fines are likely to be imposed?
- What restrictions might be imposed on our business?
- What would be the effects of bad publicity?

ETHICAL EFFECTS

Ethical difficulties can be very difficult to quantify. Customers' perceptions that a business is behaving unethically could have a negative effect on sales and share price. Internally, employees who are aware of unethical practice going on within the organization might feel disaffected, which could have a negative impact on how well they perform. Ultimately, they could choose to leave the business or even act as whistleblowers, leading to negative publicity.

Whose Problem Is It?

It is very important to give thought to who has a stake in the problem and its solution, as they will all have their part to play in the problem-solving process and in the implementation of any subsequent changes. Failing to consult with, or involve, any of these individuals or groups could make the implementation of any solution pointless.

Soft Systems Methodology suggests three groups of people who will be involved in any problem:

- *Customers* – the people who will be affected by the problem and its solution. What do they think about what is happening at the moment? What problems, if any, do they see? What would they like to be improved?
- *Actors* – the people involved in the problem area and who will be responsible for implementing any solutions. What are their perspectives on it?
- *Owners* – the people who have ultimate power over the problem area and who will give ultimate approval for making the necessary changes and providing the investment needed. What are their critical success factors?

Again, answers to these questions will all be, to some extent, culturally determined. Imagine that we are considering the problem of how to sell a specific type of food in a culture that may be hostile to it – say, France. The customers would be French consumers, the actors would be the marketing staff working for the food manufacturer – say, McDonald's – and the owners would be the burger company's senior management. The output of such an analysis could be the accommodation described in the 1994 film *Pulp Fiction*:

> *Vincent*
> *Well, in Amsterdam, you can buy beer in a movie theatre. And I don't mean in a paper cup either. They give you a glass of beer, like in a bar. In Paris, you can buy beer at MacDonald's. Also, you know what they call a Quarter Pounder with Cheese in Paris?*

> *Jules*
> *They don't call it a Quarter Pounder with Cheese?*

> *Vincent*
> *No, they got the metric system there, they wouldn't know what the **** a Quarter Pounder is.*

Jules
What'd they call it?

Vincent
Royale with Cheese.

Jules
Royale with Cheese. What'd they call a Big Mac?

Vincent
Big Mac's a Big Mac, but they call it Le Big Mac.

Tarantino 1994, *Scene 8.*

Clearly, Jules's limited perspective on the world would not have led to an effective solution. However, taking the 'Frenchness' of customers into consideration leads to a solution that recognizes the particular constraints that that imposes.

It is also important to remember that you, as the problem investigator, will not be operating in a completely neutral way. Remember the Hawthorne effect[1] – that people behave differently when they know that they are being observed. You, as a manager with your own cultural perspective, and being seen to have a particular cultural tradition, may find it difficult to formulate a truly honest picture of what is happening within a team. Your own perspectives will draw you subconsciously towards favouring certain interpretations, and hence solutions, over others. The ability to work and think in as detached a way as possible is therefore crucial.

When Does the Problem Occur?

Asking the 'when?' question can give us useful clues that will later help us find out more about the causes of the problem and how serious it might be.

Again, if we think back to the performance flowchart in Figure 2.7, we will remember that a key question to ask is: 'Did they used to be able to do it?' If someone used to be able to do something but cannot do it now, this indicates two possibilities:

---

1   The Hawthorne effect refers to conclusions drawn from studies carried out at the Hawthorne Works of the Western Electric company near Chicago in the 1920s. The original study was to see how productivity could be improved by better illumination, but the results and considerable subsequent analysis and reanalysis led to the conclusion that almost any change in the working environment can increase productivity temporarily if people know they are the subject of some experimentation.

1. they may not have enough practice in carrying out the task, so they are forgetting how to do it properly, or
2. they are doing the task often enough, but they are not receiving any feedback informing them that things are going wrong.

This analysis gives us some ideas about root causes and possible solutions.

First, think about when the problem was initially recognized. Did things suddenly start to go wrong? If so, what else happened at the same time? Perhaps there was a change in personnel, in operational practice or even some environmental change – from summer to winter or vice versa – that changed operating temperatures.

A factory manufacturing ceramic pipes was concerned that the percentage of finished pipes failing the final quality control test was increasing. When it looked back at its records, it realized that the deterioration had been slow but inexorable: over a 12-month period the reject rate had slowly climbed from an acceptable 3 per cent to the now unacceptable 10 per cent.

Several of the quality assurance managers examined the manufacturing process carefully. They looked at the quality control records for the raw materials being bought in. Machinery was inspected and kiln temperatures monitored exhaustively. Nothing seemed to have changed, and everything was operating within normal tolerances.

Attention then focused on the final inspection procedure. The official procedure was to check a random selection of pipes for length and diameter and then place them in a hydraulic press to make sure that they could withstand a specified longitudinal load. All was well.

The tubes also had to be tested for lateral strength, and the test load was 75 kg. However, to their surprise, the managers discovered that the inspector did this by standing on them. If they cracked under his weight, then he would test the entire batch and often ended up rejecting them. His managers had not known that he did this, so asked why. The inspector explained that when he had started the job, he had realized that he himself weighed 75 kg and that standing on the pipes was much quicker than putting them into the testing machine. The managers felt somewhat reassured when he told them that he had always done this throughout the five years that he had been in the job and that there had 'never been any problem'.

However, he casually mentioned that 18 months previously he had had an accident playing football which had meant that he was no longer able to play the game and, as a result, had put on a bit of weight ...

The problem was solved!

Does the problem happen all the time? If it is only an occasional problem, it might not be very serious, unless, when it does occur, it causes major difficulties. What is the pattern of its occurrence – random or regular? How long does it go on for? Is there anything changing in its environment when the problem begins or when it ends?

Starting the Problem-solving Process

Problem-solving is not something that you should do on your own, with the doors shut and the blinds down. You may have taken on individual responsibility to devise some solutions to a perceived problem, but that does not mean that you must do it all yourself. You will need other people not only to provide information about what is happening in the workplace that is, or may be, pertinent to the problem, but also to help you analyse what is happening and identify and select potential solutions.

Why? A problem is only a perception, and if you start off with just one person's definition of the problem, you will almost certainly end up with a limited range of solutions. This will happen even in culturally homogeneous settings, but when you are looking at a culturally diverse workplace, your own cultural glasses will almost inevitably bring some degree of cultural bias not only to your initial perception of the problem, but also to the analysis and identification of potential solutions.

To decide who you need in your team remember the SSM mnemonic CATWOE: **c**ustomers–**a**ctors–**t**ransformation–**W**eltanschauung–**o**wners–**e**nvironment. The three we are interested in are the customers, actors and owners.

OWNERS

First, the owners. In SSM these are defined as people who could stop the transformation that is taking place in the system. They are therefore senior management personnel who have made the decisions that have led to the initiation of the workplace activity that we are concerned about. You will need them in order to:

- establish what the desired outcomes of the workplace activity are;
- define what they would see as a successful solution to the current problem;
- identify customers that are being affected by the problem;
- identify actors who are involved in the problem;
- support your efforts to get to the root causes of the problem and to remove any obstacles that may appear;
- implement solutions that you ultimately decide are necessary.

They are therefore key players in the team, but need to be managed carefully. When questioning them on what the problem is, make sure that they concentrate on describing their dissatisfaction with *outcomes* rather than processes. As soon as they start talking about problems with the way in which things are currently being done, you will know that they already have solutions in mind. This tendency to know what a solution is before doing any detailed analysis is sometimes called 'solutioneering'. The danger with this is that owners may have their own pet solutions or hidden agendas and that they may pressurize you to identify them as a solution or even subvert your analysis activities. Alternatively, they may be worried about what you might find in case it reflects badly on them as senior managers, and so will be keen to keep your analysis as brief and as superficial as possible.

CUSTOMERS

Customers are the people who are affected by the system's transformation, which means that they may receive some of the system's outputs directly or indirectly. These outputs might be the system's intended outputs or some incidental, and perhaps even undesirable, byproducts of the transformation. What distinguishes customers from being some part of the environment is that they can provide feedback to the actors that will influence the workplace transformation. As an example, consider the department found in many organizations that is responsible for producing in-house magazines or providing 'softer' content for an intranet. Their direct customers are everyone within the organization who receives the magazine or reads the intranet materials. This will include people who work in the marketing department who are responsible for external publicity and communications. Clearly, messages distributed internally need to be completely consistent with those that are released externally, so obviously Marketing will also be indirect customers for the in-house magazine's underlying messages.

As with the owners, customers can also provide you with high-level information. They will be mainly interested in the outcomes and will probably have little interest in, or knowledge of, the processes. What a customer defines as a satisfactory outcome should be a fundamental consideration in identifying and selecting solutions. Their externality means that they are less likely to have hidden agendas or try to derail your analysis. However, you will need to avoid revealing too much about problems or inefficiencies within your organization when consulting external customers, unless the relationship between the two businesses is so strong that openness can strengthen the bond.

ACTORS

Thirdly, there are the actors – the people on the workplace stage who are directly involved in the transformation and who are, in some way involved in, or responsible for, the perceived problems. They will probably, but not necessarily, be people at a lower level in the organization and will be the group mainly responsible for providing you with the fine detail about what is happening. Getting their involvement and buy-in to eventual solutions is vital as they will also be responsible for implementing them. Failing to consult people and being seen to be 'imposing' solutions that are unacceptable for whatever reason may affect the eventual success of your solution. They may result in reduced morale or even sabotage.

FINALIZING YOUR TEAM

Now that you know the three groups of people you need to be talking to and involving in the problem-solving process, think about who they are going to be. You will probably need help from the owners in identifying them and may also need to ask the owners to give them permission to spend time helping you. The owners will also be able to arrange for you to talk to the customers and actors.

Now, start contacting these people and drawing up a schedule of meetings and other analysis activities.

Writing Your Problem Statements

Once you have identified a few people in your problem-solving team who can give you some initial help, you need to start considering what the problem actually might be. It probably currently exists as a more or less vague statement of dissatisfaction, and you need to clarify it and then explore its possibilities.

First, remember the five problem questions:

1. What is the problem?
2. Whose problem is it?
3. Where does it happen?
4. When does the problem occur?
5. How serious is the problem?

Then – enlisting your team members' help, if possible – try to write a problem statement that captures responses to each of these questions.

For example, someone came to me and said that her particular workplace concern was about internal office communications. We worked out an initial problem statement as:

'Communications within our division are often ineffective throughout the hierarchy, which is leading to strained working relationships and failure to meet objectives.'

You can see that this statement:

- describes what the problem is (ineffective communications);

- identifies whose problem it is and where it happens (throughout the division's hierarchy – in other words, everybody's problem);
- states when it happens (often);
- explains the seriousness of the problem (strained relationships and failure to meet objectives).

That is a good start, but we want to take this further. What we need to play around with it so that two things happen:

1. our imagination regarding the problem is stimulated so that we can think about it more creatively, and
2. different perspectives, particularly cultural ones, are explored.

You can do this in various ways. Jones (1998) suggests a number of methods:

- Paraphrase the initial statement, using different words to express the same meaning.
- Turn the problem on its head and state the opposite.
- Broaden the focus of the problem.
- Ask 'Why?', and write this as a problem statement.

Finally, as we are interested in problems related to differing cultural perceptions, write a problem statement that consciously addresses cultural perspectives.

A good way to come up with a number of different problem statements is to run a brainstorming session with your problem-solving team. This technique is described in more detail in Chapter 9, and it would be a good idea to read through that before trying it out here, as, in order to be effective, brainstorming needs to be done carefully, following a number of important guidelines.

PARAPHRASING THE PROBLEM STATEMENT

Looking at the original problem statement, we might consider paraphrasing into something like:

'Nobody in our division is any good at exchanging information, which means that people are irritating each other and not getting the job done.'

What different perspectives on the problem might this give us? Well:

- It is written in a more emotionally dynamic way, which might stimulate more energy for finding solutions.
- It makes us think about how 'strained working relationships' are actually manifested.

- It is a first-person rather than a third-person statement, so the writer sees themselves as being 'in there', rather than just as an observer of other people having a bad time.

TURNING THE PROBLEM ON ITS HEAD

Stating the opposite of the original problem statement often gives people involved with a problem one of those 'Ah-ha' moments, when they suddenly see something in a completely different way. For example, the person who presented me with the initial problem sat down with a colleague and came up with:

'Our division is very effective at keeping secrets in order to prevent cosy working relationships and complacency.'

Why is this so enlightening?

- 'Keeping secrets' opens up the realization that poor communications might not be an accident after all.
- Are strained working relationships such a bad thing anyway, if the alternative is complacency?

BROADENING THE FOCUS

What is the larger context of the problem? A statement expressing this might be:

'Communications within the organization are often handled poorly, leading to poor staff morale and inefficiencies'.

Rewriting the problem statement in this way:

- makes us question if what we are looking at is a local or an institutional problem, which, of course, might lead to completely different solutions.
- forces us to think about communications between departments as well as between individuals.

ASKING 'WHY?'

As we shall see later, asking 'Why is this happening?' repeatedly of a problem statement is a useful way of identifying root causes of the problem. But we can also use the technique once or twice with our original problem statement to come up with a different angle. For example, one answer to why our communications usually poor within the division might be:

'People are too busy trying to get their work done for them to take the time to pass on important operational information to other people, inadvertently making it harder for everyone to achieve.'

What have we learned from this?

- Poor communications might be a result of excessive pressure and activity.
- People do not have time to do anything properly.

EXPLORING
CULTURAL
PERSPECTIVES

The best way to get a redefinition of a problem statement from a different cultural perspective is to involve people from different cultural backgrounds in this initial discussion of the problem. The person who presented this problem initially was an American, and she was finding working with her Japanese boss particularly frustrating as she felt that she was just not being given the information she needed. Had it been possible to involve the boss in this problem restatement exercise, he might have come up with something like:

'Many people in the division need to have everything described in excessive detail, wasting time and stopping them from getting on with other important work.'

The cultural issue at work here is the conflict between high- and low-context cultures. The Japanese boss, coming from a high-context culture, probably subconsciously uses a lot of non-verbal signals to convey information, such as silences or facial gestures and subtle variations in the tone of voice. This would be fine when communicating with other Japanese people as they would recognize these other messages and would know exactly what was meant. However, our American subordinate comes from a low-context culture, where everything is much more explicit: if you want somebody to do something, you tell them exactly what they need to do. She is frustrated because she is not being told exactly what she needs to do and is having to, as she sees it, 'read between the lines'.

So rewriting the problem statement from a different cultural perspective can help us get to some initial understanding about cultural factors that might be at play.

Deciding the Next Step

You have now put together your problem-solving team and, probably with their help, have written a few different statements of the problem you are trying to solve. The next thing to do is to gather more detailed information, and this is covered in Chapter 7.

The Reliable Constructions Case Study: Step 1

The black Bakelite telephone on Barlow's desk rang. Barlow looked at it and slowly picked it up, wondering if it meant trouble again.

'Barlow? Get yourself over here quick. We've got a problem and we need you to sort it out.' Nulty in Eastern European Operations never wasted time on niceties.

Philippa Barlow was the company's problem-solver. Whenever something went wrong in the workplace, she was the person to sort it out. This was why she found herself heading out to see Reliable Construction's operations manager in its new Eastern European offices. All that she knew was that Nulty was getting increasingly worried about progress on a major construction project the company was managing. Logistics were going haywire; nothing was arriving on-site on time. And she was going to have to find out why.

'Okay, Nulty, I need a team to help me with this. Who is involved in what is going on here?'

'Well, it's the Transylvania site. Michael Antonescu is the site manager, and he's furious about the way he cannot get any of the deliveries he needs to arrive on time. You obviously need to talk to him to get his side of the story. The other key person is Stephanie Beech. She is head of the Logistics Department. They are responsible for getting the supplies into the warehouse and for arranging transport to site. She's a Brit, and she's here to make sure that the local operations run as smoothly as they do back in Britain.

'Who's the site for?' Philippa asked. 'It might be useful to get their impressions about what is happening.'

'I'd rather not at this stage,' snapped Nulty. 'I'd like them to think that we are a completely efficient outfit, and I'm not sure that we look like it at the moment.'

'Okay, I can understand that. What about staff working on-site, and those people actually responsible for the deliveries. Can you give me any access to them?' Philippa then asked.

'Sure, that's no problem. Let me know what sort of people you want to talk to and I'll arrange it.'

Philippa felt that her team was starting to take shape. The people to talk to first were Michael Antonescu on-site and Stephanie Beech down at the warehouse. She could see that they were the people who owned the problem, along with Nulty. She rang these two, and they arranged to meet the next day.

That night in her hotel, Philippa gave some thought to what the problem seemed to be. She had borrowed a flipchart pad from the one of the hotel's function rooms, and on it wrote down what seemed to be the key information:

- *What is the problem? Construction materials are being delivered late.*

- *Whose problem is it? The problem directly affects the site manager and his operations.*
- *When does the problem occur? It seems to be a constant problem, and has been since the start of the project.*
- *How serious is the problem? Potentially very serious. It threatens the profitability of this project and the likelihood of future business within the country.*

Knowing that her first flipchart sheet had been written on, Philippa turned off the light.

In next morning's meeting it was obvious that the relationship between Michael and Stephanie was strained. But Philippa knew that she was the person who could make everything alright. She showed them what she had written on her flipchart sheet and explained that she wanted to 'toss the problem around a bit and see what came out'. The first step was to write a problem statement based on her summary of what was going on. Immediately, Michael and Stephanie started arguing about a definition of the problem. Philippa smiled and let them do this for a few minutes before interrupting.

'That's great. That's just what I want us to be doing, discussing what our different perceptions of this problem are. Let's spend a bit of time trying to capture what you have just been talking about.'

The first problem statement they managed to write up was:

'Essential construction materials are regularly arriving late on-site, threatening completion of the project on time and within budget.'

'Okay', Philippa said. 'Let's first see if we can write than using some different words and see if that throws anything up.'

They had a break for coffee, and then came back and managed to agree on another statement:

'Building materials are not arriving when needed on-site, increasing costs and causing delays.'

Philippa suggested that they thought about that and whether or not it offered any new insights. Michael pointed out that there was a difference between 'arriving late' and 'not arriving when needed', and that it opened up the possibility that there might be some planning problems at his end. Stephanie smiled slightly. Philippa agreed, and said that she was also glad to have found an alternative to the emotionally-laden word 'late', which often seemed to blame somebody.

She next suggested that they tried to turn the problem on its head and see what they came up with. Both Michael and Stephanie looked rather confused at this, so Philippa suggested that they think about what the opposite of the current problem statement might be. They came up with:

'Site is asking for Logistics to deliver materials too early.'

'But I'm not sure that we are,' said Michael.

'Well, I think the way to look at this statement is to consider that "too early" might mean earlier than Logistics can respond?' Philippa suggested.

'Yes, I think there's something in that,' agreed Stephanie. 'There are sometimes things going on holding things up that we have no control over. Hey, this is a useful exercise.'

The rest of the morning moved on very quickly. Michael and Stephanie were getting the idea of redefining the problem statement, and, each time they did, it sparked off more discussions about what the problem really was and what was contributing to it. And, most importantly, the relationship between the two was distinctly warmer by the end of the day than it had been at the beginning. In fact, at the end of the meeting Michael suggested to Stephanie that the next time she visited the site he would take her to this really nice traditional restaurant that he knew. Philippa smiled to herself.

'Well, that sounds great. Look, I need to get back to my hotel room to write a few things up and make some telephone calls. I'll see you both soon. Thanks, it's been a really useful day.'

That evening, in her hotel room, Philippa reflected on how much more information she now had about what was happening on-site. Getting Michael and Stephanie together had allowed them to explore the problem from a number of different angles, and getting them involved meant that they were now both fully committed to what Philippa wanted to do. It had turned out to be a very effective way of getting her problem-solving team working together for the first time.

She rang some of the people that Nulty had suggested she talked to, and arranged to travel up to the Transylvania site the next day. Feeling excited about what lay ahead, she slid down under her duvet and thought about what the next week might bring.

Step 1: Summary

Step 1 of your problem-solving process is to:

- put together a problem-solving team, that includes people affected by the problem (customers), people who own the problem (owners) and people directly involved in the problem (actors).

- write an initial problem statement, defining what the problem is, who is involved, when it occurs and how serious it is.
- write several different definitions of the problem statement, using techniques such as paraphrasing, stating the opposite, broadening the focus, asking 'why?' and introducing cultural perspectives.

7 *Step 2: Collect Data*

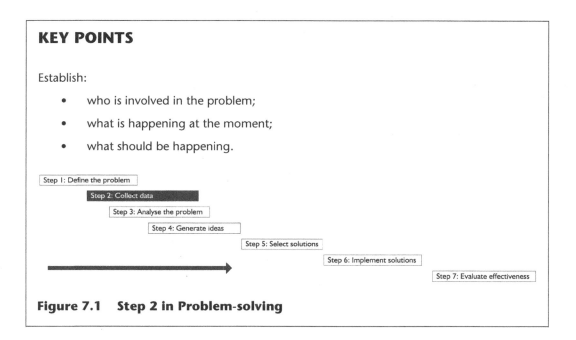

KEY POINTS

Establish:

- who is involved in the problem;
- what is happening at the moment;
- what should be happening.

Figure 7.1   Step 2 in Problem-solving

Introduction

There are a number of different ways of collecting data about a problem, each of which has strengths and advantages.

In Step 1 you will have developed a number of different problem statements, and it is likely that, in doing so, you will have started to collect useful information about what is happening. In Step 2 you concentrate on collecting more information.

What Data Do You Collect?

There are three initial questions to ask:

1. Who is involved?
2. What is happening at the moment?
3. What should be happening?

WHO IS
INVOLVED?

As the old saying goes, it takes two to tango, and, similarly, you can never have a problem with just one person or one group of people. The first question to ask therefore is: who is involved in what is going on? Who are the main protagonists? Who is affected by what they do? Who affects them?

You can get answers to this question from the problem owners or actors, and do not be surprised if different people give you different answers. Each participant in the problem will have their own perspective, so that, after talking to a few different people, you will have probably identified a number of individuals or groups that are playing some part in what is happening.

Useful questions to ask these groups or individuals are:

* Who does this job?
* Who do they report to?
* What happens after they have completed the job?
* Where do they get that information from?
* Who makes decisions about that?

By way of illustration, consider a problem presented to me by someone who had been asked to develop a training programme for guards on her country's international borders. The problem was that women passing across the border were being mistreated, and she had been asked to do something about it.

The list of people we identified as being involved in this problem was as follows:

* border guards (obviously),
* female travellers (the other obvious protagonists),
* male travellers (who would also be crossing the borders at the same time and so would, by default, be to some extent complicit in, or witnesses to, whatever happened),
* border guard supervisors (who might or might not be present at the border itself, but who would obviously be involved in whatever solution was devised),
* police (because some of what was allegedly happening at the border would be illegal),
* Ministry of the Interior (the state body employing the border guards),
* border guards of the adjoining country (because they were stationed only yards from this particular country's guards, and although we were not sure how involved they might be in the problem, ignoring them might mean that we failed to consider a potential solution).

You can therefore see that it is important at this stage to consider individuals and groups who have both direct and indirect involvement in the problem. Remember that it easier to discount people later on in the problem-solving process than to draw them in and consider their involvement later in the analysis.

As we shall see in Chapter 8, it is useful to draw a *systems map* summarizing who these people and groups are. Figure 7.2 depicts an example of a systems map for this particular problem: we shall look at how this type of diagram can be used in more detail later.

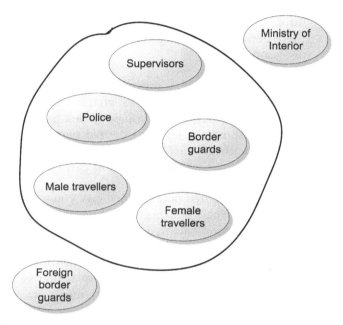

Figure 7.2 Who is involved at the border?

WHAT IS HAPPENING AT THE MOMENT?

Collect as much information as you can about what is happening at the moment. At this stage of your analysis, keep statements about this as simple as possible. For example, using the problem of the border guards, your information statements might be:

- Guards are not complying with the code of conduct they are expected to follow.
- There are no copies of the code of conduct available in the border offices.
- Supervisors are not always on duty at the border posts.
- There are no separate toilet and washroom facilities for men and women.
- There are no women available to carry out body searches of women.

Try to develop as rich a picture as possible of the existing performance. Do not worry too much at this stage about trying to make sense of all the information, as you will be doing this during

Step 3. However, as you will inevitably start to see patterns and connections in the information you collect and will be developing an understanding of what lies behind the problem, you will be tempted to do some analysis straightaway. If it feels right, do it – but make sure that you do not jump to conclusions on the basis of early, limited information.

WHAT DO YOU WANT TO BE HAPPENING?

The problem owners in particular should be able to give you information about what *should* be happening. A clear idea about these desired standards of performance is important for a number of reasons:

- When you have established what the desired performance is, you can compare this with what is happening at the moment, and double-check that you do in fact have a problem.
- Establishing the levels of desired performance and comparing them with the current performance gives you a measure of the *performance gap*. Thinking about closing a performance gap can sometimes be useful.
- Levels of desired performance give you a set of criteria that you can use when you begin to evaluate the effectiveness of the solutions implemented.

When you write down these definitions of the desired performance, try to keep them as quantitative as possible, using specific levels of performance. Statements including words such as 'better', 'improved' or 'lower' are generally fairly useless as definitions of performance.

For example, at the border it was decided that some of the desired standards of performance were:

- zero reports of women being mistreated at the border;
- border guards complying 100 per cent with the requirements of their code of conduct;
- supervisors always available in their office between the hours of 0700 and 1800.

How Do You Collect the Data?

There are various ways in which you can go about gathering information.

EXISTING INFORMATION

Information may already exist that directly or indirectly describes the problem you are investigating. Many organizations spend large amounts of time and effort reinventing their wheels, and it is possible that people before you have looked at the problem and written about it or attempted to devise solutions. So it is always a good idea to look on dusty shelves or in the bottom-most folders on shared drives and see what has been done in the past.

QUANTITATIVE
DATA

It is always very useful to collect information in numerical form – for example, how often something happens, how many mistakes are made each day, levels of customer complaints and so on. Such information is less dependent on personal opinions and comes in very useful if you try to carry out any evaluation.

Ask around to find out where such information is available. IT systems often collect a vast amount of quantitative information about what is happening.

Table 7.1   Who can provide information

Type of person	How they can help
Expert performers	They can provide information about what are the most effective and efficient ways of doing something.
Average performers	They can tell you what opportunities there are for improving what is happening, identifying the performance gap between what they and the experts do.
Low performers	They can reveal what training may be necessary, again identifying opportunities for improvement.
Managers of performers	These people can tell you what standards of performance they expect, what performers are alike and what distinguishes low, average and expert, the conditions under which people are performing and what problems they have seen in the workplace.
Customers and other people affected by the performance	These people can tell you something about the effects of poor performance.
Subject-matter experts	They can tell you a lot about how things should (in theory) be done. Note that they may not be the same as expert performers: expert performers may be able to carry out a task exceptionally well, but might not be able to do things as well if they are out of the ordinary, and they may not understand why they do, or have to do, what they carry out.

INTERVIEWS

Talking to people involved can provide a great deal of information about how they do the job and what problems they find with it. There are different types of people you can talk to, each able to give you particular types of information (Jackson, 1986).

Conducting effective interviews is a skill that needs practice. People provide more information when they feel relaxed, which happens most easily when you can conduct the interview as if it were a conversation. The best type of interview is semi-structured, where you draw up a list of questions that you want to ask before the interview, but just use these as a guide, and let the natural conversational dynamics of the interview dictate the flow and sequence of topics you explore. Keep referring back to your initial list to make sure that you cover everything and to act as a prompt if you reach the end of a line of inquiry and are not sure what to do next. One way to do this is to write the questions on a Post-it® note and stick this to one edge of your notepad. This is easy to refer to and avoids the problem of having to find a separate page of notes and hence disrupt the flow of conversation.

The repertory grid

The repertory grid is a useful technique you might also consider using during an interview. It is particularly useful for gathering information about complex tasks, where considerable analysis or judgement is necessary.

You, as the analyst, work with someone who knows people involved in carrying out the task well, such as a line manager. This person identifies three people from the group who perform well, three whose performance is average and three whose performance is below average. You then write their names on separate cards and place them in a 3 × 3 grid in front of you.

Choose three cards at random, and ask the manager to select two of the people whose performance is similar. Then ask what is different about the performance of the third person. Make a note of this, then choose another three cards and repeat this questioning.

Repeat this until you cannot find any new information. This technique makes it easier to identify subtle differences in behaviour that are affecting a performance.

Critical incidents

During the interview you may find it useful to ask people how they or others have responded to critical incidents. These are events that have had a significant impact on the workplace. They might be something positive, such as having to meet a new order or deal with a new major customer, or something negative, such as an accident or a downturn in business. Whatever the nature of the incident, the disruption that it causes will provide a lot of useful information about the performances that it affects.

| Problems with interviews | One danger with relying on interview information is bias on the part of either you, as the interviewer, or the interviewee. For example: |

- What you already know about the situation may cause you to take a particular interest in one area and neglect others.
- Interviewees may be reluctant to say something that they feel will show them in a bad light.
- Interviewees may have some kind of hidden agenda or see the interview as an opportunity to settle an old score with someone else, and so give you inaccurate information.

To minimize the effects of bias you should triangulate your questions. You can do this by asking the same people different questions about the same subject or asking different people the same questions about a subject. Comparing answers will identify areas of agreement and inconsistencies.

A significant disadvantage of interviews is the amount of time that they take up: a typical interview might last anywhere between 30 minutes and two hours, but you must also take into consideration travelling and setting-up time. For that reason you might want to consider talking to people in small groups. This does have some advantages:

- You can potentially obtain more – and more rounded – information in the same amount of time.
- The dynamics of the group might lead to the disclosure of more interesting information and the owners or actors involved in the interview might spend some time clarifying their own understanding of what is happening.

However, these advantages must be balanced against the potential disadvantage of people being reluctant to be completely open and honest in the presence of other people, particularly if there are hierarchies involved.

| QUESTIONNAIRES | Questionnaires are useful for collecting information from large numbers of people. With careful design, you may be able to collect information that is easy to analyse statistically, and anonymous questionnaires make it possible for people to be quite honest about how they see a situation. |

However, it is difficult to design a questionnaire that probes deeply into the subtleties of a performance problem. Trying to design questions that do this but which are completely unambiguous is very difficult and can also make the questionnaire time-consuming for someone to complete. Any perception that a questionnaire is complicated is going to deter large numbers of people from filling it in: social science researchers are happy if they get more than a 10 per cent return on postal questionnaires. Even with on-line availability and submission, returns are likely to be low. If you want your information to be statistically significant, you must make sure that you design and test the questionnaire very carefully before distributing it: it is incredibly easy to hand out questionnaires that you think are completely clear and unambiguous, and find that your respondents have misinterpreted vital questions.

PARTICIPATING

If the situation allows it, trying to do the performance yourself can yield information about what is easy or difficult. It can also give you the opportunity to take note of, and reflect on, other factors that might be influencing performance that people familiar with the job might have become so used to that they no longer notice them – for example, noise, poor lighting or some other distraction.

OBSERVING

It can also be useful to watch people carrying out the performance. You must, however, remember that people tend to behave differently when being watched. This phenomenon is often referred to as the Hawthorne effect, after the famous studies carried out in the Hawthorne works of the Western Electric Company in the 1920s and 1930s. The original intention of these studies was to see how performance could be improved by changing workplace variables such as lighting or rest periods, but when it was found that more or less any change improved performance, the researchers started to realize that it was the very act of observation and being regarded as a 'special group' that made the workers in the study perform better.

Interestingly, Gilbert reports that subsequent reanalysis of the original Hawthorne methodology showed that one factor not taken into consideration as potentially performance-enhancing was that the participants were given ongoing feedback about how well they were performing and that their payment system was also modified to reflect improved performance. Gilbert contends that if these variables had been taken into consideration, the Hawthorne effect would not have been identified as such, and, in his inimitable style, suggests that '… perhaps the course of industrial relations would have been different; over the years we would have worried less about such complexities as social identity and morale, and worried more about such simplicities as telling employees how well they are doing and paying them accordingly' (Gilbert, 2007, p. 184).

The Reliable Constructions Case Study: Step 2

The next morning Philippa spent some time making a list of the things that she wanted to find out and who she thought she needed to speak to. She obviously needed to spend some more time talking to Michael and Stephanie, the managers in the two principal departments involved. They would be able to tell her more about their perspectives on what was happening and could suggest the names of other people that she should talk to. As problem owners, they would also be able to help her with some definitions about what they wanted to happen, which would help her when she came to carry out an evaluation.

So she started by having a brief chat with the two of them over the telephone, and asked each one for suggestions about who she should talk to. She said she wanted to talk both to people they thought were very good and others that seemed to be struggling, as she recognized that comparing the different perspectives of these groups of people could be very illuminating. She thought that she could get most of the information she needed by interviews. The small number of people involved made it pointless to spend time and effort developing questionnaires, but she also thought that it would be useful to spend a little time just watching what happened on each site, if only to get a better understanding of the working conditions in each place.

Before leaving for the Transylvania site she made a few more telephone calls and set up some interview dates. Her experience told her that this would not be the only period when she would be gathering information. It would obviously take her a long way forward, but she knew that once she started analysing the information she had gathered, she would probably want to talk to other people, or perhaps go back to some of the first group in order to clarify points of detail. It would also be useful to explore people's reactions to her first ideas about solutions that could be implemented.

Early that afternoon she set off.

Step 2: Summary

We have looked at the type of information that you will need in order to solve your problem and also considered what different ways there are to obtain it. Bearing this in mind, here is a summary of what you need to do to gather information:

- Decide what information you need to collect.
- Work out the best ways of getting this information.
- Find out what information currently exists.
- Draw up a list of people you need to talk to.
- Plan the design and distribution of any data collection instruments you think you will need.
- Decide if there are any other activities, such as participation or observation, which would help you.

8 Step 3: Analyse the Problem

KEY POINTS

- Develop a better understanding of what is happening in a problem by using a selection of appropriate diagrams.

- Identify the root causes of the problem.

```
Step 1: Define the problem
      Step 2: Collect data
          Step 3: Analyse the problem
              Step 4: Generate ideas
                      Step 5: Select solutions
                              Step 6: Implement solutions
                                      Step 7: Evaluate effectiveness
```

Figure 8.1   Step 3 in problem-solving

Making Sense of the Data

After carrying out your research you will probably find that you have a mass of data with little structure or order. You will know that certain themes are recurring and will have some initial ideas about what the main problems are, but will want to find some way of sorting the data into a useful structure. There are a number of simple graphical tools that you can use to help you do this:

- *rich pictures* – described earlier in Chapter 4, used in Soft Systems Methodology (SSM).
- *systems maps* – where you capture the actors in the problem and group them according to their relationships.
- *influence diagrams* – a development of system diagrams, where you show which actors influence other actors.
- *multiple cause diagrams* – a powerful tool for exploring different causes to the problem you are interested in.

- *causal flow diagrams* – described earlier in Chapter 4, where you can explore relationships and feedback mechanisms.
- *process flowcharts* – simple diagrams that can show decision mechanisms within a process.
- *process flow diagrams* – which capture the flow of a process through a number of different actors.

Each of these types of diagram has its own particular value, and you can use whichever of them seems most appropriate to your particular problem. Typically:

- Process flowcharts and flow diagrams can help you to develop detail.
- Rich pictures, systems maps and influence diagrams can help establish the actors involved.
- Multiple cause and causal flow diagrams can help you explore underlying issues.

Your aim in this stage is to have developed a clear understanding of the problem and its root causes, and so you should select and use whichever of these tools will help you to do this.

Utilize cultural diversity, and involve people with different perspectives to yourself. The techniques described in this chapter are designed to stimulate thinking about a problem, and the quality of your analysis will be improved considerably if you can work with people who can think in alternative ways.

Whichever of the problem-solving tools described below that you use, you will find it important to think back to the cultural indicators described in Chapter 2, as these will give you different hooks for picking the situation apart. For example, to use just two indicators, you can think about how people with a different approach to authority (the power distance indicator) or managing time (long-term orientation), might view what is happening.

Rich Pictures

Drawing a rich picture is an essential part of conceptualizing a problem if you are following an SSM approach. However, they can also be extremely useful even if you are following a less rigorous approach. In a rich picture you use a cartoon approach to capture as much information as you can about what is happening in the situation you are examining – for example, who and what is involved, what their relationships are, what difficulties are being experienced and so on.

Do not think that you have to be an artist in order to create a rich picture: stick people are perfectly acceptable representations of individual actors! And also do not think that you need to use software to create 'professional-looking' rich pictures: they are just tools to help your thinking and are not really intended to form a part of any analysis report. A good idea is to draw them out on a large sheet of paper such as a flipchart sheet, so that, as you develop it, you can sit back, look at what it is starting to show and reflect on it. Doing it this way also makes it easier to involve other people, as asking for help and contributions in drawing a rich picture makes it more likely that you will capture different perspectives and interpretations about what is happening.

Figure 8.2 is a rich picture drawn to capture some of the issues that arose in discussions about the problem described in Chapter 7 – that of guards mistreating women passing through an international border. As you can see, the level of artistic ability needed is not high! However, it does help to illustrate what is going on. We represented a border guard by a stick figure wearing a cap. They are confronting a female traveller, and the conflict between them is indicated by the familiar crossed swords symbol. It was also reported that the guards were robbing women from time to time, so we represented this by showing a bucket with a dollar symbol on it, with an arrow to show that something was going into the bucket. There is a supervisor in an office building, and to indicate that they did not seem to be

Figure 8.2   Rich picture showing border guard situation

taking any action against what was going on we drew them wearing a blindfold. The telephone connection to the capital city is shown as broken, indicating that communications were unreliable.

Drawing this picture together with the person who came to me with the problem proved to be a very useful way for both of us to improve our understanding of the situation and to stimulate us to ask questions that we might not otherwise have thought about. The visual representation summarizing what we knew about the situation was so much more useful than pages of handwritten notes, because it made it much easier to see connections and relationships (or the lack of them).

Rich pictures are a visual and highly creative way of representing your thinking about a situation, and, as such, there are no particular 'rules' about what is right or wrong in drawing them. However, there are some useful guidelines:

- Try to represent elements (unchanging aspects such as the people, departments or organizations) as simple drawings, rather than as words.
- Keep the amount of writing on the rich picture to the minimum necessary to explain basic meanings.
- Use colours to distinguish between things and to make it more visually appealing (which also helps to make it more stimulating and useful as a thinking aid).
- Draw your elements first and then use lines and arrows to show relationships between them and processes going on.
- Add simple symbols to convey information about activity within the rich picture. For example, crossed swords are often used to show conflict and a '?' to show doubt or uncertainty.
- Record both factual and subjective information.

Drawing a rich picture will help you to check your assumptions about a situation. You may, for example, find yourself pondering the relationship between two elements and realize that you do not understand its nature as well as you originally thought. Making a mark on a piece of paper can help you appreciate your understanding of the subject, and, when you discuss the picture with someone else, can provide a starting-point for further discussion.

Most importantly of all, show your rich picture to other people and ask them to comment and ask questions. Working on a rich picture jointly is a powerful way of developing a shared understanding of a situation.

Here are some things to consider when reviewing your rich picture:

- Use your rich picture to provoke a debate about what is important or less important. Other people will ask you, or you can ask yourself, why you have drawn something in a particular way or in a specific position on the paper, for example.

- Do not worry about showing something incorrectly in a rich picture, as, in many respects, its faults will be its strengths and will encourage discussion.
- Think carefully about where you position elements on the paper. In an English-speaking culture the top-left corner is the most powerful, as this is where people instinctively look first, so elements in that position will be assumed to be the most significant. People whose first language is different may question this positioning, and, if so, use this to review assumptions you are making.
- Think about things which you have not included in the rich picture. Other people may ask you why you have not represented particular elements or connections: this may be because you have forgotten them or did not consider them to be significant, which might be an incorrect assumption. This in turn might be influenced by your own cultural perspective: involving other cultural perspectives can help increase the richness of the picture.
- Consider the size of the elements in the rich picture. Have you deliberately drawn something big or small, or have you subconsciously inflated or reduced the apparent importance of something?

Systems Maps

You can use a systems map to show who is involved in a particular situation and what their relationships are at a specific moment in time. It is very useful when you are trying to decide which different actors are involved in a particular situation, what their relationships are and what their relative significance is.

A systems map, as in Figure 8.3, has three elements:

1. a *system* – elements that interact and have a direct involvement in the performance you are interested in.
2. an *environment* – elements that are not directly involved in the performance but, because of their existence, affect it in some way.
3. a *boundary* – a line that divides the elements of the system from its environment.

To draw a systems map, start with a large sheet of paper – a minimum of A3. You may also find it useful to write the names of the actors on Post-it® notes rather than directly on to your sheet of paper, as this allows you to move them around and explore different groupings and relationships.

If you are using the Post-it® approach:

- Write the names of each individual actor (whether they be individual people, sections or departments, for example) on Post-its®.
- Stick the Post-its® on your sheet of paper, grouping together those that have a closer relationship.
- Decide which of the actors have a central role to play within the situation you are analysing and draw a line around these (your system boundary). Actors that are outside the system boundary are in the system's environment, and these will be people or groups who have some sort of influence over what is happening within the system.

Note that you might find that you have more than one system, in which case one system would be in the environment of another system. This is perfectly acceptable.

Now reflect on what you have drawn, and ask yourself questions such as:

- Does the system boundary enclose everyone who is directly involved in the workplace performance? If not, why not?
- Does the system boundary enclose anyone who is not directly involved? If so, why are they there? Should they be moved outside the system boundary?
- Is there anyone outside the system boundary who should be inside?

You might find it useful to draw different sized actors, to indicate their relative importance within the system. If you do this think about why you consider some people to be more important than others.

Figure 8.3 opposite shows a systems map for the border guard problem.

As you build up this picture, think about each group's cultural profile. How would you assess each individual or group (whichever is appropriate) in terms of the cultural dimensions discussed in Chapter 1, such as individualist or collectivist, preference for power distance and uncertainty avoidance, and so on?

In this particular case we evaluate the border guards as:

- being collectively oriented, and strongly loyal to their own ethnic group but potentially hostile to people from other groups;
- having a preference for high power distance, with a strong respect for authority and hierarchies;

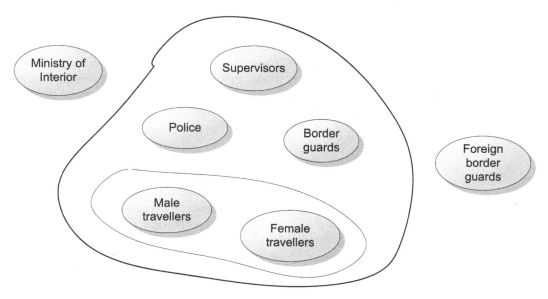

Figure 8.3 The border guard problem system map

- being ascriptive in nature, seeing status as a result of their specific ethnic group affiliation and position within its hierarchy;
- having a strong uncertainty avoidance character, preferring instructions to be clear and unambiguous.

How can we use this diagram to help us understand the problem a little more? Ask yourself the following questions:

- Have we identified everyone who seems to have a part to play in the problem? If not, why are they not there? Why did we leave them out?
- Why have we included the people that we have? Should we have included the foreign border guards? What real impact do they have on what is happening? We know that they may have some influence on the border guards in our country, so we are putting them outside the main system, identifying them as part of the environment.
- We have identified another system as the male travellers and female travellers, with the police, supervisors and border guards as part of their environment. Why have we done this? Does it help?
- The Ministry of the Interior has little direct influence on what happens at the border, so it is in the environment. But should it be in the main system? That would mean that it has a much more direct involvement in what goes on. Is that a good idea? Would it be feasible? What would the implications be?

- Depending on your analysis of the cultural profile of each group you may question whether describing each one as a single identity is valid. If, for example, border guards were made up from different ethnic groups that had different cultural values it might be instructive to draw these groups as separate items. This would encourage you to consider whether or not different ethnic groups discriminated in some way against each other.

You now see that you can identify all sorts of possible questions to ask as a result of drawing this systems map. Drawing such a diagram, adding, deleting and moving actors around is a good physical activity that will discipline your thinking and help you reflect more carefully about everyone involved. The most important part of drawing such a diagram is this modification and reflection process, rather than ending up with a definitive statement about actors and their relationships. For example, you might draw a systems map to show what is actually happening in the workplace at this moment in time, then draw a second map representing what you think should be happening, and then compare the differences.

Do this activity with other people. Different cultural perspectives can give you valuable insights into what actors are involved and where they should be.

Influence Diagrams

Influence diagrams, such as shown in Figure 8.4, are useful for exploring how the actors within a situation have influence over, or affect, each other at a specific moment in time. They can look similar to systems maps, and, indeed, you can move on from a systems map to draw an influence diagram. However, it is important to remember that an influence diagram can include *concepts* as well as physical entities.

To draw an influence diagram you might want to use the Post-it® approach, as described for drawing a systems map. If this is your choice, do it this way:

- Write the names of actors involved and relevant concepts on individual Post-its®.
- Stick the Post-its® on your sheet of paper, so that ones that you think influence each other are close together, although if there is an influential relationship between two entities that are remote from each other in some way (perhaps hierarchically or geographically), you might want to position them further apart to act as an aid to your reflection.

- Draw lines showing how the influences work. To do this draw:
  - lines with arrows to show the direction of influence (only one arrowhead per line: if influence goes in two directions draw two lines, allowing you to show that the influence in the two directions might be different);
  - different thicknesses of lines to show different levels of influence;
  - lines with different colours to show different types of influence (if this is helpful).
- Label each line with explanatory text, if this helps to make things clearer.

Influence diagrams are meant to help you think more clearly, so resist the temptation to add every single influencing connection that you can identify. Only add those that are relevant to the situation you are examining and that help clarify your thinking.

Once you have drawn your influence diagram, look at it carefully to see what it might be able to tell you:

- What are the strongest influences operating? Why is this the case? Is it appropriate or helpful that these are strong influences?
- What are the weaker influences? Is it appropriate or helpful that they are all weak?
- Are there any influences that should be present but seem to be missing? If so, why is this the case?
- Are there any strong chains of influence? Do these chains have any weak links?

Note that you should not use an influence diagram to show a sequence of activities or a flow of information or materials, although the use of arrows sometimes makes this tempting. If you want to show something like this, construct a process flow diagram instead.

Figure 8.4 shows an influence diagram for the border guard problem.

How you draw an influence diagram will be strongly affected by cultural patterns that you have identified from your analysis of the actors. So, for example:

- How will feelings about ascription in that culture affect perceived status patterns and hence influence?
- How strongly do people feel about power distance? It is high in this culture, but are the supervisors exercising the authority that they have in an appropriate way?
- How does the collectivist nature of the actors affect the dynamics between in-groups and out-groups?

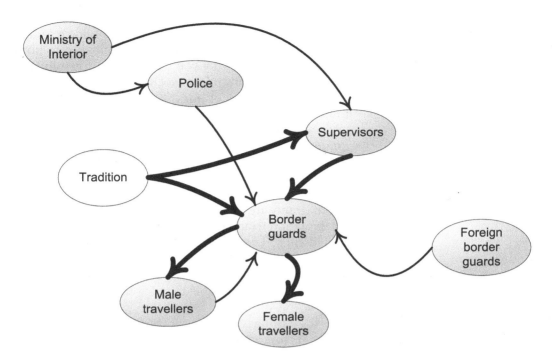

Figure 8.4   The border guard problem influence diagram

Note the similarity in Figure 8.4 above to the systems map described earlier. In fact, drawing a systems map is a good way to stimulate thinking about influences. So what does looking at this particular influence diagram make us think about?

- We have drawn the border guards in the centre. Is this justified? As they are the group whose behaviour we want to change? It might be, but let us be careful not to focus on them at the expense of other groups.
- There are two main influences acting on the guards – their supervisors and tradition. Supervisors were in the original systems map, and we have indicated that the influence is strong, but is it? Why have we drawn a thick line? Perhaps the problem lies in the fact that the influence is not strong enough.
- Tradition is a concept, and so did not figure in the systems map, but you can include concepts and ideas in an influence diagram because they do have an important part to play. It is an unfortunate feature of this particular society that women are not treated as well as they should be, so it is important to acknowledge that in an influence diagram.
- The police are shown as having a weak influence on the border guards. How true is this? Should their influence be stronger? If so, how could that happen? Why have we not shown any

connection between the police and the supervisors? Is that a valid assumption? If it is, why? Surely if there are criminal offences being committed, the police should be trying to influence the supervisors?

- Should we, then, consider the influence of tradition on the police. We should probably add a thick line connecting these two.

And so on. Again, as with systems maps and rich pictures, notice how the simple act of drawing a diagram has sparked off numerous questions, challenging our assumptions and opening up our thinking.

Multiple Cause Diagrams

You can use multiple cause diagrams to explore the different reasons *why* something is happening: they are therefore extremely useful tools for trying to uncover the root causes of a problem. Creating a multiple cause diagram will help you untangle your thinking about a particular situation and will provide you with a valuable tool that you can use to communicate this thinking to other people. Only use multiple cause diagrams to show cause-and-effect relationships, not sequences of actions or influences. If you want to show a sequence of actions, use a process flow diagram and an influence diagram to show influences.

Figure 8.5 shows a multiple cause diagram generated during the investigation of the border guard problem.

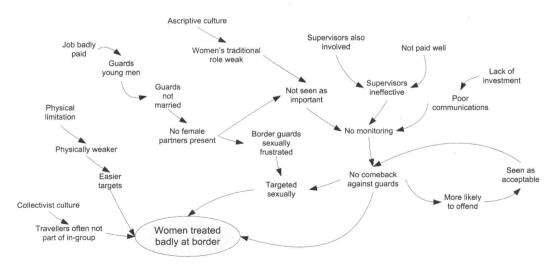

Figure 8.5   **Multiple cause diagram showing factors involved in border guard behaviour**

As with the previous diagrams, start with a large sheet of paper (minimum A3). In the middle of the sheet write one of your problem definitions. Choose whichever seems most useful, but remember that you can repeat this activity for each different problem definition in order to see what root causes emerge in each case.

When you have done this:

- Write down a statement of one factor that immediately comes to mind as being a direct cause of the problem (as with the other diagrams, you might want to do this on Post-it® notes). To do this, ask yourself: 'Why is this happening?'
- Repeat this for other direct causal factors that come to mind.
- When you have run out of these initial ideas, explore each of these separate causal factors individually. Again, ask yourself: 'Why is this happening?'
- Repeat this questioning process over and over again for each individual causal factor that you identify.
- Look out for causal factors that may have an effect on other chains of causality that you have identified. If you find any, mark them as additional causal links.

As you start work on the diagram, you may find yourself defining the causes as *states* (for example, 'No comeback against guards' or 'Easier targets'). However, as you develop the diagram and come to understand the situation better, you will find it more useful to express causality in the form of *variables* instead (for example, 'Level of sanctions applied against guards' or 'Ease of targeting'). Doing this makes it easier to think about what might happen if you explore this situation in a causal flow diagram. We have done this below for the loop containing 'No comeback against guards', 'More likely to offend' and 'Seen as acceptable' (see Figure 8.6).

Be careful when you analyse a state or level that requires two or more independent events in order for it to occur. A simple multiple cause diagram would suggest that any single cause feeding into an event can bring it about, so, if a combination of causes is needed, you should indicate this on your diagram.

If you find it difficult to think about different causal factors, remember the three elements of Gilbert's Behaviour Engineering Model (discussed in detail in Chapter 2): information, equipment and desire. Think about causal factors related to the provision or comprehension of information, the suitability and capacity to use equipment or tools and the appropriateness of incentives provided, taking into consideration the motivation of the workforce.

Make sure that you break down the chain of causality appropriately. Making a leap from one cause to a subsequent effect may lead you to overlook an intermediate cause that could have other implications. So, when you identify what you think is a causal factor, think about whether there is a direct link between the two items or if there is an intermediate factor. If there is indeed an intermediate factor, explore its causes, since overlooking intermediate factors could mean that you miss out on important root causes.

When you write down a causal factor, also consider what other effects it might have. These may create feedback loops, which are particularly important because they can result in vicious circles. If you do find any, you might want to take these specific causality chains and explore them further in a causal flow diagram. For example, one of the causal factors identified in Figure 8.5 is that no comeback or sanction being taken against guards is a contributory factor to women being treated badly. But, on reflection, we can also see that the lack of punishment means that they are more likely to do the same thing again. The more this happens, the more acceptable it becomes, and this makes it even less likely that sanctions will be imposed.

Look out for links between separate chains of causality. These can also lead to feedback loops that need further consideration.

Keep the level of detail appropriate to your area of concern. You can take a multiple cause diagrams back to the birth of the universe if you wish, but this (in most cases) is really going just a bit too far!

You can also use the multiple cause diagramming technique to explore consequences of a particular action. To do this, instead of asking 'why?' questions, ask, 'What will happen next if this happens?' It can be particularly useful to do this after analysing root causes, as you can make a change to one of these courses and explore what the consequences might be.

As with all of these diagrams, a multiple cause diagram is more of a tool to help discipline your thinking processes rather than something that will provide a definitive statement of the exact situation. You will probably find that, once you get into the rhythm of a multiple cause diagram, you will start to think about possible causes that your data-gathering has not in fact thrown up. This might be because you have not asked the right questions, because it is something that people do not want to talk about, or because you might be wrong! Your own cultural perspective will also affect your perception of what is happening, and your description of the situation may be laden with cultural values that you are not aware of. It is therefore again a good idea to share the diagram with other people, particularly those with different cultural glasses, so that they can add or amend faulty connections.

Causal Flow Diagrams

Causal flow diagrams have been described in more detail in Chapter 4, where we looked at the general ideas underlying systems thinking.

The basic principle underlying the use of systems thinking to analyse what is happening in the workplace is to consider organizational activity as if it were a system, with the transformation of an input to an output being regulated in some way by a feedback mechanism.

In practice, causal flow diagrams are often developed after a multiple cause diagram approach has been used to explore the root causes to a specific problem. In some circumstances, you might even want to take the analysis from a causal flow diagram and use it to develop some sort of quantitative model, perhaps even within a computer simulation.

Figure 8.6 is an example of where something that came to light when drawing a multiple cause diagram has been taken forward and considered within a causal flow diagram. To do this we have taken the original wordings and rewritten them in a format which suggests levels, rather than states – for example, 'Seen as acceptable' becomes 'Acceptability of behaviour'.

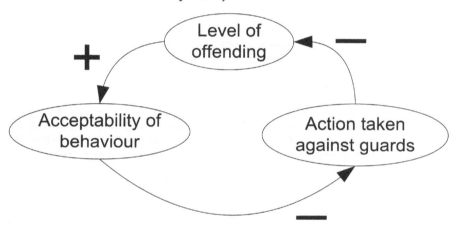

Figure 8.6   Causal flow diagram showing unstable feedback loop

Analysing the loop, as the level of offending increases, it will become more normal, and so the level of acceptability will increase (shown by a direct relationship '+'). As the level of acceptability rises, the likelihood that any action will be taken against guards decreases (an inverse relationship). As this likelihood goes down, the level of offending is likely to rise (another inverse relationship). Our causal flow diagram therefore contains two inverse relationships, revealing it to be an unstable feedback loop, and what is happening will continue to happen and perhaps get worse unless we intervene at some point. Probably the easiest way to tackle this feedback loop would be to enforce action against guards who offend. If enforcement increases, the level of offending goes down, and the acceptability also decreases. This makes taking stronger action against the guards more acceptable and likely, so that we have turned the negative, vicious circle into one that improves the situation.

Process Flowcharts

You can use simple flowcharts to capture information about decision-making processes in the workplace and to indicate consequential actions. This is sometimes described as creating an *algorithm*.

Flowcharts usually boil decision-making down to binary choices, such as 'yes' or 'no'. Real life will probably be more complicated than this, but you can use a flowchart as a comparison with reality to help develop your understanding of what is (or is not) happening in the workplace.

There are sets of standard symbols designed to be used in flowcharts, all with specific meanings, but it is not necessary or even desirable to use them when you are drawing a flowchart to help you understand a process. Keep it simple, as this will make it easier for you to draw it and then share it with other people.

At each point in the flowchart where there is a decision to be made, think carefully about the nature of that decision. Each of these points raises a number of issues that you need to consider:

- How easy is it to make?
- What information is needed at that stage in order to be able to decide between several courses of action?
- Is that information available?
- What experience or expertise is needed in order to be able to make a decision?
- What are the implications of making the wrong decision or of delaying making any sort of decision? and so on.

Analysing a process in this way, with the help of both expert and below-average performers, will help you develop a rich understanding of the complexities of what is or is not happening.

Process Flow Diagrams

You can draw a process flow diagram to show the sequence of events or movement of materials followed during a particular procedure. A finalized process flow diagram will be a rather more precise display of information than tools such as rich pictures or multiple cause diagrams, which are essentially aids to thinking. It should show precisely what is, or should be, happening in a given situation, and when you have completed it, you can use it in various ways – for example, to:

- compare reality with theory;
- identify specific stages in a process or activities in a department that you want to examine more closely.

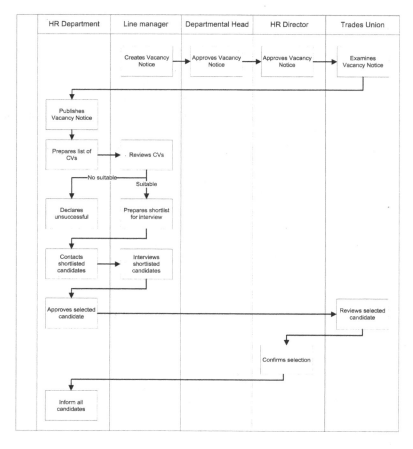

Figure 8.7   Process flow diagram showing selection procedure

Figure 8.7 above shows an example of a process flow diagram developed to show how a vacancy is filled within an organization. It shows each stage of the selection process as it moves backwards and forwards from one individual or department to another and at what stage each has responsibility.

The Reliable Constructions Case Study: Step 3

Philippa spent much of the next week talking to different people at the two sites. Her notebook slowly filled up with masses of information gleaned from interviews with managers and operators and from her observations of what was happening in each place. During this process, her mood alternated between confusion and some desperation at her inability to understand and remember all the different factors and excitement when she occasionally had some wonderful insight.

Figure 8.8   Late delivery to site: rich picture

After a couple of days she decided that she needed to try to develop some visual representations of the situation as she saw it. She found some A3 paper and sketched out a rich picture (Figure 8.8).

She first thought about what she had discovered at the warehouse. As materials and equipment were unloaded at the port they were delivered to the warehouse, where they stayed until the site ordered them up. Reliable Constructions had a contract in place with a local haulage contractor who would transport the equipment and materials up to the Transylvania site. That seemed to be one problem, in that it was difficult to find contractors to do this work. Some of the equipment needed specialist haulage vehicles, and there was something of a shortage of these. This had made it difficult to set up what the expatriate Logistics Manager, Stephanie, felt was a competitive contract. She had wanted the haulage contract to be decided on the basis of three independent companies tendering for the work, and then awarding it to the company that offered the best-value deal. However, they had only been able to find two companies prepared or able to tender for the work. Then, awarding it had caused a lot of friction in the warehouse, because one of the local supervisors felt strongly that it should be awarded to someone that he knew. Their bid was not, however, the best, and the contract had been given to another company. This supervisor had explained the situation to Philippa most emotionally: he could not understand why the logistics manager had awarded the contract to someone that he regarded as being completely unreliable. He said that he thought Stephanie was often indecisive and always wanted to ask people what they thought before making any decisions. But that hadn't stopped her from giving the contract to the wrong person, he said.

To capture this situation, Philippa had drawn the warehouse and shown the problems with the tendering process using a few boxes, and had then drawn crossed swords to show the conflict that had existed between the local and expatriate staff. It seemed significant because, by making this particular decision, the expatriate logistics manager had lost a lot of respect, even though she was completely convinced that she had done the right thing.

Philippa then thought about the haulage process. The logistics manager had said that she was disappointed with the performance of the haulage company selected, because they did not really seem to have enough vehicles in operation at any one time. Philippa had then explored this further with the managing director of the hauliers, and he explained that they had maintenance problems with the vehicles. Reliable Constructions were expecting them to make too many trips up and down the country, resulting in the lorries not being maintained properly. Back at the warehouse, the local supervisor who had never wanted this company to be given the contract in the first place said that this was because the hauliers were a 'get rich quick' outfit and paid their maintenance staff very little, so they never had enough adequately trained people to keep vehicles on the road. To make sure she remembered this problem, Philippa drew a picture of an upturned lorry with an exclamation mark.

She then looked at the situation at the construction site. She had to admit that she had not been terribly impressed with some of the people working in the site office. In her opinion, some of the people responsible for planning did not seem to have sufficient grip on the realities of the situation, and she did not think that they had been properly trained. She noted this by drawing someone with their head in the clouds. It also looked as if the planners generally had an excessively short-term attitude towards getting things on-site. Again, the site manager was not a local person and, from what several other people on-site had said, did not really understand how this country worked and that you really needed to allow more time for things to happen. This was exacerbated by the fact that priorities on-site often changed at the last minute, which, given the slow deliveries, sometimes caused serious problems.

It also looked as if communications between the site and the warehouse were poor. One of the site planners also said something that interested Philippa. Apparently, they felt that Logistics were so inefficient that they sometimes ordered things way ahead of when they were needed in order to give them what they thought would be adequate time to get things delivered. Philippa recorded this problem with time by drawing a calendar and a clock joined by a 'versus' sign to help her remember that there seemed to be some compromising taking place.

Philippa then thought that it might be useful to draw a simple systems map, even though only a limited number of people were involved in what was happening (Figure 8.9).

Once she had drawn the systems map, she thought about some of the cross-cultural issues in play.

Local people were multi-active and short-termist in nature, which meant that they were less interested in the longer-term project planning needed. They were particularist, thinking that rules should be adapted to the circumstances. They had a strong belief in power distance and a high uncertainty avoidance. Michael, although not a local person, was similar to this.

Stephanie was British, and so was linear-active, doing one thing at a time, and universalist, insisting on consistent application of rules and processes. She had a low preference for power distance, feeling more comfortable when involving other people in decision-making.

After she had drawn it, she reflected on the fact that there seemed to be two separate subsystems, Logistics and Site. This seemed to tie it in with her feeling that communication between the two was sometimes ineffectual. And there was the poor haulage contractor, left out on its own in the system environment.

It also suddenly became more apparent to her that there were expatriates managing both departments involved, and that they both inevitably had a limited understanding of the way in which the local culture worked. That prompted her to draw an influence diagram (Figure 8.10).

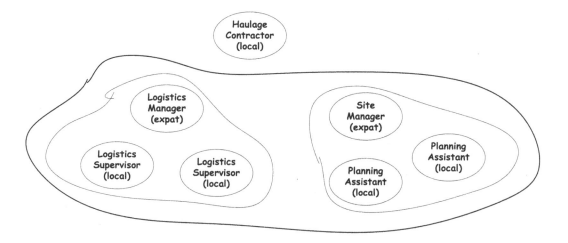

Figure 8.9   Systems map of the Reliable Constructions problem

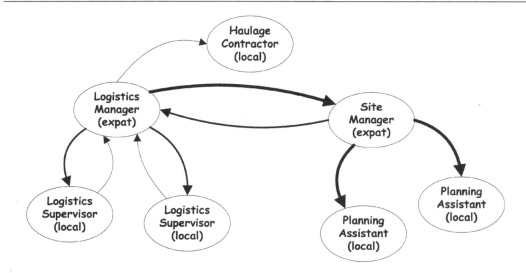

Figure 8.10 Influence diagram of the Reliable Constructions problem

The first influences she drew in were those between the logistics manager and site manager. She felt that this relationship did not work equally in both directions, in that the logistics manager seemed to have more power, and that led her to wonder about possible tensions and resentment that Michael, the site manager might be experiencing. Philippa also drew a line showing the limited influence that Stephanie seemed to have over the haulage contractor. Certainly, the limited number of haulage contractors that were able to carry out the work put the contractor into a stronger position than they would have otherwise. She also thought about the different management styles that Stephanie and Michael showed. Stephanie was more 'British' in her approach and favoured a more consultative management style, delegating responsibility to her logistics supervisors where she could, and this meant that they had a certain amount of influence over her. On the other hand, Michael, coming from a culture which valued power distance had a more autocratic management style. His two planning assistants therefore had negligible influence over him. However, that was something that they seemed to be comfortable with, and Philippa wondered whether the logistics supervisors were altogether happy with the responsibilities that they had been given. They were also multi-active in nature and placed less importance on planning and control than Stephanie's Britishness felt was appropriate.

Before moving on, she noticed that she had not drawn any lines connecting the logistics supervisors and planning assistants. Thinking about why that was the case, she realized that there seemed to be very little communication between the employees at this level, and that everything seemed to be routed through the two managers. That was something to think about later.

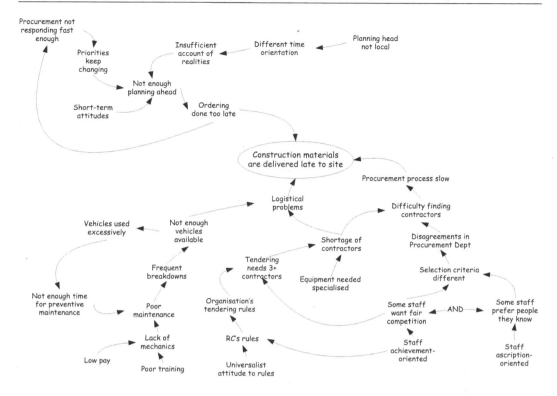

Figure 8.11 Reliable Constructions multiple cause diagram 1

Philippa then moved on to thinking about a multiple cause diagram. Looking back through her notes from her first day on the project, when she had brought Stephanie and Michael together to work on some problem statements, she saw that they had agreed on: 'Essential construction materials are regularly arriving late on-site, threatening completion of the project on time and within budget.' She wrote an abbreviated version of that in the middle of a large sheet of paper and, spreading out her notes in front of her, started to explore what was going on. What she drew is depicted in Figure 8.11 above.

She came up with three initial causes:

- Procurement processes in Logistics were slow.
- There were logistical problems in getting equipment transported.
- Site planning were ordering materials too late.

So why was the procurement process slow? Well one reason was the difficulty they had had in finding suitable contractors, and this had arisen not only because of the shortage of suitable local contractors, but also because of the disagreements there had been between Stephanie and the logistics supervisor. They had different cultural attitudes to finding a haulage contractor: with her universalist cultural beliefs, Stephanie had wanted to follow the rules and make the competition 'fair', whereas her local supervisor had felt strongly that the contract be awarded to the company that he knew he could trust to be reliable. But Stephanie had insisted on following a strict contracting process, requiring three separate competitive tenders, although the shortage of suitable hauliers had made this something of a mockery.

The logistical problems were due not only to the shortage of hauliers available, but also to the fact that the one selected did not seem to have enough vehicles available to satisfy Reliable Constructions' demands. Although, on paper, sufficient vehicles seemed to be available, they were constantly breaking down due, according to the logistics supervisor, to poor maintenance. This was because the haulage contractor did not have enough decent mechanics due to inadequate training and not paying enough to attract skilled staff. Philippa then considered the shortage of vehicles and realized that another consequence of this would be excessive use of vehicles, resulting in insufficient time for the haulier to carry out preventive maintenance. This would also contribute to poor levels of maintenance. She recognized this as a vicious circle that would need to be considered in more detail.

The third main cause was that the site office was ordering materials and equipment too late. The major reason for this seemed to be that they were not planning ahead enough, and that this was because the expatriate site manager did not seem to understand some of the local attitudes to timekeeping. That, combined with the assistants's multi-active and short-term cultural preferences meant that planning and priorities were not particularly well thought through.

All of this had given Philippa much to think about, but she remembered that during that first day with Michael and Stephanie, they had developed several other problem statements. One of those was: 'Site is asking for Logistics to deliver materials too early.' She thought it might be interesting to pull this apart, so she wrote a statement like that in the middle of a new sheet of paper and started asking 'why?' questions again. What she came up with is shown in Figure 8.12.

One issue seemed to be that the site office was not particularly aware of the problems that Logistics were having, and so sometimes made unreasonable demands. This was largely due to the poor communications between the two offices. This lack of awareness also fed into the site project planning process, weakening it. This was made worse by the planning assistants not seeming to be particularly worried about the problems being caused by them being unable to use the company's project planning software effectively.

Before she finished for the day, Philippa looked at the vehicle maintenance problem. She rewrote the states identified in the multiple cause diagram as a set of variables and drew a causal flow diagram (Figure 8.13). As vehicle availability went down, vehicle

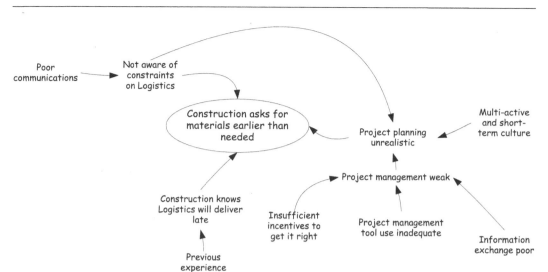

Figure 8.12 Reliable Constructions multiple cause diagram 2

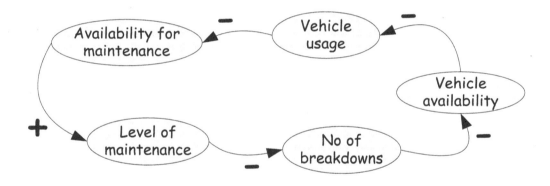

Figure 8.13 Reliable Constructions vehicle availability

usage went up, which meant that the availability for preventive maintenance decreased. That in turn meant that the level of maintenance applied also went down, so that the number of breakdowns rose, reducing the availability of vehicles. She saw that there were four inverse relationships in the loop, meaning that this was an unstable system, which would, as it currently operated, lead to an ever-worsening level of availability.

Philippa would have to think about what could be done to improve the situation in this unstable feedback loop. She drew a breath and looked at what she had achieved. She felt that the drawings she had sketched out had helped her understand the situation much more clearly than she had done before. It might be time to think about some solutions.

Step 3: Summary

We have looked at a number of different diagrams that you can use to help you analyse a particular situation. Do not think that you have to draw all of them, as each one has its own particular strengths and areas of applicability. Make sure that you are familiar with what these applications are so that you can draw the diagrams that help.

To summarize:

- Involve people with different cultural perspectives in your analysis.
- Draw a rich picture to provide a visual summary of the elements and relationships involved in a problem.
- Draw a systems map to help you make sure that you have identified all the actors within a problem.
- Take a systems map further by using it to construct an influence diagram, where you can show the pattern and strength of different influences operating within a situation.
- Use a multiple cause diagram to provide a visual representation of the different factors operating within a particular situation and to help you work your way back to find the root causes of a problem.
- Use causal flow diagrams for exploring feedback loops and for considering what changes might be made to make an unstable loop stable or to make it converge rather than diverge.
- Draw a process flowchart to capture a decision-making sequence and to help identify places where complex cognitive judgements are being made.
- Draw a process flow diagram to show how the responsibility for a complex sequence of actions moves from one part of an organization to another.

9 *Step 4: Generate Ideas*

KEY POINTS

There are a number of different families of solutions that you can apply when trying to solve a problem:

- Brainstorming is a useful way of generating solutions to problems, if carried out carefully.

- The Mager and Pipe performance flowchart is a systematic way of generating potential solutions.

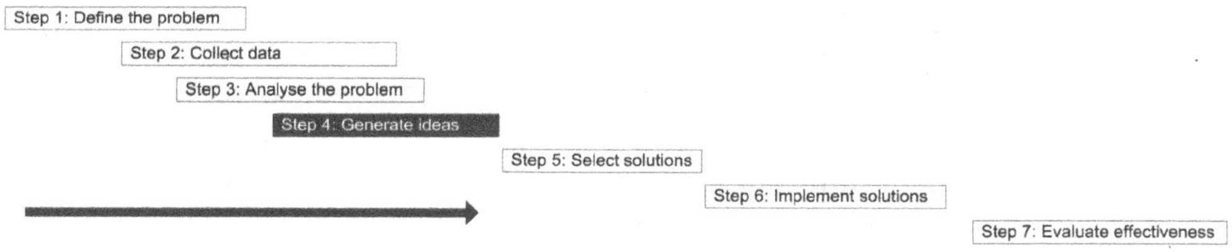

Step 1: Define the problem

Step 2: Collect data

Step 3: Analyse the problem

Step 4: Generate ideas

Step 5: Select solutions

Step 6: Implement solutions

Step 7: Evaluate effectiveness

Figure 9.1   Step 4 in problem-solving

Why is the Solution-Generation Stage Important?

If you have been reading through these chapters sequentially, you might have noticed that in Chapter 8, where we were looking at how to analyse problems, we sometimes came up with possible solutions. Why, therefore, do we have a separate step for generating ideas?

It is to be expected and perfectly acceptable that you might come up with ideas for solutions in any of the earlier steps of problem-solving. Some possible solutions will spring to mind when formulating and reformulating problem statements, and more will appear when you go out collecting information and when analysing the problem. However, this presents the danger that you will identify possible solutions early on in the process and will then close your mind to other possibilities and concentrate instead on finding arguments that justify your initial ideas. Elsewhere in this book we have mentioned how this is what we call 'satisficing'.

It is also quite possible that the first solutions you think of will be those that you are most familiar or comfortable with: for example, if you have a background in training it is highly likely that you will be instinctively looking for training solutions, whereas if you have a human relations policy background you will be thinking about changes to policies and guidelines that influence behaviour. As the old saying goes, 'If you do what you've always done, you'll get what you've always got'.

So what we need is a bit of discipline. Treat all the ideas that you come up with in the early, investigatory steps of the process as possibilities and make a note of them. Then, when you have analysed your problem to a point where you think you understand it in enough depth, move on to a more rigorous process of idea generation.

In this chapter we will look at some methods you can use to help generate a list of possible solutions in a more systematic manner.

What are Possible Solutions?

In addition to using systematic processes for identifying potential solutions, it is also a good idea to have a better understanding of the full range of interventions that are available. Hale (2007) has done a very good job in developing a comprehensive list of general interventions. She suggests that there are 15 'families' of interventions gathered in six different groups (Figure 9.2).

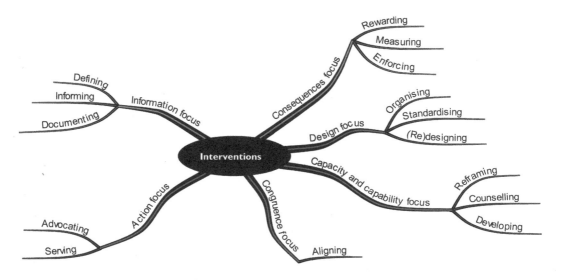

Figure 9.2   Hale's intervention families
Source: Hale (2007).

Essential characteristics of these families are described below, and later we shall see how each type can be brought out by using the systematic approach of the performance flowchart (described in Chapter 2).

INTERVENTIONS FOCUSED ON INFORMATION

In the discussion of Gilbert's Behaviour Engineering Model in Chapter 2, we saw how information was one of the three basic factors influencing performance (the other two being equipment and desire). However, of the three, information is probably the most important as it can underpin the use of both tools and equipment and be closely related to providing the connection between incentives and motivation. Without paying careful attention to the provision of information all other solutions may fail.

From a cultural perspective, information-related interventions must take into consideration the issues described in Chapter 2. These include such things as language comprehension, perception of visual data and so on.

There are three families of intervention that are focused on information: those that define, those that inform and those that document.

Providing information that defines

Using Behaviour Engineering Model terminology, these are interventions that describe what people are supposed to be achieving. These might be vision or mission statements, organizational charts to show where responsibilities lie, standard operating procedures or other guidelines that explain how particular tasks that must be carried out, standards of performance, and so on.

On the border

Thinking back to the border guard problem considered in previous chapters, here are some ways in which we could provide defining information:

- Create a mission statement that the border guard service will provide identical treatment to all travellers, regardless of gender, and that this will be in full agreement with international declarations on human rights.
- Create organization charts showing responsibilities for managing border activities.
- Draw up standard operating procedures providing detailed explanation about how to deal with international travellers.

Providing information that informs

There are two elements to providing information that informs:

- deciding what information is needed;
- developing a mechanism for making sure that the informative information is delivered.

Necessary information covers feedback on performance: how well a task is being carried out, how quickly, how accurately, how many are being produced, sold and so on. This will need to be tied in with defining information, such as required standards of performance: it is no good telling somebody that they are producing 90 widgets an hour without also telling them that the required output is 80 or 100, as clearly this extra item of information casts quite a different light on the first statistic.

Information delivery mechanisms must also be provided, and these should be designed so that the feedback is provided as quickly as possible. Telling someone in week 20 that their widget production in week 18 was below target is going to have a limited effect. Apart from making it very difficult for someone to think about what particular actions were responsible for the above- or below-average performance in order to make necessary changes, it also sends a message that this particular measure of performance is not very important.

On the border

Informing information interventions might include:

- reports sent to all border posts about incidents of mistreatment.
- communications about actions being taken to strengthen the implementation of border procedures.
- establishing weekly meetings to review what has happened at border posts.
- debriefing sessions to deal with specific incidents
- gather information about ethnicity of people being mistreated.

Documenting information

It may be necessary to take actions that record defining or informing information in appropriate ways. This might involve establishing processes to create such things as user guides or performance aids.

On the border

Documenting activities might include:

- development of checklists defining how to deal with cross-border travellers.
- developing, printing and distributing copies of standard operating procedures.
- printing posters summarizing key aspects of the United Nations Declaration of Human Rights.

INTERVENTIONS FOCUSED ON CONSEQUENCES

Consequences-focused interventions are those that suggest establishing activities that can reward, measure or enforce performance. They may therefore be closely connected with information-focused interventions.

There are cultural issues to consider here:

- Whether or not something is a reward depends on the cultural values of the person receiving it.
- You can measure many different things, but the significance of the numbers you get will vary from culture to culture: for example, what is seen as taking a long-time in one culture may seem insignificant in another.
- Enforcement measures need to be implemented in a way that suits the cultures affected. Participative approaches would be preferred by people with a low power distance preference, whereas authoritarian ones would be more appropriate where there is a preference for a high power distance.

Rewarding activities   Rewarding activities relates to the motivation–incentive nexus. These will be activities designed to encourage people to work towards achieving and then maintaining the desired levels of performance specified by definition interventions. These might typically include any of the ideas in Table 9.1.

Table 9.1   Rewards and recognitions

Rewards	Recognition
Bonuses	Praise, such as a simple 'Thank you'
Commission	Public acknowledgement
Profit-sharing schemes	Certificates
Share options	'Employee of the month' award or
Prizes	similar
Paid-for dinners or holidays	Letter of thanks from a senior manager

This is a particularly complex area to consider when dealing with cross-cultural situations. As discussed in Chapter 2, culture has a profound effect on such things as what motivates people and how rewards should be delivered. For example, for people who have collectivist tendencies, motivation will be provided by the incentives that promote the in-group as a whole, and strategies that reward individuals may be counterproductive. Similarly, public recognition of good performance by an individual who has a collectivist ethos could be profoundly embarrassing and actually result in reduced levels of performance. When working with some cultures, rewards may need to be negative – in other words punishment – since telling a Japanese person, for example, that their performance is inadequate will probably result in improved performance (Ide, 1999), whereas doing this to a British person could well result in them performing even more badly.

On the border	Rewarding solutions might include:

- public recognition of individual guards who do something positive to help travellers, particularly females.
- financial rewards to individuals or border posts where no incidents of mistreatment occur.

Measuring activities	Measuring activities involves developing and introducing systems that record levels of performance. These will be related to information/informing interventions.

On the border	Measuring activities here might include:

- recording the numbers of incidents of mistreatment each week.
- counting the numbers of days that have elapsed since the last incident of mistreatment.
- appointing a person with a specific responsibility to gather, analyse and make information available.

Enforcing activities	Enforcing activities means taking action to make sure that satisfactory performance is achieved. These will include strengthening or putting monitoring systems in place, and instigating disciplinary procedures. If threatened, disciplinary procedures must be enforced, because, if they are not, performance is likely to deteriorate further.

There may be cultural aspects to consider here, as what might be seen as a strong disciplinary procedure in one culture may be less effective in another. For example, Nisbett (2005) contrasts the different ways in which American and Japanese parents discipline errant teenagers. For the individualist American teenagers, whose focus is on relationships outside the family in-group, punishment is to confine the son or daughter to their house, and perhaps even to confiscate mobile phones so that communication with their friends is not possible for a period of time. In contrast, punishment of Japanese teenagers would be to lock them out of the house, as exclusion from the family in-group is threatening and seen as something that should be avoided at all costs.

On the border	Enforcing activities in this situation might include:

- taking steps to make sure that supervisors monitor activities and taking action in cases of mistreatment.
- implementing punishments appropriate to the level of mistreatment, ranging from warnings to withdrawal of pay to dismissal to imprisonment.
- Instigating formal review procedures to investigate cases of alleged mistreatment.

INTERVENTIONS FOCUSED ON WORK DESIGN

Work design interventions look at the way in which tasks are carried out and make improvements. These may be by organizing the way in which tasks and responsibilities are divided up and allocated, standardization of processes, procedures or equipment and redesign of the way in which tasks are carried out.

From a cultural perspective, work design interventions need to take account of cultural ergonomic issues at both macro- and micro-ergonomic levels. For example:

- How will work redesign relate to people's mental models?
- Will revised practices fit in with local circumstances?
- Will the redesign affect the cultural perceptions of the work?
- Will there be issues about usability of equipment, clothing and so on?

Organizing activities

These activities look at performance from a relatively high level and might involve:

- changing who is responsible for carrying the task out, perhaps by outsourcing.
- dividing up or grouping together work units so that they can work more efficiently and effectively.
- changing the sequence in which tasks are performed.

On the border

Organizing activities in this situation might include:

- contracting out border management duties to a private contractor.
- making border guards effectively part of the police force.
- changing recruitment policies so that there are more women border guards, and at least one at every crossing-point.
- ensuring appropriate ethnic balance of border guards to minimise in-group/out-group discrimination.

Standardizing activities

Standardizing activities means making sure that tasks are always carried out in the same way regardless of by whom, where and when. This may involve providing new tools, equipment, materials and working environment.

> In 1999 the US NASA Jet Propulsion Laboratory was eagerly awaiting the arrival of its Mars Climate Orbiter spacecraft in orbit around Mars. However, as it approached the red planet it was not travelling at the correct velocity in order to go into orbit, and, instead of settling into the planned circular trajectory, it just went straight on going, and, as far as anyone knows, is now happily in orbit around the sun and not Mars.

> After carrying out an inquiry into the reasons for the loss of the Orbiter it was concluded that one team working on the project had been using imperial units (pounds and inches), while another had been using metric units. The resulting errors had led to the spacecraft being on the wrong trajectory when it arrived at Mars (NASA, 1999).

On the border

Standardizing activities in this situation could include:

- making sure that every border post is provided with a copy of the United Nations Declaration on Human Rights.
- making one individual responsible for making sure that the UN Declaration is implemented at every border point.

Redesigning activities

Redesigning activities is concerned primarily with micro-ergonomics factors related to the detail of carrying out tasks. For example, this might include redesigning equipment so that it is easier to use, and perhaps more suitable for people with different physical characteristics such as size or strength.

On the border

Redesigning activities in this situation might include:

- building improved facilities.
- changing the layout of buildings so that it is harder to hide the mistreatment of women.

INTERVENTIONS FOCUSED ON CAPACITY AND CAPABILITIES

Capacity and capability interventions are those concerned with increasing the abilities of people within the workforce to carry out tasks to the standards required. The families of activities suggested here are those that can help people reframe their attitude towards work, counselling activities that provide support and advice to both work- and personal-related issues and development activities, which includes training.

There would be many cultural sensitivities around interventions of this type. For example, counselling activities may move beyond the realm of the workplace into people's personal lives. Training decisions may be influenced by cultural preferences.

Reframing activities

Reframing activities concerns people's attitudes to their work. Such activities will concentrate on helping people to see work from a different perspective and, perhaps, to feel more positive or confident about it.

On the border

Reframing activities might include:

- one–to–one or small group sessions aimed at trying to change border guards' attitudes towards treating women.

Counselling activities	Counselling activities look at providing people with support and advice on personal, financial or health-related issues, for example. They might focus on specific issues, such as retirement planning, pension provision or on helping people reduce the amount of alcohol they drink or stop smoking. In some cases there may occasionally be a need to provide some post-traumatic incident counselling.
On the border	Counselling activities in this situation might include:

- providing trained counsellors to work with guards on a one-to-one basis to explore issues about gender-based violence.
- offering advice about financial matters to reduce the motivation to rob travellers.

Development activities	Development activities may just be one out of the 15 families, but they are the ones that are most usually offered up as solutions to end all problems. So this includes providing training courses, mentoring, coaching, job swap opportunities and the like. These are activities that are appropriate if a lack of knowledge or skill is a cause of the problem.
On the border	Development activities that might be appropriate in this case include:

- a training programme on the United Nations Declaration of Human Rights.
- a training programme on how to deal with travellers, with special emphasis on female travellers.
- job rotation opportunities so that people can gain experience of working in different environments.

INTERVENTIONS FOCUSING ON ACTION	Action-focused interventions are those that are designed to influence people to take action about a particular issue. These can be difficult or sensitive initiatives to implement.
Advocating activities	With advocating activities, steps are taken to put pressure on relevant parts of the organization to take action. For example, if poor performance seems to be related to underinvestment in a particular area, an advocating activity might be to carry out a study looking at how this underinvestment is affecting performance and to then find ways in which the results of the study might be used to exert pressure on people who are in a position to increase investment.
On the border	Advocating activities in this situation might include:

- persuading international organizations such as the United Nations or an influential non-governmental organization (NGO) to put pressure on the national government.

- inviting journalists to investigate what is happening and write news stories about it.

Serving activities

Serving activities provide resources to individuals or groups who wish to take some part in improving performance, but are unable to do so because of particular constraints. For example, if performance is due to a shortage of labour, it might be possible to recruit temporary labour from elsewhere to help.

On the border

Serving activities in this situation might include:

- providing someone, from an external agency perhaps, to work alongside border guards to help them change their behaviour.

INTERVENTIONS FOCUSED ON CONGRUENCE

Congruence-related interventions are those that seek to ensure consistency between all levels of the organization. Congruence implies consistency, and this can be challenging where there are different beliefs and values within the workplace.

Alignment activities

Hale (2007) suggests alignment activities as the only ones within the congruence group, and says that these should focus on making sure that all activities are related to, and support, the organization's overall aims and objectives. An example of such an activity is making sure that reward structures value those behaviours that the organization's culture claims to represent.

On the border

Alignment activities in this situation might include:

- making managerial or organizational changes that help ensure that the government's promise that it is there to 'serve the people' is implemented at border posts.

How to Generate Lists of Potential Solutions

As described earlier, preceding steps in the problem-solving process will almost certainly suggest potential solutions. However, these will have been probably generated somewhat at random and will probably reflect your own particular interests, experience and existing knowledge. In this section we will look at some more or less systematic techniques you can use to help you develop a longer list of solutions to consider.

Which technique or techniques you choose to use depends on both the nature of the problem and the resources you have available to you. For example, some are more useful for looking at high-level organizational problems and others at the task-related level; some are useful for analysis when working on your own, while others allow you to take advantage of a problem-solving team. If you are able to take advantage of a small group of people to help you with generating solutions, then you should do so. You will almost certainly end up with a longer list of solutions (although they may not all be of high quality in terms of feasibility or effectiveness), but, more importantly, involving other people should help to increase their commitment to assisting with the implementation of solutions that are finally chosen. Therefore, if you work with a small team to jointly develop a list of potential solutions and then diplomatically manage the shortlisting and final selection process, you will find Step 6 of the problem-solving process, implementation, goes much more smoothly.

It is, however, pertinent to remember at this stage just how effective people working in groups can be. The concept of *synergy* (defined by the *Oxford English Dictionary* as 'increased effectiveness, achievement, etc., produced by combined action, cooperation, etc.') is often explained by saying that groups working together always produce better solutions than people working individually. However, what is often overlooked or misunderstood is that, although people working together on a common task will almost always produce a better solution *than the average* of solutions produced by people working individually, the performance of a group is usually not as good as the individual performance of the best one or two people in the group. This suggests that while there may be significant and essential political advantages to harnessing a problem-solving group to devising solutions, you should not assume that it will produce better results than you working on your own. However, this would be at the risk of ignoring different cultural perspectives.

We shall look at three methods you might consider for generating ideas for potential solutions:

- *brainstorming* – a good way of harnessing the creative energies of a group of people, particularly your problem-solving team.
- the *Mager and Pipe performance flowchart* – a systematic way of working through different elements of the factors influencing performance.
- *force field analysis* – a way of looking at the different influences acting on a situation that prompts reflection.

Each has its own merits, and you may find one more useful or easier to use than the others. However, they are not mutually exclusive, and using all three would provide a comprehensive way of coming up with ideas.

Brainstorming

Brainstorming is a technique that is often used to involve people in developing a list of responses. It is seen as an approach that utilizes the brain's ability to develop networks of ideas, so that a single stimulus can trigger off a series of associated ideas.

The technique first emerged in the 1930s and since then it has become extremely popular in many areas of management. However, this popularity has led to it being carried out in many different ways, so it would be useful here to define some essential guidelines for running brainstorming sessions. The guidelines below are based on principles defined by Osborn (1953):

- No idea offered during the ideas-gathering session should be criticized.
- Wild ideas are encouraged.
- The purpose of the exercise is to get as many ideas as possible, as increasing the number makes it more likely that some will be of value.
- Ideas already proposed and recorded can be combined, developed or otherwise improved.

Osborn also had other recommendations about how sessions should be organized and managed:

- Groups should contain between five and ten participants, and the constitution of the group should reflect the nature of the problem being considered.
- Participants should be of the same level within the organization.
- Participants should have a wide range of experience in matters related to the problem at hand.
- Gathering ideas and evaluation should be done in separate sessions.
- The facilitator should have been formally trained in creative problem-solving techniques and be expert at asking questions to encourage and elicit new responses.
- There should be a separate person with specific responsibility for recording contributions on a surface or media visible to all.
- Sessions should last between 30 and 45 minutes.

These are fairly exacting requirements, and it is doubtful that many brainstorming sessions, as generally run, follow these requirements precisely. It is therefore not surprising that the effectiveness of such sessions can vary considerably. A problem is that it seems such a simple thing to do that people often run brainstorming sessions without considering the potential pitfalls – the pitfalls that Osborn's guidelines were intended to avoid.

The popularity of brainstorming has meant that it has become a popular topic of research activity. Many studies looking at how well brainstorming works have concluded that its effectiveness is somewhat limited (see, for example, Lamm and Trommsdorff, 2006; Paulus and Paulus, 1997). Various explanations have been offered for why this is the case, such as social loafing, free riding, evaluation apprehension, production blocking, personality traits and uniformity pressure.

Groups enable *social loafing*, where individuals working in the relative anonymity of a group choose not to participate. This happens if they make judgements about how the group as a whole is performing and feel that they can get away with lower levels of performance. They can also *free ride* – that is, assume that other people will do the work for them or see no need to take any risks. Social loafing and free riding are more significant as problems with individualists, because collectivists' cultural tightness impels them to follow the group's rules closely, from fearing of sanctions if they try to take advantage (Triandis, 1995).

Although the facilitator will say that ideas will not be judged or evaluated in any way, people know that everything they say may be taken down and used in evidence against them, even in the supposed free-thinking world of the brainstorm. This has been called *evaluation apprehension.*

Individuals may have ideas that they want to suggest but, because they have to wait for others to stop talking they forget them, being distracted by other completely different ideas being shouted out. This has been described as *production blocking* and it often occurs where no additional person has been assigned to record contributions, so that the process of logging ideas takes time and slows things down.

Personality traits set a pattern for who contributes. People who, in everyday life, talk a lot and dominate proceedings often take over in brainstorms, while shyer, quieter people sit unobserved in the background.

Participants drawn from similar levels in the same organization will quite possibly have a somewhat similar set of attitudes and experiences to bring to the party, so the freewheeling nirvana that brainstorming suggests may not be achievable. Researchers have called this *uniformity pressure*, and it is obviously similar to the idea of groupthink.

Over the years there have been many criticisms levelled at brainstorming, challenging just how useful it is as a technique, particularly when compared against the effectiveness of people working individually. Although this is an important consideration, many of the studies that have questioned brainstorming's effectiveness have been criticized for the methodologies they have employed (Isaksen, 1998). It is useful to briefly consider what these studies have claimed, as this shines a useful light on what can improve or reduce the effectiveness of brainstorming sessions. For example:

- Studies have generally been made using university students as participants. They have been put together to operate as a group, but have no prior experience of working with each other.
- The subjects used to examine the effectiveness of the brainstorming sessions have been artificial (such as the usefulness of an extra thumb or unusual uses for a coat hanger), so that participants have no particular expertise in the topic of discussion.
- Evaluation has tended to focus on the number of solutions obtained rather than on their quality.
- Research methodologies have concentrated on comparing the number of ideas produced by brainstorming groups against those produced by people working individually using the same rules. This merely shows the relative effectiveness of group as against individual working, but says nothing about the absolute effectiveness of group brainstorming processes.

Brainstorming was originally conceived as an activity that would complement other creative problem-solving approaches, and so would be used alongside other techniques and at various points in the problem-solving methodology, not just at the solution generation stage. So, for example, if the technique is also used to generate alternative problem statements (Step 1 of the problem-solving process, described in Chapter 6), participants can develop a deeper understanding of the issue being investigated and will be able to come up with better-quality solutions. When used in the actual workplace setting, the sets of people that take part are real dynamic groups, composed of people who know each other and the subject under discussion and so understand where the problem has come from and where it is going, rather than being nominal groups created as part of an academic research exercise.

Essentially, brainstorming studies have removed the activity from the context within which it has been designed to operate, so it is perhaps not surprising that it has not appeared to be particularly effective. But what studies also show is that there are other benefits from large group brainstorming activities that arise from its sense of excitement, fun and involvement.

Brainstorming can be a valuable technique to use within the problem-solving process, but it must be done with care if it is to be effective. Based on the original guidelines and the criticisms of the technique as outlined above, here are some suggestions about how to make brainstorming sessions more effective:

- Use brainstorming throughout the problem-solving process.
- Manage the event efficiently.

- Train participants in the brainstorming process before starting serious work.
- Follow up on brainstorming.
- Ask people to brainstorm before the brainstorm.

USE
BRAINSTORMING
THROUGHOUT
THE PROBLEM-
SOLVING
PROCESS

Brainstorming was always intended as just one of the tools to be used during the problem-solving process, so look for ways of integrating it into other steps. For example, you can brainstorm to find redefinitions of the problem statement, to develop evaluation criteria and to work out what needs to be done in order to implement chosen solutions. A development of the brainstorm process is the nominal group technique, which is described in Chapter 10 as a method to help you prioritize potential solutions. This technique integrates brainstorming and evaluation, so is described in detail in Chapter 10.

MANAGE
THE EVENT
EFFICIENTLY

The effectiveness of a brainstorm is significantly influenced by how well it is managed. It is particularly important to have skilled facilitators manage the event, who provide the necessary training, explain the process and encourage participation.

Before the event the facilitators should find out who the participants are going to be and try to make sure that there are no hierarchical issues, since, if the group contains managers, supervisors and subordinates, there is much less likely to be a free flow of ideas. They also should define the problem in a way that engages the participants. So, for example, if the aim of the session is to identify solutions to the border guard problem, one question might be:

- How can we improve the problem at the border?

Alternatively the question could be:

- You are passing through the border and see a woman being mistreated. What could be done to stop this happening?

This second statement of the problem draws participants in and encourages them to think that they are involved in the situation, whereas the first portrays it as a somewhat academic exercise. As such, the second statement is likely to generate a better response.

During the event the facilitators must be able to think of questions to stimulate the flow of ideas whenever there seem to be breaks in people's enthusiasm or a new line of thinking opens up that needs further exploration. They must also observe the group's dynamics and look out for people who are not taking part, perhaps because they are shy, socially loafing or free riding.

Someone also needs to be given responsibility for recording ideas, because if the facilitator does this, they cannot monitor group activity and concentrate on asking questions to stimulate activity. Alternatively, each participant could have paper and a pen, so that they can you write ideas down as they think of them and then call them out when they get the chance.

TRAIN PARTICIPANTS BEFORE STARTING

Isaksen (1998) reports how various studies have shown that brainstorming produces better-quality results when the participants have received some training before starting. This does not need to be significant: there is no need to send people on a residential course on how to take part in a brainstorm; the need is for something more like a warm-up act before a television game show. Before starting on the serious business of brainstorming for ideas about the problem you are considering, it is a good idea to run through the guidelines for the event and to then practise on a harmless, but enjoyable, subject. One topic that often seems to work well is 'My pet hates'.

FOLLOW UP ON BRAINSTORMING

Many of the best ideas in a brainstorm come later on in the process. This may be due to various factors: participants may be more relaxed; initial ideas stimulate further thinking; or perhaps people are starting to have a greater understanding of the problem. The process of thinking of new ideas does not necessarily end when the formal event comes to a close, as people may continue to have ideas later in the day or even perhaps while they sleep! It is always therefore a good idea to tell people at the end of the event that if they do have any further ideas, they should pass them on to you.

ASK PEOPLE TO BRAINSTORM BEFORE THE BRAINSTORM

One way of getting around the evaluation apprehension problem to some extent is to brief people a few days beforehand about what you want to achieve from the event, and to ask them to start putting together a list of solutions that they would like to propose. As with traditional brainstorming, you give them the brief that you want as long a list of potential solutions as possible and do not want them to evaluate their ideas in any way and so eliminate them from their list.

Away from the pressure of perceived judgement, people are much more likely to write down ideas that come into their head. This does not, of course, mean that they will express them during the event, but the very act of putting them down on paper makes it more likely that they will be made public. Even if people do not pluck up the courage to do this during the event, they can always give you their written list at the end.

This method also fits in well with the nominal group technique used for evaluating potential solutions, as described in Step 5 (Chapter 10).

PAIRED BRAINSTORMING

Building on this idea of pre-brainstorming brainstorming, it has been shown that you can get a larger number of ideas covering a wider range of themes by asking people to work on the problem before the event in pairs. When two people work together, they can spark ideas from each other, and a pair is a small and secure enough group to prevent people feeling that they need to censor themselves.

Using the Performance Flowchart

Mager's and Pipe's performance flowchart was discussed in Chapter 2, where we saw how it provides a systematic way of looking through the factors that Gilbert identified as key factors affecting performance in the Behaviour Engineering Model. The generating ideas stage of the problem-solving model is where you can make effective use of this.

As you work through the decisions in the flowchart, you will find yourself coming up with a number of different solutions. It is worth reflecting back on the families of interventions described earlier in this chapter, as each of the questions is particularly likely to suggest certain families. Although it is important not to see this as a rigorous and exclusive set of possibilities, Figure 9.3 shows how this may well happen.

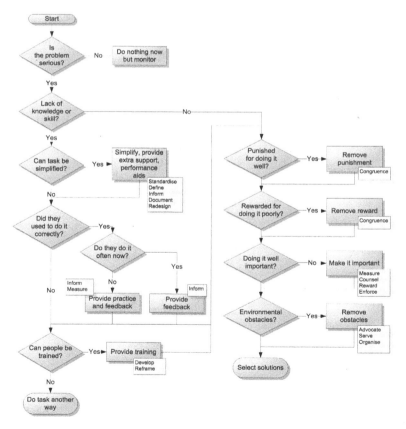

Figure 9.3   The performance flowchart with intervention families

To see how this works, let us apply it to our analysis of the border guard problem.

Table 9.2   Using the performance flowchart to analyse the border guard problem

Flowchart question	Answer	Possible solution
Is the problem serious?	Yes, women are being badly treated to the extent of being robbed and sexually abused. There is definitely a need to deal with this problem.	
Is there a lack of knowledge or skill?	Yes, although the problems are probably largely caused by attitudes, there are some knowledge and skill issues that need to be tackled as well.	
Can the task be simplified?	The task of regulating travellers as they pass through the border is not in itself complicated, but there could be scope for issuing all border guards and supervisors with a simple rule book or checklist that they would need to observe when processing people. This would define a standard for the behaviours required and would make any contravention of acceptable procedures explicit, removing ignorance as a potential defence. Similarly, making sure that the United Nations Declaration on Human Rights was available and visible would be at the very least a statement of intent. Trustworthy guards could be deployed to work alongside guards suspected of unsatisfactory behaviour to act as coaches and encourage good practice. Women guards could be appointed and deployed to every border crossing to have responsibility for processing female travellers.	Rule book or checklist observed when processing people. Poster of United Nations Declaration on Human Rights. Appointment of trustworthy guards as supervisors. Appointment of women guards.
Did they used to do it correctly?	No, this has always been a problem.	
Can the people be trained?	Yes, some training might be appropriate. A more detailed training needs analysis would be	Deliver training on the United Nations Declaration of

Table 9.2   *Continued*

	necessary, but it should probably cover such topics as the United Nations Declaration on Human Rights, the government's own guidelines on dealing with members of the public and procedures for stopping and searching people. This would provide the guards with the background knowledge that they would need in order to carry out their work correctly. However, the problem is largely attitudinal, and so this training might be largely ineffectual at changing behaviour. Effective training would need to work on changing personal attitudes at a deep level.	Human Rights. Deliver attitudinal training.
Are they punished for doing it well?	The guards do not seem to be punished in any particular way by their employers if they do the job well, but a major factor is that they are poorly paid. Not extorting money from travellers may therefore seem like a punishment. Within the guards' male culture, harassing female travellers may bring prestige, so treating them decently may lead to teasing and a loss of status.	Institute punishment for unacceptable behaviour. Review salary levels.
Are they rewarded for doing it poorly?	Mistreating women may be enhancing the macho reputation of the men doing it. This would need to be dealt with by actions to devalue machismo, perhaps by improved supervision or attitudinal training. Extorting money improves the guards' income, so is a reward. Treating people who are outside the in-group (in other ethnic groups) badly would improve their feeling of superiority and higher status.	Training of supervisors to identify and deal with displays of macho behaviour. Attitudinal training to discourage this activity. Appoint women border guards. Make border guard postings for married men only, which would mean that men's actions would be monitored and hopefully regulated by a wife. Ensure that border posts are operated by guards representing a mix of ethnic groups.

Table 9.2 *Concluded*

Is doing it well important?	The lack of sanctions or punishment, and perhaps even observation that it is happening, may be normalizing the behaviour, in that mistreatment of female travellers is acceptable. To change this, the guidelines that prohibit such behaviour must be promoted and shown to be essential. This would require a campaign to promote the desired standards, and, as identified previously, institution of appropriate rewards for the desired behaviour and/or sanctions and punishment for not doing this.	Campaign to publicize the United Nations Declaration of Human Rights. Implement reward scheme to acknowledge compliance. Institute punishment for unacceptable behaviour.
Are there any environmental obstacles?	The physical conditions under which the guards work does not help. Communications with the capital city are poor, and so there is little sense that what they are doing is accountable or being monitored. Living conditions are low-quality, which discourages men from asking their wives to accompany them.	Improve communications with the capital city. Improve living conditions.

This analysis has shown how you can use the performance analysis flowchart to work through a situation and identify possible solutions, but it is not necessarily a comprehensive analysis. You may reflect on how this compares with the list of solutions described in the earlier section looking at Hale's families of interventions, but this comparison shows the value of using different approaches to solution identification. For example, when considering the question about simplifying the task, you could review your list of solutions and consider to what extent you have covered standardizing, defining, informing, documenting and redesigning – the families of particular relevance to this question.

And, of course, if you were to run a brainstorming session you could quite possibly come up with yet more solutions.

Force Field Analysis

Force field analysis is a technique attributed to the German psychologist Kurt Lewin. The technique centres on the idea of a field – your area of interest where you want to introduce some change – and the forces acting on that field, particularly those opposing or restraining any change and driving change – moving the field in the direction you want it to go.

The technique is useful as a tool for both identifying potential solutions and analysing their likely effectiveness. To see how it works, consider the border guard problem. A force field analysis of the situation might provide Figure 9.4.

Vertically, we have a line that represents the current situation or level of mistreatment of women. To the right-hand side of this we draw arrows representing the restraining forces. Our analysis of the current situation has identified tradition, acceptability of the situation, the level of supervision, the isolation and the ignorance of desired performance as being key restraining forces.

On the left-hand side we draw the driving forces, those forces that could make a change to the position of the equilibrium – in other words, to move it to the right. These would seem to be the level of sanctions applied, the quality of supervision, communications with the outside world and the provision of information.

We next think what we can do to move the equilibrium to the right. There are two ways of doing this:

- Increase the strength of the driving forces.
- Decrease the strength of the restraining forces.

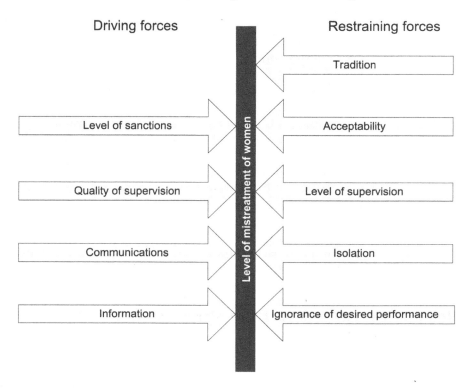

Figure 9.4   Force field analysis of the border guard situation

One of the strengths of force field analysis is that it helps us visualize the interplay between driving and restraining forces. So, for example, we have drawn the 'level of sanctions' driving force directly opposite 'acceptability', suggesting that increasing the level of sanctions might make mistreatment less acceptable and so reduce the force that it exerts. But increasing the level of sanctions is not the only way of reducing acceptability, so the diagram prompts us to think about other ways in which we can make mistreatment of women less acceptable.

Now consider the effect of tradition. This is a very strong restraining force, and against it we have no driving forces. Now, we might be able to think of some driving forces that would directly push up against tradition, but, remembering Newton's Third Law of Motion – that to every force there is an equal and opposite force – this might have the effect of hardening opinions and increasing the forces of tradition. After all, although the last 20 years have seen increased globalization, more international travel and easier communications, this has been accompanied by more religious fundamentalism and stronger nationalism in many parts of the world, and a strong argument can be made that the former has promoted the latter. So initiatives to point out to the border guards that their tradition of paying women little respect is unacceptable or an anachronistic hangover from a bygone age are likely to have little effect. In such circumstances we need to look at what we can do to reduce the effect of tradition, which is likely to need much longer-term action.

We can continue the use of the force field analysis by considering restraining and driving forces in greater levels of detail and using the diagram to reflect on appropriate strategies to take with these forces.

Although the technique has been used here to help us identify potential solutions, it can also be used to help select options. One way of doing this is to assign some quantitative value to each force and to see how the total level of forces on each side balances. For example, here we might say that the tradition force represents ten units, the acceptability force six units, the level of supervision three units and so on. If you were to do this for every force identified, you could end up with a better quantitative estimate of the level of action you would need to take to achieve a change in the equilibrium. This numerical approach is obviously going to be easier to use in some circumstances than others, where assigning quantitative levels could be effectively arbitrary.

The Reliable Constructions Case Study: Step 4

Philippa's desk was now covered with sheets of paper and her walls by sheets of flipchart paper, representing the notes she had taken in a dozen or so interviews and her systems maps, multiple cause and causal flow diagrams. She realized that she was finding the detective work fascinating, but that Nulty would be calling her soon to find out what she had discovered. The time for analysis was over, and she needed to start coming up with some solutions.

She reflected on how she might go about that. Brainstorming had some attractions, but she realized that it would be difficult to bring together a suitable group of people. There were not that many people involved in the problem and arranging it to avoid the constraints that would be created by the different hierarchies would be very difficult. She was operating in a country with a high power distance culture, and she recognized that subordinates would never say anything to challenge what they thought their supervisors opinions might be. However, it might be worthwhile to approach each person that she had spoken to quietly and individually, and ask them to spend a little time drawing up a list of solutions that they thought might be effective. If she stressed to them that the source of these ideas would be kept completely confidential, they might be able to provide some useful ideas that she could take forward and evaluate when she moved on to the next step in her problem-solving approach.

But, for now, she was on her own. She made herself a cup of coffee and pulled out a copy of the Mager and Pipe performance flowchart. 'There has got to be something in this that will help me,' she thought. She found a blank sheet of paper and a pencil and started to write.

From her analysis she had decided that there were three areas that needed some attention. These were:

- the poor communication that existed between sight and the Logistics function,
- how people approached project planning in the two parts of the business, and
- the availability of vehicles, which, although this was a problem affecting a contractor, needed to be sorted out in some way.

She decided to look at the problems with communication first (Table 9.3).

She repeated the process for the problems with project planning (Table 9.4).

Philippa finally turned her attention to the problem of vehicle availability. This was not a problem that the performance flowchart was designed to help with, so she instead looked at the causal flow diagram that she had developed in order to understand the dynamics of the problem with vehicle availability and maintenance (Figure 9.5).

She could see that the best way to break this vicious circle would be to provide more mechanics and so increase the level of maintenance. That should reverse the downward spiral, but, of

Table 9.3   Using the performance flowchart to analyse the Reliable Constructions communications problem

Flowchart question	Answer	Possible solution
Is the problem serious?	Yes, the delays threaten the completion of the project on time which would have a bad effect on the reputation of Reliable Constructions in the country.	
Is there a lack of knowledge or skill?	Yes, there are some issues to do with language problems. We should therefore consider the left side of the flowchart.	
Can the task be simplified?	There are some areas of confusion caused by lack of language skills. One quick solution to help with this would be a phrasebook of important words or phrases used in everyday communications.	English–local language phrasebook.
Did they used to do it correctly?	No, this is the first time that the local members of staff have had to use English regularly in a work setting.	
Can the people be trained?	Yes, local staff all have basic English skills, but are not confident in some of the workplace-specific language that they need. But they are all capable of improving. Expatriate staff have the ability to learn some basic local language, which would probably be more useful for team morale purposes than for practical communication, but valuable nonetheless.	English-language training for local members of staff. Training in the local language for expatriates staff.
Are they punished for doing it well?	The site manager has a high power distance culture and so behaves in an autocratic, hierarchical way. This makes it difficult for his assistants to challenge problems that they see, as they feel that if they bring problems to his attention, they will be criticized or punished.	Checklists stating required service levels to reduce ambiguity. Team-building activities to clarify cultural issues.

Table 9.3   *Concluded*

Flowchart question	Answer	Possible solution
Are they rewarded for doing it poorly?	Yes, by not communicating with their counterparts, the planning assistants do not have to deal with the problems they are causing. Someone else is sorting the mess out for them, so the assistants' jobs are easier.	Clearer management delegation of responsibilities.
Is doing it well important?	The logistics manager believes in delegating responsibility, but her assistants find this difficult to understand culturally and have interpreted this as meaning that making decisions about deliveries is not a priority. They also see her as a weak leader.	Improved communication within the team. Team-building activities to clarify cultural issues. Stephanie to attend cross-cultural management training.
Are there any environmental obstacles?	There are some language difficulties, with the mixture of English and other local language being used at different times. This is particularly a problem with voicemail messages. There are also ambiguities introduced by people with high- and low-context styles of communicating, so that sometimes people receive what they feel is incomplete information, while others feel patronized by excessive focus on specifics. There are incompatibilities in the degree to which people feel comfortable about expressing emotion, leading to misunderstandings.	Standardization on a specific language. Standard procedure that voicemail messages are supported by e-mail. Improved and increased communication within the team. Team-building activities to clarify cultural issues.

Table 9.4   **Using the performance flowchart to analyse the Reliable Constructions project planning problem**

Flowchart question	Answer	Possible solution
Is the problem serious?	Yes, as noted before.	
Is there a lack of knowledge or skill?	Yes, there are knowledge and skill issues contributing to the problems with project planning.	

Table 9.4   *Concluded*

Flowchart question	Answer	Possible solution
Can the task be simplified?	Yes, there are things that could be done to simplify the process of project planning. The planning assistants would benefit from having a step-by-step guide to the planning process and some simple guidance to using their project planning software.	Planning step-by-step guide and checklist. Guide to key tasks carried out using project planning software.
Did they used to do it correctly?	No, this is a new task for them.	
Can the people be trained?	Yes, they are capable of being trained and would benefit from some training in project management and planning skills.	Commission or send staff on a project management and planning course.
Are they punished for doing it well?	Yes, they feel that the site manager likes to see them apparently working under stress, so there is little incentive for them to get systems working smoothly. If they did get things working smoothly, he would possibly accuse them of not working hard enough.	One-to-one session with the site manager to discuss managerial issues.
Are they rewarded for doing it poorly?	Yes, the site manager feels that they are working hard.	As above.
Is doing it well important?	This seems to be clear enough.	
Are there any environmental obstacles?	The planning assistants' culture is multi-active and short-term-oriented. They are therefore not naturally inclined to think and plan ahead.	Team-building to develop shared culture

course, this was with an external contractor, not her own company. She would have to think about how to approach this with the haulage company, but that was for another day.

Step 4: Summary

This chapter has looked at a number of different ways of generating ideas for potential solutions in Step 4 of the problem-solving process.

The different methods have their particular strengths and weaknesses, and you may well find it useful to employ several of them, as each will stimulate different ideas. To summarize:

- Hale's intervention families break down the possible solutions into a number of discrete areas. You can consider each small area and think of potential solutions.
- Brainstorming provides a way of utilizing the enthusiasm and creativity of a number of people in order to come up with potential solutions.
- The Mager and Pipe performance flowchart offers a way of systematically working through the factors affecting performance in order to identify solutions in knowledge and skill and organizational areas.
- Force field analysis is a graphical way of looking at influences on a particular situation so that you can consider where to place an emphasis on remedial action.
- Utilizing cultural diversity will make the identification of different potential solutions to a problem more likely.

Finally, it is probably worth mentioning the subject of discipline again. First thoughts about solutions may be right, but quite possibly they will not be. Avoid the temptation of the quick fix and always be prepared to spend time doing some thorough analysis.

10 *Step 5: Select Solutions*

KEY POINTS

- Involve people with different cultural perspectives in the process of selecting solutions.

- In order to select appropriate solutions you need to decide what criteria are important.

- Weighted pair ranking is a technique that helps you make considered comparisons between different types of solution.

- The Nominal Group Technique is a way of obtaining a democratic consensus about suitable solutions.

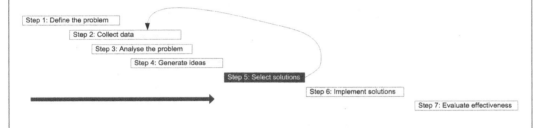

Figure 10.1 Step 5 in problem-solving

Criteria for Selecting Solutions

If you have carried out Step 4, generating solutions, carefully and thoroughly you will probably have ended up with quite a list of potential solutions, and these will cover a wide spectrum of activities. Some will be simple and others complex, some easy and inexpensive to implement and others more costly. You may therefore need to prioritize these solutions so that you can decide which ones to implement first and which to leave until later.

In order to prioritize your solutions you need some criteria against which to judge them. What these are will vary from situation to situation, but there are some core criteria that will be applicable in most cases:

- how the costs and benefits of the solution compare;
- how acceptable a solution is;
- how effective a solution is;
- how quickly the solution can be implemented.

COST–BENEFIT

The cost–benefit ratio of a solution is the comparison between how much it costs and what benefits it brings. Calculating cost–benefit ratios is a standard procedure followed when making investment decisions, but, while calculating costs is generally relatively easy, estimating the financial value of benefits can be very difficult, particularly when considering the 'soft' area of performance improvement. And, unfortunately, the process we have been following for developing a comprehensive suite of solutions to improve performance does not help very much, as it can be very difficult to separate out the influence of one particular solution from that of the others. In many cases, it is the application of the complete set of solutions that provides the power, as they may all be interlinked in some way.

However, one starting-point that we have for calculating the potential benefit of our set of solutions is to go back to Step 1 of the problem-solving process and review our answer to the question 'How serious is the problem?' When we first discussed this question in Chapter 2, when analysing the Mager and Pipe performance flowchart, we introduced the idea of the cost of doing nothing. Now, if we have done our job properly and analysed the problem thoroughly, so that our solutions taken in their entirety will solve the initial problem, hopefully this cost will be significantly reduced by what we propose. This, therefore, can be our proposed benefit.

But what about costs? These will depend on the solution proposed, and we can consider these under several different headings.

Cost of organizational changes

There will be two elements to these organizational costs:

- the cost of making any necessary changes, such as designing new processes, introducing new payment schemes and creating new infrastructure.
- the opportunity costs incurred while changes are being made, during which time performance may suffer.

Obviously, how significant these are will depend very much on the nature of the changes.

Cost of training

Training can be a very expensive solution. In order to develop an effective training solution there are several different activities that need to be paid for. Phillips and Stone (2002) suggest the following list of costs:

- *Conducting a needs assessment.* Although our problem analysis should provide a good start to the process of specifying the training requirements, it will still be necessary to do a further task analysis and decide on the appropriate blend of the training needed.
- *Design and development.* The training solutions identified will need to be designed and developed, and if e-learning solutions are suggested, the development costs can be high.
- *Acquisition.* It may be possible to buy a suitable training programme off-the-shelf, which will probably prove cheaper than commissioning a bespoke solution.
- *Delivery costs.* If the programme involves face-to-face training there will be costs of trainer's time (on a per trainee basis), the hire of facilities, travel and subsistence costs for trainees, opportunity costs incurred while trainees are away from their workplace and so on. E-learning solutions minimize these costs, but investments in infrastructure, such as Learning Management Systems,[1] may still be required.
- *Evaluation.* In an ideal world the effectiveness of the training programme should be measured, and this will incur costs.
- *Overheads.* Running the training programme will incur some extra administrative costs.

Cost of simplification and providing information

At last some good news. In most cases, the cheapest (and often the most immediately effective) solution is to simplify working processes in some way and give people information about their performance. Chapter 2 suggested some ways in which this can be achieved:

- Tasks can be broken down and made easier.
- People can be given performance aids to help them with what they do.
- People can be given some extra support with parts of the task that they find difficult.
- Information systems can be set up so that people have feedback about how well they are doing.
- Instruction manuals and guides defining required procedures can be produced.

These will clearly incur some costs, but they will typically be considerably less than the cost of making major organizational changes or designing and implementing training.

---

1   A Learning Management System (LMS) is software that is designed to deliver and monitor the use of training within an organization. It is often associated with e-learning, but can also be used for managing other types of training.

Sadly, solutions such as these lack the glamour of the other two types of solution, and so their effectiveness is often queried. Attitudes such as these reveal a lack of understanding of what really causes poor performance.

ACCEPTABILITY

From your, perhaps detached, perspective as a problem-solver, you may be able to see the eminent logic in the solutions that you have identified, but you must think about how the organization and the individuals involved may react to them.

From the perspective of the individuals involved you again need to think about their cultural values: are there elements to a solution that they would find uncomfortable or even unacceptable? From the perspective of the organization, are the solutions politically acceptable? Are they congruent with the organization's vision? Do they touch on any taboos that cannot be touched or even acknowledged?

If at all possible, you should seek opinions about the potential solutions from people with different cultural perspectives. Although there are techniques you can use to select solutions that try to make the process as rational as possible (and several of these are explained in this chapter), the evaluations you make are ultimately determined to a greater or lesser extent by your own cultural perspective. So look for extra opinions.

Making judgements about acceptability can be difficult, but one way is to try to think through the implications of a particular solution. A useful technique for this is a diagram such as that shown in Figure 10.2. This resembles a multiple cause diagram turned around, where instead of repeatedly asking the question 'Why does this happen?', we ask 'What would happen if?' over and over again. Diagrams of this type are sometimes known as concept fans, cause-and-effect or Ishikawa diagrams.

Figure 10.2 explores the possible implications of limiting border guard postings to married men only. Our first two thoughts are that this would probably raise the average age of the men on duty and that there would be more women around. Older men would probably be more expensive and might be less flexible about moving to take up a post at a border. However, they would probably also be more experienced and more capable, so they might not need as much supervision. With their extra maturity, they might also be less likely to harass women travellers.

More women being around would mean that extra facilities would be needed, in terms of living accommodation and the like, and there would be more children who would need school facilities or similar. However, because in this particular culture women tend to be commercially very active there would economic development at the border would probably increase as a result of increased trading

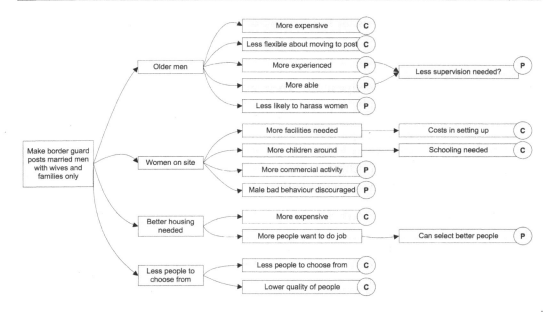

Figure 10.2 Implications of limiting border guard posts to married men only

activities. Having more women around might also discourage men from behaving badly.

Better housing would be needed and this would be expensive. However, this would make the posts more attractive so that more people would want to do the job and therefore you could select better people.

On the other hand, by saying that you will only accept married men, you are reducing the number of potential candidates and so you might find the quality of people is actually lower. And so on, repeating this for each potential solution identified.

Diagrams such as this are very good at stimulating creative thoughts and helping our minds to explore new possibilities and implications of potential solutions. The trouble is that we are now faced with a problem that has a number of pros and cons. How do we reach any kind of conclusions about the acceptability of the solution?

Jones (1995) suggests a technique he calls pros, cons and fixes. This is a five-step process:

1. Draw up a list of all the pros (shown in Figure 10.2 by 'P').
2. Draw up a list of all the cons (shown by 'C').
3. Consolidate the list of cons by identifying and pulling together duplications.
4. Neutralize as many cons as possible by seeing whether anything can be done to reduce or eliminate them.
5. Evaluate what you are left with.

Let us see how this works with the border guard problem.

Step 1: Draw up a list of the potential pros

The pros are:

- You have more experienced border guards.
- You have border guards who are more able.
- There is less need for strong supervision.
- Older men are less likely to harass women.
- There is more commercial activity in the area.
- Bad behaviour by men will be discouraged.
- You can select better people.

Step 2: Draw up a list of the cons

The cons are:

- Limiting border posts to married men will be more expensive.
- Married men will be less flexible about moving to a border post.
- Setting up the new arrangements will cost money.
- Schooling will be needed for the extra children.
- The housing will be more expensive.
- There will be fewer people to choose from.
- The quality of person you can find will be lower.

Step 3: Consolidate the list of cons

To consolidate the list of cons, look to see if there are any duplicates (which there usually are, because we generally find it much easier to think of cons than pros):

- Limiting border posts to married men will be more expensive.
- Married men will be less flexible about moving to a border post.
- ~~Setting up the new arrangements will cost money~~. (Extra costs already considered)
- Schooling will be needed for the extra children.
- ~~The housing will be more expensive~~. (Extra costs already considered)
- There will be fewer people to choose from.
- The quality of person you can find will be lower.

Step 4: Neutralize as many cons as possible

You now look at the remaining cons and see if there is anything you can do to either reduce their significance or eliminate them:

- Limiting border posts to married men will be more expensive. (Inevitable.)
- Married men will be less flexible about moving to a border post. (Fix: offer incentives to move.)
- Schooling will be needed for the extra children. (Fix: This will have future benefits.)

- There will be fewer people to choose from. (Fix: make border guard posts available to either married men or women (married or single).)
- The quality of person you can find will be lower. (Fix: make border guard posts available to either married men or women (married or single).)

So, by seeing what we can do to eliminate or neutralize the cons we can see that the situation is not as bad as we thought. It has also encouraged us to think of another solution. We had in fact identified this as a potential solution before, but, because it has now emerged from this analysis, we can see that the two solutions could work well together.

You could repeat this analysis using the concept fan and pros–cons–fixes techniques for each solution. You would be then in a much better position to compare the acceptability of all the potential solutions.

Force field analysis is another technique which may help here. This was discussed in more detail in Chapter 9, where we saw how it could be used as a way of identifying potential solutions. However, if you bear in mind that it provides a useful way of looking at how the forces driving and restraining change can interact, you should be able to see how you can use it to come up with some judgements about what effects particular solutions might have.

EFFECTIVENESS

Obviously all the solutions you have identified will be effective in some way, but clearly some will be more effective than others and may target different areas of the performance problem. You should give some thought to this, as it will help you with your prioritization.

You could use the concept fan and the five-step pros, cons and fixes technique explained earlier to evaluate solutions from an effectiveness perspective as well.

SPEED OF
IMPLEMENTATION

Different solutions will take varying amounts of time to implement. Here, again, solutions designed to simplify or provide information on performance can often be the quickest to implement, adding to their advantages.

Conversely, implementing training solutions and organizational changes can take a considerable length of time to happen.

Methods for Selecting Solutions

Having considered some of the criteria that you need to take into consideration when selecting potential solutions, you now need to start the potentially difficult task of making decisions. There are two ways you can do this:

- Select the ones that your instincts tell you will be the most effective and provide quick results.
- Systematically compare and evaluate the solutions so that you end up with a rational listing of what should be done.

The choice is yours, but remember that you *do* have the choice. As with finding solutions to problems in the first place, this part of the process is often driven more by emotion than reason, and so even if you want to make an emotional decision, you may find it useful to try to confirm it by using one of these more systematic methods. If you do choose on the basis of your instincts, beware of confirmation bias – that having made your initial choice, you will then look for information that supports this choice and interpret it in such a way that it justifies the selection. Remember this line from Kahlil Gibran's *The Prophet*: 'Therefore let your soul exalt your reason to the height of passion that it may sing.'

We shall look at two specific methods here:

1. weighted pair ranking, which simplifies the comparison process by making you look at only two options at a time, and is a technique you can use on your own.
2. the Nominal Group Technique, which is a method you can combine with some form of brainstorming session and introduces a measure of democratic consensus into the decision-making process.

Weighted Pair Ranking

Weighted pair ranking is an effective way of sorting a list of possible solutions using a structured and rational approach. It simplifies the problem of comparing a large number of items by just making you compare two things at a time and, at each point, thinking about why you are making that particular decision.

To illustrate the principle of how it works, we can apply it to the problems of deciding what my favourite fruit is. Suppose I am presented with a banana, an apple, an orange, a pear and a plum. How might I sort these into an order of preference?

First, prepare a simple table listing the fruits (Table 10.1) with the other headings as shown.

Also prepare a chart to help remember which comparisons we have made and what our reasons were (Table 10.2).

Now ask the first pair-ranking question: 'Which do I prefer, an apple or a banana?' The answer is a banana, but why? Well, I like the soft sweetness. This question is important to ask, as otherwise there is a danger that we will make an irrational, emotion-based decision or make one without really thinking about it. That means that the banana has won one round, so we give it a score of 1 (Table 10.3).

Table 10.1   Scorecard for ranking fruit

Fruit	Score	Total	Ranking
Apple			
Banana			
Orange			
Pear			
Plum			

Table 10.2   Justifications for ranking fruit

	Apple	Banana	Orange	Pear	Plum
Apple	–	Banana: soft sweetness	Orange: juiciness	Apple: ripeness easier	
Banana		–			
Orange			–		
Pear				–	
Plum					–

Table 10.3   Ranking fruit scores so far

Fruit	Score	Total	Ranking
Apple	1		
Banana	1		
Orange	1		
Pear			
Plum			

Next we compare an apple with an orange. I prefer the orange's juiciness, so the orange scores 1. Apple or pear? The apple has it, as it always seems difficult to catch a pear when it is not rock hard or squishy and over-ripe. Apples get off the mark. The situation so far is summarized in Table 10.3.

We carry on with these paired comparisons, and each time a fruit wins a comparison we give it a score of 1 in the table. When we have made all the comparisons we end up with Tables 10.4 and 10.5.

Table 10.4 Completed Justifications for ranking fruit

	Apple	Banana	Orange	Pear	Plum
Apple	–	Banana: soft sweetness	Orange: juiciness	Apple: ripeness easier	Apple: bigger
Banana		–	Banana: sweeter, more energy	Banana: sweeter, more energy	Banana: more to eat
Orange			–	Orange: juicier	Orange: sweeter
Pear				–	Plum: juicier
Plum					–

Table 10.5 Completed scorecard for ranking fruit

Fruit	Score	Total	Ranking
Apple	11	2	3rd
Banana	1111	4	1st
Orange	111	3	2nd
Pear		0	5th
Plum	1	1	4th

There we have it: my ranking for liking these fruits is banana first, followed by orange, apple, plum and pear in that order.

Now that might look rather trivial, and it is. I only have five items and the decisions are quite simple. However, as a methodology it is quite rigorous. I have avoided trying to make comparisons of more than two things at a time and have kept it as rational as possible. We can therefore use this, in theory, to draw up a ranking list of any number of items. But there is one problem. Comparing fruit is simple, but what about ranking items where each item has advantages and disadvantages?

Well, we can adapt the method to take into account different aspects of the set of items. To show how this works, let us take a slightly more complicated issue: where to go on holiday. My choice is between a cycling and camping tour in my home country, Britain; renting an apartment in Tenerife; scuba diving in Honduras; doing an overland trek through the desert of the northern Sudan; or driving and camping around France. These are all very different, and each has its own set of advantages and weaknesses. What I need to do next is to work out what those criteria are and what their relative importance is. After some reflection, I come up with the following (Table 10.6)

Table 10.6   Relative importance of criteria for choosing a holiday

Criteria	Weighting (per cent)
Cost	30
Environmental friendliness	15
Excitement	25
Sunshine	30

This is going to be a rather more complex procedure, so I shall open up a spreadsheet in order to calculate the ranking of the holidays. Using a spreadsheet has another advantage in that I can later play around with the weightings, so I can see what effect the relative importance of each has. If I lose my job, cost becomes more important, whereas if I win a lot of money on the lottery it ceases to become such an issue.

We simply repeat the paired comparisons as we did for the fruits, but do it for each criterion in turn. So let us first compare each one from a cost perspective (Table 10.7).

Table 10.7   Comparing costs for different holidays

Holiday A	Holiday B	Winner	Reason
Cycling and camping tour in Britain	Renting an apartment in Tenerife	Britain	Obvious
Cycling and camping tour in Britain	Scuba diving in Honduras	Britain	Obvious
Cycling and camping tour in Britain	Trekking through Sudan	Britain	Obvious
Cycling and camping tour in Britain	Driving and camping in France	Britain	Obvious
Renting an apartment in Tenerife	Scuba diving in Honduras	Tenerife	Closer, mass tourist destination
Renting an apartment in Tenerife	Trekking through Sudan	Tenerife	Air fares cheaper
Renting an apartment in Tenerife	Driving and camping in France	France	No air fares, car-sharing
Scuba diving in Honduras	Trekking through Sudan	Sudan	Daily costs in Sudan lower
Scuba diving in Honduras	Driving and camping in France	France	No air fares, daily costs lower
Trekking through Sudan	Driving and camping in France	France	No air fares

When we enter these results into our spreadsheet we get Figure 10.3.

We then repeat this for all of the other criteria. When we have done this, we find that we have the following results (Figure 10.4).

So we can see that, based on the criteria and weightings we have chosen, our best choice for the holiday is trekking in the northern Sudan. How does that feel emotionally, and does it seem like a reasonable result? Given that I gave considerable weight to excitement and sunshine, the idea of bouncing in a bus across the Sahara Desert does sound about right.

When you take pair ranking to this level of sophistication, you can begin to see how useful it is. We have taken five very different holidays and analysed them from different perspectives in order to end up with a quantifiable ranking.

Let us apply this to evaluating solutions to the border guard problem. In Chapter 9 we came up with a considerable number of ideas about how we could deal with this situation. For simplicity we can look at six of these ideas here:

1. standard operating procedures for dealing with travellers;
2. distributing posters about the United Nations Declaration of Human Rights;
3. financial bonuses to border posts where there are no reports of mistreatment;
4. removing all single, unmarried men from border-post positions;
5. running training sessions on how to deal with female travellers;
6. inviting journalists to visit border posts and write stories about what is happening.

Next, we need to decide on our criteria for evaluating these solutions. There are many different criteria that you could consider, but, in this example, we shall use the ones discussed earlier:

- cost–benefit ratio (the likely benefits from the solution must be greater than the costs of implementing it);
- likely effectiveness (the solution must be effective in reducing the amount of mistreatment);
- acceptability (the solution needs to be acceptable to the border guards so that it has a chance of changing their behaviour);
- speed of implementation (it is important that some change is seen as quickly as possible).

Now, we need to decide on some weighting to apply to each of these four criteria. One way of doing this would be just to consider what seems right, as we did in the case of the holiday planning example. However, if we are going to keep the selection process as rational as possible, we should try to do this in a more organized way,

Holiday decisions

Criteria weightings	
Cost	0.3
Environmental friendliness	0.15
Excitement	0.25
Sunshine	0.3

	Criteria													Total weighted score	Ranking
	Cost			Environmental friendliness			Excitement			Sunshine					
Holiday option	Score	Total	Weighted score	Score	Total	Weighted score	Score	Total	Weighted score	Score	Total	Weighted score			
Cycling and camping tour in my home country, Britain	1111	4	1.2			0			0			0		1.2	
Renting an apartment in Tenerife	11	2	0.6			0			0			0		0.6	
Scuba diving in Honduras		0	0			0			0			0		0	
Doing an overland trek through the desert of the northern Sudan	1	1	0.3			0			0			0		0.3	
Driving and camping around France	111	3	0.9			0			0			0		0.9	

Figure 10.3 Spreadsheet comparing scores for cost criteria

Holiday decisions

Criteria weightings	
Cost	0.3
Environmental friendliness	0.15
Excitement	0.25
Sunshine	0.3

Holiday option	Criteria													Total weighted score	Ranking
	Cost			Environmental friendliness			Excitement			Sunshine					
	Score	Total	Weighted score	Score	Total	Weighted score	Score	Total	Weighted score	Score	Total	Weighted score			
Cycling and camping tour in my home country, Britain	1111	4	1.2	1111	4	0.6	1	1	0.25		0	0		2.05	3
Renting an apartment in Tenerife	11	2	0.6	11	2	0.3		0	0	111	3	0.9		1.8	4
Scuba diving in Honduras		0	0		0	0	111	3	0.75	11	2	0.6		1.35	5
Doing an overland trek through the desert of the northern Sudan	1	1	0.3	1	1	0.15	1111	4	1	1111	4	1.2		2.65	1
Driving and camping around France	111	3	0.9	111	3	0.45	11	2	0.5	1	1	0.3		2.15	2

Figure 10.4 Completed spreadsheet comparing all criteria

and one method for doing this is a simple pair ranking comparison of the four criteria.

So, which is more important, cost–benefit ratio or effectiveness? In reality, you would, at this stage, have to give some thought to the available budget, but, for the sake of the example, let us say that effectiveness is more important. Effectiveness therefore scores one point. We are now familiar with this method, so let us assume that we work through each of the comparisons and end up with the following ranking:

1. Effectiveness.
2. Cost–benefit ratio.
3. Acceptability.
4. Speed of implementation.

Note that, in doing this, we might feel that some criteria are of equal importance: if this happens, it is acceptable to give each criterion in the pair half a point.

On the basis of this ranking, the weighting given to each is:

Effectiveness 40%
Cost–benefit ratio 30%
Acceptability 20%
Speed of implementation 10%

We now work through the paired comparisons each solution, considering each of the different criteria in turn. Note that cross-cultural issues become particularly important when considering the Acceptability criterion in particular. Depending on the decisions we make in each question, this could give us the final result as shown in Figure 10.5.

We can see from Figure 10.5 that, according to the results of our paired comparisons and the weightings applied, the best solution is to offer financial bonuses to border posts where there are no reports of mistreatment. Producing standard operating procedures and inviting journalists are joint second, and the least attractive solution is training – which interestingly, was the solution that had been initially proposed for this particular problem.

At this stage it is interesting to reflect on the process and the outcome. One of the things that the process brings out is your depth of understanding as an analyst of the situation, because, to get to this position, you have to consider some difficult questions. For example:

- Do you know if the border guards want to be there? Perhaps they like being there because of the opportunity for corruption, in which case they would prefer solutions that maintain the status quo. On the other hand, if they generally dislike the posting, they would prefer a solution that moves them away.

Solving the border guard problem

Criteria weightings

Criteria	Weighting
Effectiveness	0.4
Cost-benefit ratio	0.3
Acceptability	0.2
Speed of implementation	0.1

Solution	Criteria												Total weighted score	Ranking
	Effectiveness			Cost-benefit ratio			Acceptability			Speed of implementation				
	Score	Total	Weighted score	Score	Total	Weighted score	Score	Total	Weighted score	Score	Total	Weighted score		
Standard operating procedures for dealing with travellers.	111	3	1.2	111	3	0.9	111	3	0.6	111	3	0.3	3.0	2=
Distributing posters about the United Nations Declaration of Human Rights.		0	0	1111	4	1.2	111	3	0.6	1111	4	0.4	2.2	4
Financial bonuses to border posts where there are no reports of mistreatment.	11111	5	2	1	1	0.3	111111	6	1.2	1	1	0.1	3.6	1
Removing all single unmarried men from border post positions.	1111	4	1.6	1	1	0.3		0	0		0	0	1.9	5
Running training sessions on how to deal with female travellers.	1	1	0.4	1	1	0.3	11	2	0.4	11	2	0.2	1.3	6
Inviting journalists to visit border posts and write stories about what is happening.	11	2	0.8	11111	5	1.5	1	1	0.2	11111	5	0.5	3.0	2=

Figure 10.5 Spreadsheet comparison for border guard solutions

- How does acceptability to the border guards compare to acceptability to the government?
- Just what would the organizational issues be in limiting border guard postings to married men or women only?
- Are the criteria you have selected valid? Do they need to be refined in any way? Do you need to introduce additional criteria?
- How morally acceptable does it feel to be dealing with this problem by making financial payments? What does that say about your initial criteria?
- How well do you understand the cross-cultural issues? How clear are your cultural glasses regarding the different actors in the problem?

So you can see that, even at this point, you may need to go back and collect more information and analyse the situation a little more carefully. Pair ranking therefore provides a very powerful tool for checking your understanding of what is happening.

Second, how does the outcome compare with what your initial instincts told you would be the best plans of action? If the final ranking just does not seem right, take a closer look at the weightings you have given. One of the beauties of using a spreadsheet to do this is that you can analyse the sensitivity of the final result and see what happens if you adjust weightings slightly.

The Nominal Group Technique

The Nominal Group Technique is a method originally developed by Delbecq and Van de Ven (1971) that brings together the power of brainstorming with the fairness of a proportional voting system. It is worth considering as a method of evaluating different solutions if you have a problem-solving team available to you, as it enables even quite large groups to discuss an issue and then rank the suitability of particular solutions. It is particularly useful where:

- relationships within the group make simple voting potentially biased because of such factors as evaluation apprehension.
- you have a relatively small number of solutions.
- levels of knowledge and experience in the group are very different.

Here is how you would run a Nominal Group Technique session.

ASK THE GROUP
TO GENERATE
THEIR IDEAS
SILENTLY

If you have the group in a room with you, make sure that they all have a piece of paper on which they can write their ideas. Alternatively, if you can plan in advance, you can tell people before the event what you want them to do so that they can prepare a list of potential solutions quietly and on their own. In this respect, this part of the process resembles the pre-brainstorm approach, described in Chapter 8.

COLLECT EACH PERSON'S LIST OF IDEAS

When everyone has had a chance to produce a list of ideas, collect them in. There are several different ways in which you can do this, depending on the nature of the group and how you have organized the idea-generating stage.

Here are some ideas:

- Ask each person to read out one of their ideas and write it up on a flipchart, then move to the next person, and so on, going round and round until everyone has read out all of their ideas. This works well if people are comfortable with each other and will not withhold their ideas out of shyness or diffidence. It also makes it possible for people to come up with additional ideas as you are go round the circle.

Or:

- Collect each person's list and write it up on the flipchart. This eliminates the possibility of people deciding to withhold their ideas because they feel that they do not fit in with what other people are suggesting, but can take a lot of time. This approach is most feasible if people have generated their list before the meeting, in which case you collect them and write the ideas up before the meeting starts.

Or:

- Provide people with Post-it® pads and asked them to write one idea on each note. You can then collect them in and quickly stick them up on the flipchart. This makes the next stage of sorting ideas about easier.

While you are doing this, do not discuss, evaluate or judge the ideas in any way.

SORT THE IDEAS

Working with the group, reorganize all the ideas into a manageable list. Combine any duplicates, but make sure that the people involved are happy with the standardized wording for the solution.

Make sure that each idea in your final list is expressed clearly, so that everyone knows exactly what it means.

FACILITATE A DISCUSSION ABOUT THE IDEAS

Now allow some time for the group to discuss the ideas in the list. They might want to seek some clarification or even to refine some of the ideas in some way. This means that you may need to add some items to the list, or reword some. People may also want to discuss the advantages and disadvantages of individual ideas.

However, to avoid the danger that more vocal members of the group or a small clique might try to impose their own thinking on what is happening, you should have a rule that changes can only be made if every member of the group agrees, and that, if even just one person disagrees with a proposed change, the item must stay as it is.

IDENTIFY EACH
ITEM ON THE LIST

When you have your final list, give each one a letter of the alphabet to identify it.

ASK PEOPLE TO
VOTE

Next, make sure that everyone has a piece of paper they can write on. Ask them to select their top five solutions and put them in order, writing down the letter representing their best solution and giving it five points, then writing down the letter for their second-best solution and giving it four points and so on until all five solutions have been ranked.

COLLECT THE
VOTE IN

You should now collect each person's voting paper. It is best to do this anonymously to minimize the chances of people changing their vote when they hear what other people are saying.

Take each paper and write the score given for each solution next to the solution written on the flipchart. When you have done this for each voting paper, add up the scores for each individual solution and work out the final ranking.

This may sound complicated, but in practice the Nominal Group Technique is a simple, enjoyable and effective way of using a group to arrive at a considered decision. Following the guidelines described above minimizes the risk that powerful individuals or cliques will influence the final outcome.

The Reliable Constructions Case Study: Step 5

Philippa had developed three lists of solutions for the different problem areas that she had identified. She looked at the sheet of paper on which she had written down the solutions that she thought would be effective in helping solve the problems with project planning:

1. a step-by-step guide and checklist to help with planning.
2. a booklet explaining key tasks carried out using project planning software.
3. sending staff on a project management and planning training course.
4. running a one-to-one session with the operations manager to discuss managerial issues.
5. setting up some team-building activities to develop a shared culture.

She felt that getting people together to run some sort of brainstorming or Nominal Group Technique session was not going to be possible, so she decided to use the weighted pair ranking method instead.

The first thing to do was to decide what her criteria would be. She knew that Nulty was getting impatient and wanted to see some results from her analysis, so getting things moving quickly was a priority. Cost was an issue, but she also wanted things to be effective, as implementing something that proved ineffectual would reflect badly on her abilities. And, of course, it had to be acceptable. She did a simple pair ranking exercise to confirm this and ended up deciding that the weighting for her solution evaluation would be:

Speed of implementation 0.4
Cost–benefit 0.25
Effectiveness 0.25
Acceptability 0.1

Philippa started the process of comparing the solutions. She knew that, although it seemed rather laborious, it would be worth doing. The first criterion to consider was the speed of implementation. The checklist would be easier and quicker to produce than the project planning booklet, and it would certainly be quicker than finding some suitable project management training for the planning assistants However, she knew that she could very quickly set up one-to-one sessions with Michael and Stephanie to discuss their managerial issues. But the checklist also scored highly when compared to the team-building activities solution. That meant that the step-by-step guide and checklist had scored three points and the one-to-one sessions one point for speed of implementation. She carried on and then entered the results in a spreadsheet. When considering the acceptability, she took great care to think about the cross-cultural issues involved, such as power distance, time orientation and linear/multi-active. Figure 10.6 shows the result.

As she had suspected, the one-to-one sessions came out as the best solution, followed by the step-by-step guide and checklist. The team-building solution that she thought was necessary in order to develop a shared culture came out last in the list, but this did not really surprise her, as she recognized that this was more of a longer-term strategy.

The exercise had also helped her think about some of the issues surrounding these solutions. For example, she realized that she would need to sell the benefits of the team-building to everyone involved and that the project management training would have to be carefully tailored to their needs if it were to justify its ranking.

The next area she needed to consider was the list of solutions she had developed for improving communications. That was a

Project planning solutions

Criteria weightings

Effectiveness	0.25
Cost-benefit ratio	0.25
Acceptability	0.1
Speed of implementation	0.4

Solution	Criteria												Total weighted score	Ranking
	Effectiveness			Cost-benefit ratio			Acceptability			Speed of implemenation				
	Score	Total	Weighted score	Score	Total	Weighted score	Score	Total	Weighted score	Score	Total	Weighted score		
Checklist	11	2	0.5	111	3	0.75	111	3	0.3	111	3	1.2	2.8	2
Key project planning tasks booklet		0	0	11	2	0.5	11	2	0.2	11	2	0.8	1.5	4
Project management training	11111	5	1.25	1	1	0.25	1111	4	0.4	0	0	0	1.9	3
One-to-one sessions	11	2	0.5	1111	4	1	1	1	0.1	1111	4	1.6	3.2	1
Teambuilding activities	1	1	0.25	0	0	0	1	0	0	1	1	0.4	0.7	5

Figure 10.6 Evaluating project planning solutions

much longer list, and the weighted pair ranking process would take quite some time. But this morning's session had been useful. She now had a list of solutions that she could take to Nulty that not only tackled the problem of poor project planning, but could also be implemented quickly and relatively cheaply.

She felt that she deserved a cup of coffee.

Step 5: Summary

In this chapter we have looked at what you need to do in order to evaluate and select solutions to a problem. To summarize:

- Decide what criteria you need to evaluate your solutions against.
- Decide what method you are going to use to evaluate your solutions.
- Use weighted pair ranking as a systematic way of comparing different solutions.
- Use the Nominal Group Technique with a problem-solving group to help evaluate solutions.

11 *Step 6: Implement Solutions*

KEY POINTS

- Organizational changes must take into account what the organizational culture is.
- Potential Problem Analysis is a technique that will help you think about what might go wrong.
- Training solutions need to take cultural preferences into consideration in both their design and delivery.

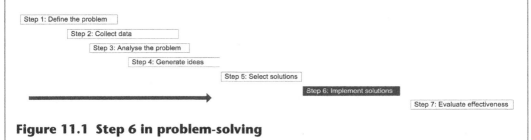

Figure 11.1 Step 6 in problem-solving

Cultural Aspects to Implementation

In Step 6 you need to put into place the solution or solutions that you have identified as being most appropriate for solving your performance problem. By definition, implementing a solution implies making a change, so a key part of this step is in having some understanding about how to facilitate change.

The implementation process needs to pay careful attention to cultural issues within the workplace. Here are some potential issues to consider, presented under the relevant cultural indicators.

Individualism and collectivism:

- How will these solutions affect individuals or in-groups? The solutions and their implementation need to take these preferences into consideration.

- If there is a preference for collectivism, how can the implementation harness the power of people working together?

Power distance:

- In low power distance cultures, solutions that are perceived to be imposed from the top down may be rejected, especially if there has been no participation in the problem-solving and decision-making process.
- In high power distance cultures, the top-down method may be preferred.

Uncertainty avoidance:

- Very few cultures like change, but in cultures that have high uncertainty avoidance, any change is likely to provoke greater levels of anxiety. This may dictate the pace at which changes can be introduced and will certainly mean that there will need to be clear communication about what is going to happen.

Long-term orientation:

- If changes being introduced are intended to be effective over a different timeframe to that which people expect, this needs to be explained. So, for example, if the workforce has a short-term orientation, changes that will only bring benefits in the longer term may need to be justified more clearly.

Change management is a management subject in its own right, and its complexities are beyond the scope of this book. However, a key issue is to be aware of the norms that an organizational works to, because these may have implications for the ease of implementing a solution and its likely success.

We shall consider here two main types of implementation:

1. issues surrounding the implementation of some kind of organizational change.
2. what to do to ensure that training solutions are implemented successfully.

Implementing Organizational Changes

Hicks (1991) suggests that there are four principal types of organizational change:

1. *Structural.* We change how departments or divisions are structured, change lines of command, make physical changes or move things around.
2. *Procedural.* We change the way things are done, by altering processes, procedures or how information moves around.
3. *Policy.* We make changes to policies, goals or visions.
4. *Attitudinal.* We change the way people feel about some aspect of their work or their place within the organization.

Within each of these categories, the changes might be small or large, but, however big or small they are, we can expect resistance.

Any major changes we are planning to make in any of these areas may have an impact on the organizational culture. Our emphasis in this book has been on the cultures espoused by individuals, and we defined this as the pattern of behaviour shown by a particular group. Organizations are groups, and they have their own pattern of behaviour. There are various ways in which organizational behaviour is manifested, such as:

- the pride displayed by the organization in what it is and does,
- whether it focuses on excellent or adequate performance,
- how clear its goals are,
- its philosophy on leadership and supervision,
- the relative emphasis placed on collaboration and teamwork as opposed to individualism,
- the openness or secrecy of its communications,
- whether it encourages supportive and trusting or competitive relationships,
- its approach to training and development,
- the relative importance placed on group responsibility and autonomy,
- whether the management style encourages participation and involvement or is autocratic,
- how tolerant the organization is of dissent and differences of opinion,
- whether it welcomes change and innovation or prefers stability and conservatism,
- what approach it takes to learning from problems and difficulties,
- its attitude to relationships with its customers,
- the approach it takes to profitability and cost effectiveness (Hicks, 1991).

You can see how a number of these aspects of organizational culture mirror dimensions of national culture that we have focused on in this book. Therefore, you need to consider the extent to which any solutions you need to implement will fit in with these organizational norms. If you anticipate any problems, you may need to think again about which solutions to implement or to devise a strategy that will help you make the necessary changes.

MAKING
CHANGES AT
THE WORKPLACE
LEVEL

The types of change that you will most likely be interested in implementing, given the focus of this book, will be at relatively local levels, perhaps even at an individual workplace. Even so, you will still encounter some resistance. This will come in two forms, both arising from fear:

- *cognitive fear* – where someone feels that they do not have the necessary knowledge or skill to be able to make the change required.
- *emotional fear* – a simple fear of the unknown and what it might bring.

Cognitive fear is relatively easy to deal with. Once you have carried out your analysis you should have a fairly good idea about the different abilities of people in the workplace and, in all probability, your suite of solutions will include something that is designed to give people the knowledge or skill that they are going to need. But you must still make sure that people know that this will be provided in order to help dispel this cognitive fear.

Emotional fear is harder to deal with, as it is quite possible that people will be reluctant to admit to experiencing it. This reluctance may be due to an organizational culture that makes it difficult to admit any weakness or to a national culture where, for example, admitting fear may be thought to cause a loss of face for that particular group.

Planning for Implementing Changes

So far in our discussion of what we need to do to implement our solutions, we have focused largely on resistance to change. That is certainly a key factor to consider, but we must not lose sight of the fact that there will also be simple organizational problems that we need to take into consideration: for example, getting materials printed, arranging meetings and the like.

So, when faced with the challenge of implementing your solutions, what can you do? Well, you can spend a little time thinking about what might go wrong. Kepner and Tregoe (1981) describe a formal process for doing this, which they call Potential Problem Analysis. Their method has four stages, but, as with the problem-solving approach described in this book, it is not necessary to follow them in a strict order.

| STAGE 1: IDENTIFY AREAS WHERE THINGS MAY GO WRONG | Think about the steps you need to take in order to implement your solutions, perhaps by drawing up a plan. Then look at these steps and identify those points at which things are most likely to go wrong. For example, look for points where: |

- something will be done for the first time in the business;
- more than one person will be needed in order to make something happen;
- deadlines are tight;
- things must be coordinated from a distance.

| STAGE 2: IDENTIFY WHAT SPECIFIC THINGS MIGHT GO WRONG | For each of these points think about what could go wrong and draw up a list. For example, if something is going to happen for the first time, you might be afraid of: |

- someone doing it incorrectly;
- it not being done at all;
- it taking longer than expected;
- an unexpected problem arising.

And so on.

| STAGE 3: DECIDE WHAT THE LIKELY CAUSES OF THESE PROBLEMS WOULD BE | Having identified what might go wrong, think about what might cause this to happen. For example: |

- someone doing it incorrectly (they do not have the correct information or training);
- it not being done at all (they forget to do it, accidentally or deliberately);
- it taking longer than expected (poor estimating);
- an unexpected problem arising (lack of planning or preparation).

For each of these decide what you can do to prevent it happening – for example, providing information, setting up reminders, practising beforehand and son on.

| STAGE 4: IDENTIFY CONTINGENCY PLANS | Working on the assumption that if anything can go wrong, it will and that, however well you plan ahead, the unexpected can be expected, develop contingency plans that you can draw on if necessary. |

Implementing Training Successfully

If your analysis has led you to the conclusion that training is necessary, then be aware that, if you are to provide effective training, you have another period of analysis ahead of you. Learning design is a major subject in its own right, so we will not attempt to cover it here, but we will look briefly at aspects of the training design process that relate to cultural diversity.

There are various ways of approaching the learning design process to take cultural diversity into consideration (Henderson, 1996):

- The *perspectives* approach – the overall approach used within the training reflects the dominant culture, but minority cultural perspectives are presented. This can be criticized as being tokenistic.
- The *inverted curriculum* approach – the learning design is based on the needs of minority cultures, but excludes perspectives of the dominant culture. This might be described as creating a training ghetto.
- The *culturally unidimensional* approach – a 'one size fits all' approach is followed, denying cultural diversity and providing everyone with the same learning experience.
- The *multiple cultural* model – the materials are designed to be used flexibly, taking into account preferred ways of learning and teaching, and so ensuring equal outcomes for all learners.

In Henderson's terms, the ideal way to develop training programmes is to follow the multiple cultural model. To do this, the training needs analysis target group description needs to have a clear definition of the varied cultural preferences, and the design of the training materials needs to support both behaviourist and constructivist pedagogies. McLoughlin (1999) suggests a number of questions that the learning designer needs to ask:

- What kind of learning environment are the learners most familiar with?
- What is the learners' attitude to time?
- How do the learners perceive the trainer's role?
- What kinds of motivation are appropriate to the learners?
- Is the balance of control over the learning process appropriate to learners' expectations?
- What cognitive styles do the learners have?

WHAT KIND OF LEARNING ENVIRONMENT ARE THE LEARNERS MOST FAMILIAR WITH?

Most people will be familiar with the classroom setting, although even this may not be the case for unskilled workers in low-income countries.

E-learning is more of an unknown. In economically developed countries it is growing in importance and, in many applications, is regarded as potentially more effective and efficient than face-to-face training. However, it is not uniformly accepted in these countries: it appeals more to individualist cultures, as it often removes, or at least reduces, the social contact that can be valued as part of the learning process; also, in organizations with clear hierarchies and separations of roles, managers may have less experience of using computers, being used to delegating computer-based activities, such as e-mailing or correspondence, to secretaries.

The use of e-learning may also discriminate against people from economically disadvantaged backgrounds, who may have had less experience of using computers.

WHAT IS THE LEARNERS' ATTITUDE TO TIME?	Trainers who come from linear-active cultures, which see time as a commodity, can often find running training events where participants do not share this perspective as frustrating. Courses start late, breaks extend past the stated 15-minute length and the lunch interval may stretch into the afternoon. In many cultures, a timetable is not a rigid prescription that must be followed – more a general statement of intent that helps people plan how to integrate the different aspects of their lives during that particular day.
HOW DO THE LEARNERS PERCEIVE THE TRAINER'S ROLE?	There is a trend in individualist cultures, with their general dislike of rigid hierarchies, for trainers to act less as 'instructors' and to be more facilitative in style. This fits in well with a preference for a more consensual approach to management. However, this is not a popular approach in high power distance cultures. Here, the trainer needs to show their authority and experience, and will, for example, open a workshop by stating their academic qualifications and work experience in order to reassure the participants that they are qualified and definitely in charge (Lim and DeVries, 2003). Such cultures also prefer training to be achieved by a delivery of information rather than through a more constructivist approach, and expect less interaction with the trainer (Mercer Bing et al., 2000).
WHAT KINDS OF MOTIVATION ARE APPROPRIATE TO THE LEARNERS?	In individualist and work success cultures, people are motivated by the perception that training will help them perform better, improve their chances of promotion or earn more money, whereas in collectivist cultures people are more interested in activities that strengthen relationships or benefit their in-group in some way.

Triandis quotes research by Earley suggesting that self-focused learning methods are effective in individualist cultures, but less so in collectivist cultures, and that, in those situations, group-focused training is more effective at improving performance (Earley, 1994, reported in Triandis, 1995).

The pace at which a training programme starts will need to be tailored to the nature of the participants. Career success and individualist people with their task-orientation will be keen to make the most of the time available and move quickly on to learning new skills and knowledge that they can make use of, whereas people oriented towards quality of life or a with a collectivist background will be keen to spend time getting to know other participants.

Activities within a training programme also need to take these cultural differences into consideration. Individualists generally enjoy competition, so activities that set individuals or groups into competition with others or against a clock or other measurement will be motivating. Collectivists, on the other hand, would rather work on collaborative or cooperative group tasks. For this reason, brainstorming – a popular activity in North American and British training – can be unpopular with such people. Identifying individuals who have made a good contribution will also encourage people. However, this would be counterproductive with people from a collectivist background. Singling them out as in some way 'better' than other participants would be embarrassing.

IS THE BALANCE OF CONTROL OVER THE LEARNING PROCESS APPROPRIATE TO LEARNERS' EXPECTATIONS?

Trainers from individualist cultures can find delivering training to people with a collectivist outlook somewhat unnerving due to the lack of questions and other overt feedback. In fact, these participants are simply showing their respect for the trainer: asking questions would imply that the trainer has not explained the subject well enough, and would therefore cause them to lose face.

In high power distance cultures the trainer is expected to push the learning process along in an authoritative style, and not to allow participants to dictate the process. The trainer should also think carefully about how to ask questions and where they should be directed: if there is a hierarchy within the room, subordinates will feel very uncomfortable if they are expected to provide answers in front of more senior members of staff.

Cultures with an aversion to uncertainty will expect there to be a clearly defined timetable or structure for the training programme. They will also be looking for clearly presented course materials for reference and for the trainer to follow a more directive style.

WHAT COGNITIVE STYLES DO THE LEARNERS HAVE?

Participants from collectivist backgrounds may feel uncomfortable acting as individuals to answer questions or complete activities and will prefer working together in small group activities that will allow them to discuss questions and agree answers consensually.

Cultural Preferences and E-learning

The use of e-learning presents a specific set of challenges. Most e-learning materials rely quite heavily on reading and may present difficulties in cultures where people are less accustomed to this activity. This can be complicated further if the language used on-screen is not the person's first language. Here, voice-overs supporting on-screen text can be very useful. Screen ergonomics need to take cultural preferences into consideration. For example, as discussed in Chapter 2, different cultures attach very different meanings to particular colours; in Muslim countries graphics that show men and women interacting may be completely unacceptable; and in India a photograph showing a woman wearing a red dress may confuse people, because this would indicate that she is a bride or taking part in some special occasion (Daftuar, 1975). The often unsupported nature of e-learning means that everything presented on-screen must be completely clear and unambiguous to the learner, so learning designers must take great care to avoid using analogies and metaphors that might be incomprehensible to someone from another culture (Timm, 1999).

The Reliable Constructions Case Study: Step 6

Philippa looked at the lists of solutions that she had developed and started to think about implementation issues. To solve the problems with project planning she had come up with:

- Running one-to-one sessions with the operations manager to discuss his managerial style. This was going to need an attitudinal change and could be potentially challenging.
- Developing a step-by-step guide and checklist to help with the planning process. This was procedural and probably relatively straightforward, but she realized that she would need to think about the planning assistants' cultural preferences to make sure it worked properly for them. For example, their preference for uncertainty avoidance would affect the level of detail that it should contain.
- Arranging some project management training. She knew that back in Britain there were plenty of off-the-shelf courses covering project management, but that they would be tailored for the domestic market, and the delivery style of the trainers in the classroom-based courses might not be particularly suitable for her location. The training should acknowledge the assistants's multi-active and time orientations. She would have to do some careful research.
- Developing a booklet explaining how to carry out key tasks in their project planning software. As with the checklist, this should be relatively straightforward, but she needed to make sure that whoever designed it carried out a thorough task analysis and understood the target group well, so that it would be structured and written in an easy-to-use way again, it should consider the uncertainty avoidance preference of the target group.

- Running team-building events to develop a shared culture. This was another attitudinal change issue and could, again, be quite challenging. However, she knew that the organization took a lot of pride in what it did and was keen to develop in this particular regional market. It was also an organization that welcomed change, so she knew that the senior management back home would probably support something of this kind. Also, having come to know many of the people working in Reliable Constructions in the country, she felt confident that they would welcome it as well.

Table 11.1 Potential problem analysis of providing project management training

Where might things go wrong?	What might go wrong?	What might cause this?	What can we do to prevent this?
Identifying the training provider	Might not find a suitable provider. Chosen trainer might not be suitable. Might choose the wrong blend of training.	Not doing enough research. Not having the right contacts. Not being aware of the strengths and weaknesses of different approaches.	Look through my network to find a trusted consultant to advise me. Contact the big training provision companies. Do some thorough Web searching.
Customizing the training	Customizing not done correctly.	Selecting the wrong training provider. Not giving the training provider enough information. Training provider not doing their job properly.	Make sure we select the right training provider. Look within the country to find a training provider. Negotiate payment to include an element payable after satisfactory completion.
Delivering the training	Training delivered poorly. Difficulty of finding dates for delivery.	Not selecting the right training provider. Not enough importance attached to the training.	Selecting the right training provider. Getting senior managers to let people know that they see this as very important.

Before moving on to look at her second list of solutions, Philippa thought it would be useful to do a quick Potential Problem Analysis looking at the project management training. She drew up a table (Table 11.1).

She thought that was a good start. But it was now getting late in the day, and she decided to leave things until the morning when she could return to her planning activities with a fresh mind.

Step 6: Summary

This chapter has looked at some of the issues associated with implementing solutions to problems.

To summarize:

- Structural, procedural and policy changes are the easiest to implement, but much will depend on the organizational culture.
- Attitudinal changes are the hardest to implement.
- It is often a good idea to give careful thought to the potential problems that might arise during implementation in order to prevent them happening.
- The design and delivery of training activities needs to take into consideration the target group's cultural preferences.

12 *Step 7: Evaluate Effectiveness*

KEY POINTS

- Evaluate effectiveness by comparing the size of the problem after implementing solutions against the original size estimated in Step 1.

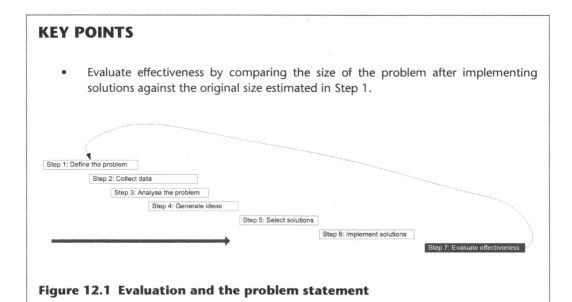

Figure 12.1 Evaluation and the problem statement

How to Approach Evaluation

It may have been a long journey, but hopefully at some point you should find yourself in a position where you need to evaluate how successful the solutions you identified and implemented have been. To consider how to do this, we need to review the problem-solving process again (Figure 12.1).

Looking at Figure 12.1, you can see that our seven-step problem-solving process is presented as cyclical rather than linear. Right back at Step 1 we looked for answers to the question, 'How serious is the problem?', and this is what should be driving our evaluation.

So, in that respect, evaluation should be a relatively simple activity. We know how big the problem was initially, and now, after a decent amount of time, we can see what is happening. Hopefully, problems will be much smaller.

You now need to decide what to do next. You can either:

- review the problems that now exist and see whether improvements need to be made to the solutions you have already implemented or if you need to identify any new solutions; or
- move on and find some more problems to solve.

When doing your evaluation there are a few useful things to remember. The passage of time may have changed the factors influencing the performance, and this may have affected how well your solutions have worked. Try to find out what these changes have been and make any necessary adjustments.

Avoid trying to determine the relative effectiveness of each of the individual elements of your solution. The problem-solving process we have followed is a holistic one, and it is important that the effectiveness comes from implementing the entire range of solutions. Solutions will probably interact with each other to some extent, so it is meaningless to try to make such statements as: 'The training accounts for 25 per cent of the improvement.'

The Reliable Constructions Case Study: Step 7

The black Bakelite telephone on Barlow's desk rang. Philippa wondered who it might be and picked it up.

'Hey, Philippa. It's me, Nulty. How's things?'

Philippa wondered why Nulty sounded in such a good mood. 'I'm fine thanks. You still over in Eastern Europe?'

'Yes, I certainly am. Look, I just wanted to tell you. We've just handed over the Transylvania site to the client, a week ahead of the deadline and under budget. Everybody is really pleased with how well the last six months have gone, and Stephanie said how much it all owed to the work that you did with them. You know, we were worried that if this project went badly it would make expanding our Eastern European operations much harder, but those few simple things you did with the guys turned things around, and it looks as if we've got some other projects lined up as well. So thanks, Philippa. Just one thing. How did you do it?'

Philippa smiled. 'I'll tell you that some day,' she said and put the phone down.

Step 7: Summary

The key thing to remember about evaluation is to make sure that you know what the size of the initial problem was. Just what was the cost of doing nothing?

If you have that information, you can judge the effectiveness of your problem-solving activities by looking at the size of the problem post-implementation and comparing it with how big it was initially.

Further Reading

When coming to the end of a writing project, it can sometimes be hard to know what to say next. So an easy way out is to use what someone else has said. For example, Isaac Newton said, 'If I have seen further, it is by standing on the shoulders of giants', so, while hesitating to say that I have indeed seen further than others, it is definitely time for me to draw your attention to some of the giants upon whose shoulders I have stood.

If you are interested in finding out more about cross-cultural issues, I would draw your attention to three books in particular.

Geert and Gert Jan Hofstede have written a number of books on cross-cultural issues, and the cultural indicators they have put forward are used time and time again in other derivative work (my own included). These indicators provide an invaluable way of helping pull apart and analyse cross-cultural dynamics. Their book that has been my source of inspiration is *Cultures and Organisations: Software of the Mind* (McGraw-Hill, 2005).

Second, I would recommend Richard Lewis's *When Cultures Collide: Leading across Cultures* (Nicholas Brearley International, 2006). This is an encyclopedic look at countries around the world and how their peoples think and behave. I have always found it to be an essential read before an international journey.

Finally, I have found Nancy Adler's *International Dimensions of Organizational Behavior* (South-Western College Publishing, 2008) to be the most useful book for looking at cross-cultural issues from an academic managerial perspective. It is also extremely readable.

Leaving cross-cultural issues behind and moving on to performance engineering, the essential read in this topic is Robert Mager's and Peter Pipe's *Analysing Performance Problems* (Kogan Page, 1990). Their approach to performance analysis and their development of the performance flowchart should really make this subject easily accessible to managers throughout the world. I find it a great personal disappointment that there is generally so little awareness of how to take these ideas and apply them to workplace problems, as they do offer enormous possibilities.

To round off this suggested reading list, I would recommend a careful study of Peter Senge's *The Fifth Discipline* (Random House, 1990). Although I have been somewhat critical in this book about the limitations of much of Western management literature, Senge's book has been a great inspiration to me in writing my own. His encouragement for organizations to adopt a more holistic and systems-based approach to reviewing their operations has, in many ways, underpinned everything in my writing. Western his book may be, but limited it certainly is not.

References

Adair, W., Tinsley, C. and Taylor, M. (2006), 'Managing the Intercultural Interface: Third Cultures, Antecedents, and Consequences', in E. Mannix, M. Neale and A. Tenbrunsel (eds), *Research on Managing Groups and Teams*, Vol. 7 (Kidlington: Elsevier).

Adler, N. (2008), *International Dimensions of Organizational Behavior*, 5th edn (Cincinnati: South-Western College Publishing).

Berkowitz, L. (1977), *Advances in Experimental Social Psychology*, Vol. 10 (New York: Academic Press), pp. 173–220.

Bernstein, B. (1971), *Class, Codes and Control. Vol. 1: Theoretical Studies towards a Sociology of Language* (London: Routledge & Kegan Paul).

Birdseye, M. and Hill, J. (1995), 'Individual, Organizational/Work and Environmental Influences on Expatriate Turnover Tendencies: An Empirical Study', *Journal of International Business Studies*, 26(4), pp. 787–813.

Brookfield Global Relocation Services (2008), *Global Relocation Trends: 2008 Survey Report*, at: http://www.brookfieldgrs.com/knowledge/grts_research.

Casmir, F. (1997), 'Ethics, Culture and Communication: An Application of the Third Culture Building Model to International and Intercultural Communication', in F. Casmir (ed.), *Ethics in Intercultural and International Communication* (London: Erlbaum).

Chan, J. (2005), 'Confucianism and Human Rights', in R. Smith and C. van den Anker (eds), *The Essentials of Human Rights* (London: Hodder).

Checkland, P. and Scholes, J. (1990), *Soft Systems Methodology in Action* (Chichester: Wiley).

Crookes, D. and Thomas, I. (1998), 'Problem Solving and Culture – Exploring Some Stereotypes', *Journal of Management Development*, 17(8), pp. 583–591.

Daftuar, C. (1975), 'The Role of Human Factors Engineering in Underdeveloped Countries, with Special Reference to India', in A. Chapanis (ed.), *Ethnic Variables in Human Factors Engineering* (Baltimore, MD: Johns Hopkins University Press).

Dalacoura, K. (2005), 'Islam and Human Rights', in R. Smith and C. van den Anker (eds), *The Essentials of Human Rights* (London: Hodder).

Davis, F. (1989), 'Perceived Usefulness, Perceived Ease of Use and User Acceptance of Information Technology', *MIS Quarterly*, 13(3), pp. 319–40.

Delbecq, A.L. and Van de Ven, A.H. (1971), 'A Group Process Model for Problem Identification and Program Planning', *Journal of Applied Behavioral Science*, VII, pp. 466–91.

Demyttenaere, K., Bruffaerts, R. and Posada-Villa, J. (2004), 'Prevalence, Severity, and Unmet Need for Treatment of Mental Disorders in the World Health Organization World Mental Health Surveys', *Journal of the American Medical Association*, 291, pp. 2581–90.

Earley, C. and Mosakowski, E. (2004), 'Cultural Intelligence', *Harvard Business Review*, October, pp. 139–46.

Flood, R. and Jackson, M. (1991), *Creative Problem Solving: Total Systems Intervention* (New York: Wiley).

Freeman, M. (2005), 'The Historical Roots of Human Rights before the Second World War', in R. Smith and C. van den Anker (eds), *The Essentials of Human Rights* (London: Hodder).

Gabrenya, W. and Barba, L. (1987), *Cultural Differences in Social Interaction during Group Problem Solving*, at: http://eric.ed.gov/ERICWebPortal/contentdelivery/servlet/ERICServlet?accno=ED283 111.

Gallagher, T. (2001), 'The Value Orientations Method: A Tool to Help Understand Cultural Differences', *Journal of Extension*, 39(6), at: http://www.joe.org/joe/2001december/tt1.html.

Gardner, H. (1983), *Frames of Mind: The Theory of Multiple Intelligences* (New York: Basic Books).

Gelfand, M. and Christakopoulou, S. (1999), 'Culture and Negotiator Cognition: Judgment, Accuracy and Negotiation Processes in Individualistic and Collectivistic Cultures', *Organizational Behavior and Human Decision Processes*, 79(3), pp. 248–69.

Gilbert, T. (2007), *Human Competence: Engineering Worthy Performance (Tribute Edition)* (San Francisco: Pfeiffer).

Goleman, D. (1996), *Emotional Intelligence* (London: Bloomsbury).

Hale, J. (2007), *The Performance Consultant's Fieldbook* (San Francisco: Pfeiffer).

Hall, E. (1976), *Beyond Culture* (New York: Anchor Books).

Halversen, C. and Cuellar, G. (2001), 'Diversity and Team Development', in E. Biech (ed.), *The Pfeiffer Book of Successful Team-building Tools* (San Francisco: Jossey-Bass).

Harless, J. (1986), 'Guiding Performance with Job Aids', in National Society for Performance and Instruction (ed.), *Introduction to Performance Technology* (Washington, DC: NSPI).

Helmreich, R. and Merritt, A. (1998), 'Aviation and Medicine: National, Organizational and Professional Influences', in R. Helmreich and A. Merritt (eds), *Culture at Work: National, Organizational and Professional Influences* (Aldershot: Ashgate Publishing).

Henderson, L. (1996), 'Instructional Design of Interactive Multimedia', *Educational Technology Research and Development*, 44(4), pp. 85–104.

Hersey, P. and Blanchard, K. (1977), *Management Organizational Behaviour: Utilizing Human Resources* (Englewood Cliffs, NJ: Prentice-Hall).

Hicks, M. (1991), *Problem Solving in Business and Management* (London: International Thomson Business Press).

Hill, C., Loch, K., Straub, D.W. and El-Sheshai, K. (1998), 'A Qualitative Assessment of Arab Culture and Information Technology Transfer', *Journal of Global Information Management*, 6(3), pp. 29–38.

Hofstede, G. and Hofstede, G. (2005), *Cultures and Organizations: Software of the Mind* (New York: McGraw-Hill).

Howell, P., Strauss, J. and Sorensen, P. (1975), 'Research Note: Cultural and Situational Determinants of Job Satisfaction among Management in Liberia', *Journal of Management Studies*, 12(1–2), pp. 225–27.

Hsee, C. and Weber, E. (1999), 'Cross-national Differences in Risk Preference and Lay Predictions', *Journal of Behavioral Decision Making*, 12(2), pp. 165–79.

Huer, M.B. (2000), 'Examining Perceptions of Graphic Symbols across Cultures: Preliminary Study of the Impact of Culture/Ethnicity', *Augmentative and Alternative Communication*, 16, pp. 180–85.

Ichheiser, G. (1970), *Appearances and Realities* (San Francisco: Jossey-Bass).

Ide, Y. (1999), 'The Cultural Differences in Motivation between North Americans and Japanese', at: http://bespin.stwing.upenn.edu/~upsych/Perspectives/1999/ide.htm,

Imai, M. and Gentner, D. (1994), 'A Cross-linguistic Study of Early Word Meaning: Universal Ontology and Linguistic Influence', *Cognition*, 62, pp. 169–200.

Isaksen, S. (1998), 'A Review of Brainstorming Research: Six Critical Issues for Enquiry', at: www.cpsb.com/resources/downloads/public/302-Brainstorm.pdf.

Jackson, S. (1986), 'Task Analysis', in National Society for Performance and Instruction (ed.), *Introduction to Performance Technology* (Washington, DC: NSPI).

Jackson, T. (1998), 'Foreign Companies and Chinese Workers: Employee Motivation in the People's Republic of China', *Journal of Organizational Change Management*, 11(4), pp. 282–300.

James, O. (2007), *Affluenza* (London: Vermilion).

Janis, I.L. (1972), *Victims of Groupthink* (Boston, MA: Houghton Mifflin).

Jarvenpaa, S.L. and Leidner, D.E. (1998), 'Communication and Trust in Global Virtual Teams', *Organization Science*, 10(6), pp. 250–67.

Jehn, K. and Weldon, E., (1996), 'Conflict Management in Bicultural Teams: Cultural Dimensions and Synergistic Problem Solving', Knowledge@Wharton, at: http://knowledge.wharton.upenn. edu/paper.cfm?paperid=621.

Jones, M. (1995), *The Thinker's Toolkit* (New York: Three Rivers Press).

Kedia, B.L. and Bhagat, R.S. (1988), 'Cultural Constraints on Transfer of Technology across Nations: Implications for Research in International and Comparative Management', *Academy of Management Review*, 13(4), pp. 559–71.

Kennedy, K. (1975), 'International Anthropometric Variability and its Effects on Aircraft Cockpit Design', in A. Chapanis (ed.), *Ethnic Variables in Human Factors Engineering* (Baltimore, MD: Johns Hopkins University Press).

Kepner, C. and Tregoe, B. (1981), *The New Rational Manager* (London: John Martin Publishing).

Kitayama, S., Duffy, S., Kawamura, T. and Larsen, J.T. (2003), 'Perceiving an Object and its Context in Different Cultures: A Cultural Look at New Look', *Psychological Science*, 14(3), pp. 201–206.

Klein, H., Pongonis, A. and Klein, G. (2000), 'Cultural Barriers to Multinational C2 Decision Making', at: http://www.scribd.com/doc/1463057/US-Air-Force-2000ccrts-klein-culture.

Kluckhohn, F. and Strodtbeck, F. (1961), *Variations in Value Orientations* (Evanston, IL: Row, Peterson).

Lamm, H. and Trommsdorff, G. (1973), 'Group versus Individual Performance on Tasks Requiring Ideational Proficiency (Brainstorming): A Review', *European Journal of Social Psychology*, 3(4), pp. 361–88.

Laurent, A. (1983), 'The Cultural Diversity of Western Conceptions of Management', *International Studies of Management and Organization*, 13(1–2), pp. 75–96.

Lewis, R. (2006), *When Cultures Collide: Leading Across Cultures*, 3rd edn (Boston, MA: Nicholas Brealey International).

Lillrank, P. and Kano, N. (1989), *Continuous Improvement: Quality Control Circles in Japanese Industry*, Michigan Papers in Japanese Studies (Ann Arbor: University of Michigan Press).

Lim, G. and DeVries, J. (2003), 'The Cultural Component of Global Distance and On-line Learning', at: ole.tp.edu.sg/courseware/teaching_guide/resources/article/Grace/culturalcomponent.pdf.

Lord, R. and Maher, K. (1991), *Leadership and Information Processing: Linking Perceptions and Performance* (Boston, MA: Unwin Hyman).

Luft, J. (1961), 'The Johari Window', *Human Relations Training News*, 5(1), pp. 6–7.

Luft, J. (1970), *Group Processes: An Introduction to Group Dynamics* (Mountain View: Mayfield).

Mager, R. and Pipe, P. (1990), *Analysing Performance Problems* (London: Kogan Page).

Maznevski, M. and Peterson, M. (1997), 'Societal Values, Social Interpretation and Multinational Teams', in C. Granrose and S. Oskamp (eds), *Cross-cultural Work Groups* (London: Sage).

McLoughlin, C. and Oliver, R. (1999), 'Instructional Design for Cultural Difference: A Case Study of the Indigenous Online Learning in a Tertiary Context', at: http://www.ascilite.org.au/conferences/ brisbane99/papers/mcloughlinoliver.pdf.

Mercer Bing, C. et al, (2000), 'More than Handbook Translation: Making Training Programs Work Everywhere', *Princeton Business Journal*, 18–20 July. Available at: www.itapintl.com/facultyandresources/articlelibrarymain./makingtrainingprogramswork.html.

Meshkati, N. (1991), 'Human Factors in Large-scale Technological Systems Accidents: Three Mile Island, Bhopal, Chernobyl', *Organization & Environment*, 5(2), pp. 133–54.

Moxon, P. (1993), *Building a Better Team* (Aldershot: Gower).

Murithi, T. (2005), 'Ubuntu and Human Rights', in R. Smith and C. van den Anker (eds), *The Essentials of Human Rights* (London: Hodder).

Nakamura, K., Newell, A.F., Alm, N. and Waller, A. (1998), 'How Do Members of Different Language Communities Compose Sentences with a Picture-based Communication System? A Cross-cultural Study of Picture-based Sentences Constructed by English and Japanese Speakers', *Augmentative and Alternative Communication*, 14, pp. 71–79.

NASA (1999), 'Mars Climate Orbiter Team Finds Likely Cause of Loss', at: http://marsprogram.jpl.nasa.gov/msp98/news/mco990930.html.

Nevis, B.C. (1983), 'Using an American Perspective in Understanding Another Culture: Toward a Hierarchy of Needs for the People's Republic of China', *The Journal of Applied Behavioral Science*, 19(3), pp. 249–64.

Nisbett, R. (2003), *The Geography of Thought* (London: Nicholas Brealey International).

Obama, B. (2006), *The Audacity of Hope* (Edinburgh: Canongate).

Oberg, K. (1954), 'Culture Shock', at: http://www.amazines.com/Kalvero_Oberg_related.html.

Osborn, A. (1953), *Applied Imagination: Principles and Procedures of Creative Thinking* (New York: Charles Scribner's Sons).

Park, D. and Gutchess, A. (2006), 'The Cognitive Neuroscience of Aging and Culture', *Directions in Psychological Science*, 15(3), pp. 105–108.

Paulus, P.B. and Paulus, L.E. (1997), 'Implications of Research on Group Brainstorming for Gifted Education', *Roeper Review*, 19(4), pp. 225–29.

Philips, J. and Stone, R. (2002), *How to Measure Training Results* (London: McGraw-Hill).

Piamonte, P., Abeysekera, J. and Ohlsson, K. (2001), 'Understanding Small Graphical Symbols: A Cross-cultural Study', *International Journal of Industrial Ergonomics*, 27(6), pp. 399–404.

Rinpoche, S. (1992), *The Tibetan Book of Living and Dying*, ed. P. Gaffney and A. Harvey (San Francisco: HarperOne).

Ross, L. (1977), 'The Intuitive Psychologist and his Shortcomings', in L. Berkowitz (ed.), *Advances in Experimental Social Psychology*, Vol. 10 (New York: Academic Press), pp. 173–220.

Said, E. (2003), *Orientalism* (London: Penguin).

Senge, P. (1993), *The Fifth Discipline* (London: Century Business).

Shahnavaz, H. (n.d.), *Cultural Differences*, at: http://www.ilo.org/safework_bookshelf/english?content&nd=857170348.

Tarantino, Q. (1994), *Pulp Fiction: Screenplay*, at: http://www.godamongdirectors.com/scripts/pulp.shtml.

Timm, J. (1999), 'Selecting Computer Programs and Interactive Multimedia for Culturally Diverse Students: Promising Practices', *Multicultural Education*, 6(4), pp. 30–31.

Torrance, E. (1970), 'Influence of Dyadic Interaction on Creativity Functioning', *Psychological Reports*, 26, pp. 391–94.

Triandis, H.C. (1994), *Culture and Social Behavior* (New York: McGraw-Hill).

Triandis, H.C. (1995), *Individualism and Collectivism* (Boulder, CO: Westview Press).

Trompenaars, F. (1993), *Riding the Waves of Culture* (London: Nicholas Brealey International).

Trompenaars, F. and Hampden-Turner, C. (2004), *Managing People Across Cultures* (Chichester: Capstone).

Tuckman, B. (1965), 'Development Sequence in Small Groups', *Psychological Bulletin*, 63, pp. 284–499.

Usunier, J.C. (1996), 'Cultural Aspects of International Business Negotiations', in P.N. Ghauri and J.C. Usunier (eds), *International Business Negotiations* (Oxford: Redwood Books).

Veiga, J., Floyd, S. and Dechant, K. (2001), 'Towards Modelling the Effects of National Culture on IT Implementation and Acceptance', *Journal of Information Technology*, 16, pp. 145–58.

Weber, E. and Hsee, C., (1998), 'Cross-Cultural Differences in Risk Perception, but Cross-Cultural Similarities in Attitudes towards Perceived Risk', *Management Science*, 44, pp. 1205–17.

West, M. (1996), 'Working in Groups', in P. Warr (ed.), *Psychology at Work* (London: Penguin).

Williams, L., and Bargh, J. (2008), 'Experiencing Physical Warmth Promotes Interpersonal Warmth', *Science*, 322, 24 October, pp. 606–607.

Wilson, M. and Dalton, M. (1999), 'What Every Leader Should Know about Expatriate Effectiveness', *Leadership in Action*, 19(3), pp. 1–9.

Witkin, H.A. and Goodenough, D.R. (1977), 'Field Dependence and Inter-personal Behaviour', *Psychological Bulletin*, 84, pp. 661–89.

Wyndham, C. (1975), 'Ergonomic Problems in the Transition from Peasant to Industrial Life in South Africa', in A. Chapanis (ed.), *Ethnic Variables in Human Factors Engineering* (Baltimore, MD: Johns Hopkins University Press).

Yang, K.S. and Bond, M.H. (1990), 'Exploring Implicit Personality Theories with Indigenous or Imported Constructs: The Chinese Case', *Journal of Personality and Social Psychology*, 58, pp. 1087–95.

Yates, J.F. et al. (1998), 'Cross-cultural Variations in Probability Judgement Accuracy: Beyond General Knowledge Overconfidence?', *Organizational Behavior and Human Decision Processes*, 74, pp. 89–117.

Zakour, A. (2004), 'Cultural Differences and Information Technology Acceptance', *Proceedings of the 7th Annual Conference of the Southern Association for Information Systems*, at: http://sais.aisnet.org/2004/.\Zakour.pdf.

Index